Samuel Johnson

AND THE LIFE OF READING

Samuel Johnson

AND THE LIFE OF READING

Robert DeMaria Jr.

The Johns Hopkins University Press
Baltimore and London

© 1997 The Johns Hopkins University Press
All rights reserved. Published 1997
Printed in the United States of America on acid-free paper
2 4 6 8 9 7 5 3

The Johns Hopkins University Press
2715 North Charles Street
Baltimore, Maryland 21218-4363
The Johns Hopkins Press Ltd., London
www.press.jhu.edu

LIBRARY OF CONGRESS CATALOGING-IN-PUBLICATION DATA

DeMaria, Robert.
    Samuel Johnson and the life of reading / Robert DeMaria, Jr.
        p.   cm.
    Includes bibliographical references and index.
    ISBN 0-8018-5479-2 (alk. paper)
    1. Johnson, Samuel, 1709–1784—Books and reading. 2. Books
and reading—England—History—18th century. 3. Authors,
English—18th century—Biography. 4. England—Intellectual
life—18th century. I. Title.
PR3537.B6D45 1997
828'.609—dc20   96-38636

A catalog record for this book is available from the British Library.

FRONTISPIECE: *Samuel Johnson,* c. 1775, by Sir Joshua Reynolds
(courtesy of the collection of Loren and Frances Rothschild).

For my parents

It is strange that there should be so little reading in the world, and so much writing.

SAMUEL JOHNSON,
in conversation, 1 May 1783

CONTENTS

PREFACE

$\mathcal{I}$n his novel *If on a Winter's Night a Traveler*, Italo Calvino attempts a striking reversal of traditional practice by making the reader both the source and the focus of his presentation. He shines the spotlight of attention and celebrity on the figure traditionally meant to pay attention and give celebrity. Readers are principal actors in Calvino's book, and much of the narrative is addressed to the reader in the second person. There is a surplus of novelists in the book, but readers are rare, and the "you" of the book is singular. At one point you are accosted by one of the many novelists; the novelist is honored, star-struck, and nearly overcome with pleasure when you declare, "I'm a reader, only a reader, not an author." He replies, " 'Oh, really? Good, good! I'm delighted!' And the glance he gives you really is a look of friendliness and gratitude. 'I'm so pleased. I come across fewer and fewer readers.' "[1] The complaint that there are too many books is ancient—"Of making many books there is no end," says the preacher in Ecclesiastes (12.12). But Calvino's sense that reading has changed fundamentally and that readers are actually being replaced by writers is more recent. The historical origin of Calvino's perception is the background of my inquiry in this book.

If it did not originate in the eighteenth century, the idea that readers and reading might actually disappear gained important momentum at that time. Among those who perceived this dire possibility most clearly was Samuel Johnson. In 1753 he wittily foresaw the time imagined in Calvino's novel when "writers will, perhaps, be multiplied, till no readers will be found, and then the ambition of writing must necessarily cease."[2] Johnson's most famous critical construct, the abstract "common reader," acknowledges the growing importance of the reader in literature. Yet the invention is also a sign that at least some kinds of reading were felt to be at risk. By elevating and exalting the reader, Johnson erected a defense against the frightening possibility that England, as he said in 1756, was becoming a "nation of authors" in which "every man must be content to read his book to himself."[3]

Johnson's "common reader" bears some resemblance to Calvino's "other reader," a woman in the novel who plays a part like that traditionally assigned to the muse. The common reader is an "other reader" to Johnson—one with whom he sometimes but not always agrees—but Johnson was a real reader, and it is such real readers whom Calvino makes his heroes rather than his muses. Samuel Johnson in particular, and real readers in general, are also my heroes in this book. My goal is to describe Johnson's life of reading and in doing so to develop a language for describing other lives of reading. The sum of the lives of reading equals the real history of reading; this is distinct from the history of remarks about reading, which is a branch of literary criticism. A literary critic is a writer, and his or her works should be studied as contributions to a philosophical literary genre. A real reader is not a writer, as Calvino understands.

How, then, does one get to know a real reader? A writer is known through writing, so a reader should be known through reading. But the act of reading leaves no traces, and writing about reading is writing. One solution to the problem is clear; Calvino provides it when he addresses the reader and enters the reader's house. He attends carefully to the kitchen for signs of personality, but then he gets to the point: "Let's have a look at the books." He is able to deduce quite a lot, and it is noteworthy that his deductions involve a rough categorization of reading practices as well as readers:

The first thing noticed, at least on looking at those you have most prominent, is that the function of books for you is immediate reading; they are not instruments of study or reference or components of a library arranged according to some order. Perhaps on occasion you have tried to give a semblance of order to your shelves, but every attempt at classification was rapidly foiled by heterogeneous acquisitions. The chief reason for the juxtaposition of the volumes, besides the dimensions of the tallest or the shortest, remains chronological, as they arrived here, one after the other; anyway, you can always put your hand on any one. . . . In short, you don't seem to be a Reader Who Rereads. You remember very well everything you have read.[4]

We cannot enter his room and see how Samuel Johnson arranged his books, but it is possible to make some explorations of his library and to glean from these a sense of him as a reader. Although it is not a very good one, there is a catalogue of the sale of Johnson's books (those that remained in his estate) in 1785, the year after his death. The late David Fleeman and several other Johnsonians painstakingly augmented the list with notes and further information on the books that passed through our hero's hands.[5] Many of the books that Johnson owned survive, and some have marks in them that Johnson made while reading; precious few of these are of much interest, but Johnson's marginalia are obviously important to a study of his reading habits. To the extent that it is really private, this form of writing would seem to provide evidence of reading that is unsullied by being part of the history of writing; I will have more to say about this in chapter 2.

Although they provide less-pure evidence than his marginalia, Johnson's extant notebooks and diaries, some of his writings, and the many reports of his conversations all add to our knowledge of what books passed through his hands and of how he read, reread, and remembered them. The overall impression one gets from an acquaintance with Johnson's books and other reading materials is that he had tremendously varied reading habits. Calvino could not categorize him so easily as he does the reader whom he addresses in *If on a Winter's Night*. Johnson used books both for "immediate reading" and as "instruments of study." His collections and his reading habits were "heterogeneous" but also ordered. He remembered everything he read, and merely scanned a great many books, but he also read some books over and over throughout his life. There is no easy way to order his library or his life of reading. However, even if order does some injustice to the heterogeneous reality of what Johnson once called his "fortuitous and unguided excursions into books,"[6] order must be made for the sake of understanding. In this subject as in every subject that touches the variety of life itself, we need, to borrow Robert Frost's description of his own artifices, "a momentary stay against confusion."

Samuel Parr, an impressive scholar who accepted the awesome responsibility of composing the epitaph for Johnson's monument in Westminster Abbey, once began collecting books in preparation for writing a biography of Johnson. He made a place for the books in his library. This library within his library soon grew unmanageably large and Parr abandoned his task, remarking only, "It would have contained a view of the literature of Europe."[7] This is true, but had Parr's biography done justice to every aspect of Johnson's life of reading, it would have covered more than the literature (by which Parr probably meant the learning) of Europe. It would also have contained references to the magazines and newspapers that Johnson read; the various books he reviewed; the pamphlets that passed through his hands; the advertisements, book catalogues, novels, and even the signs, lottery tickets, invitations, and announcements that passed before his eyes every day of his life. Even if it could all be known, to read everything that Johnson read in his life would be impossible; every day one would lose ground. It makes more sense to set aside spaces, as Samuel Parr did.

In my view, at least four rooms are needed, one for each of four main kinds of reading. I describe Johnson's life of reading by talking about the contents of these four imaginary rooms, and I do this by discussing elements in each that seem to me representative of the whole roomful of texts. Because Johnson was such a great reader and read in so many different ways, I venture the further hypothesis that the categories I use to describe his life of reading are adequate for describing any other life of reading. In other words, I think these four kinds of reading are the four kinds of reading we all do: study, perusal, mere reading, and curious reading. As rash and speculative as this system may seem, it has proved workable. At least, the fourfold distinction is a useful instrument for discussing Johnson's life of reading. At most, it provides a pattern for assessing other lives of reading, including, dear reader, your own.

ACKNOWLEDGMENTS

*J*ohnson's life of reading has interested me for more than twenty years. When I set out to write about it, I found I could not do so without reading his *Dictionary*; that turned out to be a ten-year project, culminating in *Johnson's Dictionary and the Language of Learning* (1986). Soon afterward, I agreed to write *The Life of Samuel Johnson: A Critical Biography* (1993), with the understanding that I would spend a good deal of effort on Johnson's intellectual life, and so his reading. Writing both those books prepared me to write this one, and I am indebted to everyone who helped me with them. For the opportunity finally to write this extended essay I am especially indebted to the Guggenheim Foundation and to the Center for Advanced Study in the Behavioral Sciences. With special support from the Mellon Foundation, I spent my year as a Guggenheim fellow at the Center, as a member of the class of 1993. Although I had contemplated it for a long time, the book took shape as it did partly because of the unusual community in which it was written. I particularly wish to acknowledge the help I received from my colleagues in a group study project: Elizabeth Eisenstein, Richard Bauman, and Michael Schudson. Our weekly discussions on the history of political reporting touched on many aspects of the current study, and the group was kind enough to read some parts of the work in draft. Beyond my group the Center provided a community of scholars from various disciplines, most of them in the social sciences. The presence of this community vastly increased my sense of the diversity of intellectual excellence, and this confirmed the utterly simplistic but important insight at the heart of this study: that reading itself is a complex, diverse activity.

I finished work on this book back home at Vassar College, where I have received unflagging support for my scholarship for twenty-one years. One of my colleagues there for a short time, John Scanlan, suggested I write this book.

Among the many scholars in the Johnsonian community who assisted me, I wish especially to thank Bruce Redford, who helped me decipher some of Johnson's marginalia. I also received help and encouragement from the late David Fleeman, who was the greatest authority on Johnson's books. Johnsonians who combine their intellectual interest in the man with a love of books also provided help. Mary Hyde Eccles's permission to consult the great Hyde Collection was crucial to my research. I also benefited from hours spent in the interesting and extensive private libraries of Loren Rothschild and Gerald M. Goldberg. Part of the reason I wrote this book is that I love to go to libraries, and I am indebted to many librarians for their help, particularly Nancy Mackechnie of the Vassar College Special Collections, Vincent Giroud and Stephen Parks of the Beinecke Rare Book and Manuscript Library, Robert Parks of the Morgan Library, Julian Roberts, Keeper of Printed Books at the Bodleian Library, Charles Greene of the Firestone Library, and G. W. Nicholls of the Lichfield Birthplace Museum. I received generous assistance at numerous other libraries, including the Pembroke College Library, the British Library, the Folger, the Huntington, the Clark, the Lewis Walpole Library, Stanford University Special Collections, and the British Art Center in New Haven.

For all its reliance on institutions and their directors, this book was still written at home, and I have learned the most from the other readers in the house, each of whom is living a unique and varied life of reading: Alex and Davy, and especially Joanne.

I also want to pay homage to a couple of my favorite readers who died while I was working on this book and whose passionate lives of reading I admired deeply: Loretta Bulow and Ken Smith.

THE LIFE OF READING

*W*hile Samuel Johnson was making his farewell visit to his hometown of Lichfield in 1784, his ailments worsened, and Johnson's doctor ordered his famous patient to return to London for observation and treatment. Johnson was happy to obey the doctor's orders, because he loved London; as all students of Johnson know, he found the full tide of life at Charing Cross and declared that he who is tired of London is tired of life. But one of the reasons he was eager to return to London had little to do with the social life and stimulation of the metropolis. He wrote to Dr. Brocklesby to signify his compliance with the doctor's orders and added, "The town is my element, there are my friends, there are my books to which I have not yet bidden farewell, and there are my amusements."[1] To judge by this statement, books occupied a place in Johnson's life similar to that of his most valued friends.

Given the well-known realism of Johnson's literary criticism (his impatience with pastoral and other fantasies), the animism Johnson expressed about his books is surprising. Indeed, the remark makes him sound like that great, empathic reader of the next generation, Samuel Taylor Coleridge, who identified with the speakers of poems and called his pocketbooks (notebooks and other books he carried around) his only friends. Johnson's remark to Brocklesby suggests that we cannot trust the famous dicta of Johnson's literary criticism to tell the whole story of a life lived among books. Although he made his living writing books and writing about them, Johnson, like all of us, also had a silent, more private life in his conversation with books. The purpose of my book is to make Johnson's silent life of reading audible and to relate it to the silent lives of reading led by others in his time and in other times, including our own.

The silent life of reading is a part of personal rather than public life, although it is not always possible to make a clear distinction between the two. The evidence for lives of reading, then, should not come from the public, published statements of writers but rather, wherever possible, from documentary sources: marginalia, notebooks, commonplace books, diaries, anecdotes, letters, and casual, conversational remarks—in short, many of the usual sources of reports on private life. In addition, the books themselves are a source of information on a life of reading.

Knowing what books Johnson read and when he read them constitutes an important part of the biographical knowledge about him, but, for all the biographies of Johnson, relatively little attention has been paid to his reading. The reasons for this are not far to seek: the dramatic story of his professional rise to fame and the equally appealing tales of his tempestuous conversations and personal relations are more available and more colorful than his silent life of reading. Moreover, the main evidence available for reconstructing Johnson's life of reading is provided by a collection of books that is daunting in its size, diversity, and difficulty. This collection of books, partly registered in the sale catalogue of his library published in 1785, a year after his death, and further gleaned in a thorough reading of the works by and about Johnson, is the most material link between Johnson and the high Latin culture of European humanism. In my biography of Johnson I tried to show the important place of European culture in Johnson's sense of himself, as a young man especially, and throughout his life.[2] But the collection of books that Johnson left and those that passed through his hands has greater depth and diversity than it would be convenient (or possible) to explore in a book devoted primarily to his life and works.

The books themselves, most of which I have consulted in the

same editions (if not in the original copies) owned by Johnson, allow one to get close to parts of his life of reading. Other parts are not adequately registered in the books that the cataloguer noted for sale, in those on which Johnson commented publicly or privately, or even in books at all, for Johnson read all kinds of irrecoverable, ephemeral printed and written material on a daily basis; newspapers, magazines, letters, advertisements, and even street signs engaged him in ways that it is difficult but important to consider. Even the books and other recoverable texts will not directly render their secrets. The kind of consultation they offer is limited; they cannot tell us truly what Johnson or any reader other than ourselves picked up, heard, and felt in perusing their pages. But the books are not merely relics, and going over them is not the same as numbering the beads of the saint's rosary. The orphaned books do have a talismanic quality and their physical properties are important, but in addition to their look and feel they contain meaning: their words provide more voluble clues to the life of reading we wish to recover than the truly silent beads of a rosary. Reading the same words that Johnson read contributes to an understanding of his life of reading, and not merely to the process of cataloguing it.

However, an assemblage and rereading of Johnson's books, even if it could be completed, would not tell us the whole story of his life of reading. Too much has sometimes been made of this idea, but different readers, especially those separated by time and place, do not read the same text in the same way. As literary theory has been at pains to show over the past fifteen or twenty years, differences in readers and readings mean that texts actually change, because the ontology of a text includes a dependence on being read. One "reader-oriented" critic describes the existence of a literary text in this way: "Severed from the biography of the author, it begins its history within the biographies of countless readers."[3] Yet there are limits to this phenomenological approach, as the best of the "reader-based" theorists acknowledge, and texts are stable enough to permit us to examine readers by looking at them.

As Janusz Slawinski points out, one of the ways of viewing

the reader is "from the perspective of literature. We see him here as a historically defining hitching- or collection-point for a varied multitude of texts. Viewed in this light—and this is the aspect the historian must place in the foreground—he is simply the representative of the pyramid of texts he has absorbed, or could have absorbed, in his literary cultural situation."[4] Johnson is a character of such magnitude and liveliness that it would be folly to see him simply as "the representative of the pyramid of texts he has absorbed," even if we think texts can form a pyramid or be absorbed. In order to avoid this folly it is necessary to attempt to reconstruct not only Johnson's library but his "imaginary library," to adapt a phrase used by Alvin Kernan,[5] and to present his books as products of Johnson's activity and style of reading. Even when this is done, it is not the whole person of Johnson but simply the reader who will be only partially recovered. But Johnson was a reader of such range and greatness that even a partial recovery of his life of reading constitutes an important chapter in the history of reading, which is, in turn, a crucial element of cultural history.

I I

In constructing Johnson's imaginary library it is important to reveal not only what he read but how he read. By "how" I mean something less cerebral than interpretation; my interest is not so much in what Johnson made of his reading as in what he did in the act of reading, beginning with how he managed the physical activity itself. Eyewitness accounts of Johnson reading, in addition to the evidence of his library, suggest that, like most of us, Johnson read in several ways. This is an obvious perception, but I think it is important. Reading is not a single activity; there are many kinds of reading, and philosophical approaches to the subject sometimes seem to forget this. In order to make sense of the variety of reading, I propose that Johnson read in four distinct ways. Adopting Johnson's own terminology, I call these ways "study" or "hard reading"; "perusal"; "mere reading"; and "curious reading." Certain kinds of books are associated with each of the types of reading, so books can be used to organize both the manner and the material of Johnson's reading, even though the kinds of reading are, to a degree, independent of the books associated with them. The Bible, for example, can be read in any of the four ways, but it is most closely associated with study. As is the case with most systems of classification, the truth of my little taxonomy is hard to prove; it vindicates its adoption by being useful rather than true. It is useful for describing Johnson's life of reading, and it promises to be adaptable for use in describing other lives of reading as well as larger movements in the history of reading.

Johnson's life of reading began where most do, in a relaxed posture on a woman's lap. Even in the eighteenth century, although men taught writing, women introduced children to reading. Johnson's friend and confidant Hester Thrale reported that

> Dr. Johnson first learned to read of his mother and her old maid Catherine, in whose lap he well remembered sitting while she explained to him the story of St. George and the dragon. . . . The recollection of such reading as had delighted him in his infancy, made him always persist in fancying that it was the only reading which could please an infant; and he used to condemn me for putting Newbery's books [which had clear pedagogical purposes] into their hands as too trifling to engage their attention. "Babies do not want (said he) to hear about babies; they like to be told of giants and castles, and of somewhat which can stretch and stimulate their little minds."[6]

Another tale about Johnson's childhood reading experiences suggests how great was his capacity for "stimulation," even when the text he read was not designed primarily for children: "When he was about nine years old," according to Hester Thrale, "having got the play of Hamlet in his hand, and reading it quietly in his father's kitchen, he kept on steadily enough, till coming to the Ghost scene, he suddenly hurried up the stairs to the street door that he might see people about him."[7] He evidently both believed the fiction, momentarily, and was lost in it. This is a kind of reading that Johnson did all his life, but it is only one kind. In *Lost in a Book,* one of the few attempts to write a psychology of reading, Victor Nell describes this kind of reading as characteristic of one of his two types of readers.[8] Nell's "type A" reader requires that reading matter be at hand at all times, takes books to the dentist's office (right into the dentist's chair), and loads his or her suitcase with a back-breaking assortment when heading off for even a short holiday. "Type B" readers, although less compulsive about having books at hand, are more likely to enter into a trancelike or dreamlike state of enjoyment while reading. Johnson was mainly a type A reader, but he was also at times a dreamy type B reader, especially when he indulged himself, as he did all his life, in reading romances and romantic novels. Following some eighteenth-century readers and using definitions in Johnson's *Dictionary,* I call this "curious reading."

In the eighteenth century the word *curious* contained suggestions of both illicit and compulsive inquiry. The first definition in Johnson's *Dictionary* is "inquisitive; desirous of information; addicted to enquiry." His illustrative quotations warn of the dangers of curiosity; the first citation is from Ecclesiasticus and says bluntly, "Be not curious in unnecessary matters." It was as true in the eighteenth century as it is today that the principal vehicle for curious, absorbed, addicted reading was the unnecessary but perhaps harmless genre of fiction. Although some forms of nonfiction, including travel narratives and biography, may also provide the experience of being lost in a book, the novel, the romance, science fiction, and fantasy are the forms with which such curious transport is usually associated. The obvious suggestion, asserted by some studies and once maintained by the National Council of Teachers of English, is that reading in these paradigmatic cases is akin to dreaming. In this conception the association with romance, which is often framed by a dream, is most pronounced. As some studies of contemporary reading habits suggest, this kind of reading is also more common among women and perhaps among young readers than among adult men.[9]

One of the key elements that distinguishes genres of reading is the amount and kind of credence that the reader extends in the experience. In curious reading, ideally, the reader extends credence generously, even if he or she knows at the same time that what is being credited is fiction. The most characteristic experience of reading in this category is that of entering an intangible aesthetic world in which the fantasy is thoroughly admitted but also thoroughly accepted. Credence does not waver, because one is not testing the fiction against reality—as one is constantly testing in reading the newspaper—but accepting it as a "true fiction." Although Johnson was a curious reader all through his life, he also struggled against such noncritical absorption in a book. As James Boswell said, Johnson had a great deal of the *incredulus odi* (disbelieving, I despise it); he was disgusted by mere fictions once his absorption in them ceased, but he kept returning to them. Boswell was surprised to learn from Bishop Percy that the Great Cham of literature late in life read such childish romances as *Felixmarte of Hircania, Don Bellianis of Greece,* and *Il Palmerino d'Inghilterra.* Moreover, most of the books that he called his favorites are works of fiction. Telling Mrs. Thrale a story about being made to read a manuscript play and not getting past the dramatis personae, Johnson said, "Alas, Madam! . . . how few books are there of which one ever can possibly arrive at the last page! Was there ever yet any thing written by mere man that was wished longer by its readers, excepting Don Quixote, Robinson Crusoe, and the Pilgrim's Progress?"[10] Johnson's attraction and resistance to curious reading was certainly one of the most productive antagonisms in his life of reading, a notion I explore in chapter 6.

Almost as early as he began to read and hear romances, Johnson began to study. Study is a kind of reading he did with male teachers, and primarily in Latin and Greek. The best story about the origin of Johnson's life as a student (or hard) reader is that he discovered Petrarch while searching the upper shelves of his father's bookshop for an apple. The real story is that he went to school. Like other grammar school students, he began studying Latin, and he learned the habit of close, critical reading, which he applied to classical texts and sacred writings but which was available for application to all kinds of other works. It is mostly as a hard reader that Johnson is known, but he did a great deal of his hard reading in a relatively short period of his life, from the age of about fourteen to twenty-one, from the time he began thinking he would lead a life of Latin scholarship to the time when he began to realize that financial and other personal circumstances would not allow it. Johnson continued to study all his life, but never with the same intensity and devotion that he had cultivated in his teens. He studied more towards the end of his life, when he no longer had to write for a living, than in his prime working years. He wrote late in life, "I can apply better to books than I could in some more vigorous parts of my life, at least than I *did*."[11] But by then most aspects of Johnson's life, including his life of reading, had become more diverse and more flexible than they were in his youth.

One of the reasons Johnson did not apply himself to hard reading in his prime working years is that he was simply too busy writing to read anything that did not contribute to production: an eye for immediate use invariably diminishes the purity and intensity of study. Another reason he studied less in his prime is social. An important and partially defining aspect of every kind of reading is that one joins an implicit community of other readers. In the early years, study united Johnson with a community of relatively elevated people, such as those he met at Pedmore on visits to his well-to-do cousins. With his talent for study, however, Johnson sought more-exclusive, more-learned, and more-imaginary communities of fellow readers as he progressed. Even at Oxford he tried to distinguish himself by his learning from his local and even his distant friends; he imagined himself as part of a European community of neo-Latin poets, only a few of whom were among the living. He longed to join an elite world peopled by great scholar-poets such as Angelo Poliziano and Joseph Scaliger. But Johnson did not want to be known as a "grind." He offhandedly quoted Macrobius to his astonished tutor, but he resisted being seen studying. Johnson's friend Edmund Hector reported that when

the young man was in Birmingham working for Thomas Warren, "he would sometimes steal an hour and read but had a
vanity in concealing that he ever studied. It was all to be from
his own mind."[12] Early in his life Johnson tried to cultivate a
kind of *sprezzatura* and elitism that forbade the appearance of
drudgery. Later, when the years of higher aspirations and hardest reading were past, he could court the image of the "harmless
drudge," as he styles himself in the *Dictionary*, without danger.

If Johnson was anxious about being seen studying, he certainly did not want to be seen engaged in curious reading. In
his private accounts with himself and in his advice to others
Johnson constantly urged study, just as he generally derided
romance and other absorbing reading material. Bennet Langton, a close intellectual friend of Johnson's to the end of his life,
told Boswell that Johnson "used to quote with great warmth,
the saying of Aristotle recorded by Diogenes Laertius: that
there was the same difference between one learned and un-
learned, as between the living and the dead."[13] Johnson wrote
to his servant and young charge, Francis Barber, "You can never
be wise unless you love reading," and he advised his goddaughter Queeney Thrale to read when alone, warning her that "they
who do not read can have nothing to think, and little to say."[14]
But Johnson did not mean to encourage just any reading. He
may have had study primarily in mind, but he certainly meant
to exclude the reading of romances and other extreme kinds of
curious reading. When he encountered a "lady's closet" full of
romances and fairy tales in a French mansion on his one trip to
the Continent, Johnson "in contempt shewed them to Mr
T[hrale]." According to Hester Thrale, the inhabitants of the
house "would not let us see the upper apartments because they
saw us laughing & handling their Books."[15]

For different reasons at different stages of his life, Johnson
was embarrassed to be seen doing two kinds of reading that
he truly loved: hard reading and curious reading. Moreover,
there is an antagonism between these two that understandably
caused a rift in Johnson's life of reading. One sign of this rift is
that Johnson considered it dissolute to read in bed in the re-

cumbent position that he must have associated with his child-hood reading or listening. One of the only times he speaks of reading in bed, he says he "read like a Turk," which is about as dissolute a state as he could imagine.[16] He declared that Robert Burton's *Anatomy of Melancholy* was the only book that ever got him out of bed early.[17] Presumably, too, it was out of bed that he reread the *Aeneid* late in life, one book a night, as he reported.[18] In her characteristic reading pose, Molly Bloom in bed, eating chocolates and reading Paul de Kock, is at the other end of the spectrum from Samuel Johnson sitting at his desk on Good Friday, reading his Testament in Greek and later marking down in his journal his achievement for the day. But Johnson had an inclination to be like Joyce's pleasure-seeking reader, and he needed some intermediary reading experiences to bridge the gap between his antagonistic inclinations.

Boswell observed Johnson at study on Good Friday, but most of the images of Johnson reading in front of others show him reading in a way that is intense but different from hard reading. I call this kind of reading "perusal." In his *Dictionary* Johnson defined *perusal* as "the act of reading," and he is equally unhelpful in defining *to peruse* as "to read." However, his illustrative quotations suggest the required nuances. The kind of reading described in these passages is careful, attentive, and purposeful. For instance, Johnson quotes the naturalist John Woodward: "As pieces of miniature must be allowed a closer inspection, so this treatise requires application in the *perusal*." Such inspection and application are also called for in the quotation from Bacon that Johnson selected to illustrate the meaning of *to peruse*: "The petitions being thus prepared, do you constantly set apart an hour in a day to *peruse* those petitions." The other quotations support the idea that perusal is suitable for legal and critical examination.

In his life of Isaac Watts, Johnson used the word *peruse* to describe his experience of reading a book that I think is most closely associated with this kind of reading. Of Watts's *Improvement of the Mind,* he said, "Few books have been perused by me with greater pleasure."[19] This work, from which Johnson took many quotations for the *Dictionary*, would be classified today as a self-help book. Both study and perusal are intensive kinds of reading, but perusal is somewhat easier, and it is directed to a definite purpose: to improve oneself in specific ways or to find the answer to a particular problem. Encyclopedias, dictionaries, reference books of all kinds, self-help books like Watts's, religious manuals, and even do-it-yourself books are the characteristic subjects of perusal.

Johnson's most famous reading experience was an act of perusal. He told Boswell that he picked up William Law's *Serious Call to a Devout and Holy Life* expecting to scoff at it, but found himself overmatched and overwhelmed to such a degree that he was ever after devoted to religion. Johnson truly did admire Law. He quoted him from memory (with slight inaccuracies) several times in the first edition of the *Dictionary,* and when he was collecting additional quotations for the second edition, Johnson either reread him or had his amanuenses read him to collect more wisdom for his great book. On the other hand, there is plenty in Law that Johnson did not find agreeable—his insistence, for example, that prayer should begin with singing. This and some other parts of Law Johnson chose to ignore. He read Law for the sake of taking away what was valuable to him and leaving the rest, which is in the nature of perusal. Johnson did not study Law as he studied the Bible or even Vergil, granting to those texts, as he read, a kind of sacredness or at least inviolability.

Perusal, the kind of reading that Johnson did of Law's *Serious Call,* is also the kind of reading described by many eyewitnesses of Johnson's reading habits. The descriptions are not all the same; they evidently cover a range of reading behaviors, but all of these are forms of perusal. Some of the descriptions also make it clear that symptoms of Johnson's nervous disorder (possibly Tourette's syndrome) emerged while he read.[20] According to one account, his head "swung seconds" as he read; more generally, the report goes, he "never thought, recollected, or studied, whether in his closet, on the street, alone, or in company, without putting his huge unwieldy body in the same rolling, awkward posture, in which he was in use, while conning his grammar, or construing his lesson, to sit on the form [bench] at school."[21] Johnson was studying at these moments, but it seems likely that he was also seeking relief from his nervous anxieties (or expelling them).

Frances Burney supplies evidence of the therapeutic value of reading for Johnson. In the midst of one of his fits, Johnson "pulled out of his pocket Grotius *De Veritate Religionis* . . . over which he seesawed at such a violent rate as to excite the curiosity of some people at a distance to come and see what was the matter with him."[22] This manual of simple, fundamental religious tenets, originally written for the use of sailors, provided Johnson with the type of reading experience that offered him the most relief. He could read it quickly and relatively uncritically. It is the kind of reading I think he is probably doing in Sir Joshua Reynolds's famous portrait of him reading—the so-called blinking Sam portrait, of which there are many imitations. In the original and the imitations, Johnson is virtually consuming his reading matter, which he holds folded, half-crushed, before him. The book must be either broken or disbound; it is certainly not his Greek New Testament, and the reading he is doing is not study, although it is highly attentive, engaged, and searching. His posture and intensity suggest that it is not curious reading; he is not lost in a book, but rather, as his Quaker friend Mary Knowles said in one of the most memorable descriptions of Johnson reading, he is "tearing out the heart of it,"[23] and presumably leaving the rest alone.

In his description of Johnson reading, his old friend John Hawkins begins with Joseph Spence's characterization of the Italian bibliophile Antonio Magliabecci:

> "A passion for reading was his ruling passion, and a prodigious memory his great talent: he read every book almost indifferently, as they happened to come into his hands; he read them with surprising quickness, and yet retained not only the sense of what he read, but often, all the words and the very manner of spelling them. . . ." A like propensity to

reading, and an equal celerity in the practice thereof, were observable in Johnson: it was wonderful to see when he took up a book, with what eagerness he perused, and with what haste his eye . . . travelled over it: he has been known to read a volume, and that not a small one, at a sitting.[24]

The comparison is not so unqualified in its flattery as it seems, because Magliabecci was the Dr. Oddity of his nation, an eccentric librarian and antiquarian who was known for his slovenliness and his peculiar personal habits as much as for his prodigious learning. But as the descriptions of both Magliabecci and Johnson suggest, Johnson was an "eye-reader."

Frances Reynolds also noticed Johnson's powers of retention and that "Johnson read with amazing rapidity, glancing his eye from the top to the bottom of the page in an instant."[25] A friend similarly described the American Reverend William Bentley (1759–1819), whose "glancing eye and quick perception enabled him to run with rapidity through a book."[26] Like other great readers of his day, Johnson evidently did not have to sound out the words as he read; he told Bennet Langton, "A man must be a poor beast that should *read* no more in quantity than he could *utter* aloud."[27] Boswell noticed this to his amazement when he once offered to read some papers to Johnson: " 'No, Sir, (said he,) I can read quicker than I can hear.' So he read them to himself."[28] This is true for most of us, but it was evidently unusual in Johnson's, William Bentley's, and Magliabecci's day. Although Isidore of Seville suggests that silent reading was preferred as early as the sixth century, the old-style, subvocal reading habits persisted.[29] But this is only one of the ways of reading that Johnson had available to him. His remarks on the sound of what he read, whether he was discussing Milton's prosody or the correct pronunciation of the Ten Commandments, show that he sounded out his text at times. To their delight, Johnson sometimes read aloud to friends in his "forcible melodious manner"; "his recitation was grand and affecting," but silent perusal, with its searching speed, was mainly what his friends saw Johnson doing over a book.[30]

Perusal was becoming more prominent in Johnson's day, and it was certainly spread by the increasing volume of reading matter. Both Johnson and Goethe shocked their admirers by declaring openly that they did not read books through to the end. The new, speedier, silent kind of reading was inimical in many ways to the old style of study, which was designed for classical languages. It is notoriously difficult to scan a work in Latin or Greek. But the speed of perusal is compatible with curious reading to a degree, and with a fourth kind of reading that emerged in the eighteenth century, largely conditioned by the growth of the periodical press. I call this kind "mere reading," following Johnson's description of the activity in *Idler* 30. Living up to his periodical identity as the Idler, Johnson comments: "One of the amusements of idleness is reading without the fatigue of close attention, and the world therefore swarms with writers whose wish is not to be studied but to be read."[31]

As the tone of the *Idler* suggests, Johnson was easy on consumers of such stuff but harder on those who produced material for mere reading. Such material is mechanically produced, miscellaneously presented, and often unreliable. It fosters a habit of reading that resembles random access, scanning, and browsing of the kind that now seems foremost in screen-oriented reading. The system of text and reader in this kind of reading may have best been described by Italo Calvino's witty version of Descartes: "I read, therefore *it* writes."[32] Mere reading is a background or foil for the more intensive kinds of reading. It is also, even more than perusal, a kind of reading suitably done in public. In fact, much newspaper reading in the eighteenth century took place in coffeehouses, and it was both an extension of and a replacement for coffeehouse chat and gossip. This public, impersonal quality is essential to the experience.

Although it is difficult to know precisely how much of this mere reading Johnson or anyone else did or has done, a little evidence survives. Johnson's own periodical essays show that he read specific newspaper stories; he includes general endorsements of mere reading in his work on the Harleian Library and in his advice to students; and he occasionally censures the material in newspapers with a memory of particulars that shows he read the papers with some attention.

One of the qualities of newspaper reading is negligence, which is fostered in part by the heterogeneous mixture of news and advertisements in the papers. Another quality of the experience is the problem of credibility. More than other kinds of reading, mere reading is a test of credibility, and the reader's credence wavers more in this form of reading than in others. We do not have to believe everything we read in the papers, but we have to feel there is a chance that it is true. Readers of conventional dailies such as the *New York Times* must feel there is a good possibility that what they are reading is true, but they are sophisticated enough to know that opinions are sometimes embedded in news stories, that there are significant omissions, and that sources can be wrong at times. Certain kinds of curious reading, like that encouraged by eighteenth-century travel books, create a similar problem of credence. However, when it is clear that the narrative is fictional, credence ceases to matter in curious reading. It usually does not matter, for other reasons, in study. In perusal credence is extended voluntarily, but in newspaper reading credence wavers, ebbs, and flows. In his public statements about newspapers and about reporting of all kinds, Johnson usually issued warnings about such instability. He was following Lockean precepts, but it was his own experience above all that he described when Johnson said in the preface to his *Plays of William Shakespeare*, "the mind can only repose on the stability of truth."[33]

The scheme of reading I propose here derives primarily from my study of Johnson's life of reading. It provides a way of organizing that large and immensely varied part of his experience. The story of Johnson's life involves a great deal of compromise and accommodation, as well as growth and achievement, but his life of reading is more simply a tale of synthesis and integration. Beginning with a dual and somewhat antagonistic life as a hard reader and a curious reader, Johnson gradually found a middle ground in his reading: he became a more public reader, a peruser, and even a mere reader. Moreover, he got progressively better at reconciling his curious reading habits with his habits of study. The intellectual vehicle that corresponds to Johnson's achievement and, to a degree, expresses it is the notion of the "public" or the "common" reader, whose demand for engagement and entertainment Johnson elevated to a test of time. In his mature criticism, Johnson rewrote the classical dictum that literature should instruct *and* please to read that it should instruct *by* pleasing.[34] This represents an acknowledgment of psychological and social realities, but it also suggests a reconciliation of the secretive, elite student of the classics and the closeted, self-critical curious reader of romances. The grounds of this reconciliation were the relatively public ground of perusal and the truly public sphere of mere reading.

I I I

The pattern that Johnson's life of reading makes in terms of my scheme of reading is one in which the extremes gradually come to mingle in the center. Other lives of reading, almost all of which are less rich than Johnson's, may take place largely within one or two of the four categories, or start in one place and end in another. At almost any time in the history of reading, an individual life of reading might take almost any shape. Almost any kind of reading is possible for some individuals at any time in history, but some are more likely at some times than at others, and some kinds of reading predominate in certain periods. Patterns of likelihood or predominance are a way of representing the cultural history of reading, an elusive subject on which a growing number of scholars in America, England, France, and Germany have been individually and collectively at work over the past twenty years.

The chief model of interpretation to which most of the documentary findings have been applied was developed by Rolf Engelsing, a German historian. In a number of books and, in particular, in his influential article "Die Perioden der Leser- geschicte in der Neuzeit" (The periods or phases of reading in the modern age), Engelsing argues that a shift in the nature of reading took place towards the end of the eighteenth century.[35] Before that time, he maintains, most reading was "intensive," which means that people read a relatively small number of books and that they read them many times over rather than "consuming" them and shelving them or passing them on. The quintessential text of the intensive reading period in the West was the Bible, and Engelsing cites the feats of some Bible readers, including several who read the book fifty times and one who made the complete circuit 134 times, surely leaving little time for reading much else. Engelsing's intensive reading corresponds to both study and perusal in my scheme, although perusal is less intensive than study.

Sometime in the eighteenth century, says Engelsing, reading became increasingly "extensive." Readers read more and different books, and they read in a way that permitted greater consumption of the more widely available printed product. The rise of the novel and the spread of advanced literacy among women and the middle class are parts of the story, but Engelsing gives pride of place in the development of extensive reading to newspapers and other kinds of periodical literature. My categories of mere reading and curious reading correspond to Engelsing's extensive reading.

Providing ever deeper contexts for the reading revolution, Engelsing links newspapers (*Zeitungen*) with the increased availability of clocks and watches. He also links the availability of timepieces with the astronomical findings of the new science. More-local events, such as the Thirty Years' War, play their part too, and reading fits into a larger social and economic framework. Fortunately, it is beyond the scope of the present study to assess the validity of such wide-ranging social connections, but I do not wish to slight Engelsing's work. As his critics fail to point out, Engelsing is certainly not Procrustean in the application of his scheme. For example, he both admits and documents the persistence of intensive reading habits through the nineteenth and twentieth centuries. The critical approach to texts classical and modern is intensive, he says, and he cites instances of modern, multiple, intensive readings, from the *lesemut* (reading frenzy) over Goethe's *Werther,* to the craze for personal letters, to an instance of a German youth who memorized Adam Smith's *Rights of Nations,* to Karl Hillebrand's memorization of *Wilhelm Meister,* to Engelsing's own reading fifteen times a novel called *Altaich* by Ludwig Thomas. Nevertheless, I think the changes in the history of reading perceived by Engelsing might be somewhat better described by the four-part classification I propose.

Using my scheme to describe the history of reading, I follow Engelsing and say that the cultural emphasis in reading has moved historically downward from study and perusal to mere reading and curious reading. But I also think that reading has, especially of late, moved from study and curious reading to perusal and mere reading. This is the movement that Johnson's own exemplary life of reading primarily describes.

Unfortunately, the broader cultural life that Johnson's individual life of reading typifies is less successful than his in its integration of the various kinds of reading. The kind of random access, scanning, and browsing used by Johnson to bridge the opposite ends of study and curious reading in his lifetime seem to be usurping the places of study and truly absorbed reading in ours. In a concluding chapter I examine this movement and suggest that the impression of failure it renders may be false. Even if it is not, however—even if we miss the heights of reading as we occupy ourselves on its plateaus—that we have been led to this pass by a great reader may offer some consolation, and the way he managed the same journey may offer inspiration.

Taken strictly as a reader, Samuel Johnson is more a participant in the history of reading than a shaper of it. However, his life of reading displays nearly all the possible modes and configurations of reading. He dealt successfully with many of the antagonisms and contrarieties that perplex reading today, and he may be regarded as a model reader partly because of his success. Just as it is better to know anything than not to know it, it is better to read anything than not, but we fear that some kinds of reading will drive others out of existence. The fear may be justified with respect to many individuals, but Johnson's life of reading shows that it is not always justified. Few readers have Johnson's scope or intelligence, but we might all appreciate the variety of his activities as a reader and take heart from his capacity to combine them for his own pleasure, improvement, and satisfaction.

NOTES AND MARGINALIA

*R*ecent work by historians and critics on the history of books—or *histoire du livre,* as it is called in the country where it has been most systematically pursued—has given renewed prominence to the longstanding assumption of bibliographers and bibliophiles that the study of the physical life of books makes an important contribution to intellectual history generally and in particular to the history of reading. In his Panizzi lectures of 1985, for example, the brilliant bibliographer D. F. MacKenzie showed how New Criticism's and other formalist schools' assumptions about standard and standardized texts have led to many mistaken readings and a false sense of homogeneity in the experiences of readers over the centuries.[1] In an article published seven years later an equally impressive American bibliographer, Thomas Tanselle, describes the way in which the *histoire du livre* movement has put "rare-book collections . . . in the unaccustomed position of being central to a branch of scholarship that is in fashion."[2] Part of the "fashionable" theory, which is not really new at all, is that readers are influenced by the physical objects on which they practice their art; it follows that the attitudes readers take towards physical books are aspects of their experience, or at least provide important clues to the nature of that experience. Therefore, it is important to see what can be learned from our knowledge of how Johnson handled his books, how he responded to their material aspects, and what he did physically while reading.

As Thomas Tanselle suggests, the notion that kept bibliographers and rare-book collections off the current scene for so long is probably as old as books themselves. An age-old argument pits the true student against the mere book collector, and the suspicion of those who care about the material aspect of books goes back at least as far as Seneca and Lucian. In *De tranquillitate animi,* Seneca ridicules the

> man who collects the works of unknown or discredited authors and sits yawning in the midst of so many thousand books, who gets most of his pleasure from the outsides of volumes and their titles. . . . Consequently it is in the houses of the laziest men that you will see a full collection of orations and history with the boxes piled right up to the ceiling; for by now among cold baths and hot baths a library also is equipped as a necessary ornament of a great house.[3]

A hundred years after Seneca, in the third century A.D., Lucian directed a characteristically fierce invective against "the man who is ignorant and buys many books." The target in this satire is incapable of talking back; he is only allowed to nod his head yes or shake his head no a couple of times. The sin for which he is made to suffer countless abuses is that he confuses owning books with having knowledge:

> On that theory, collect and keep all those manuscripts of Demosthenes that the orator wrote with his own hand, and those of Thucydides that were found to have been copied, likewise by Demosthenes, eight times over, and even all the books that Sulla sent from Athens to Italy [Aristotle's library]. What would you gain by it in the way of learning, even if you should put them under your pillow and sleep on them or should glue them together and walk about dressed in them? . . . If possessing books made their owner learned, they would indeed be a possession of great price, and only rich men like you would have them, since you could buy them at auction, as it were, outbidding us poor men. In that case, however, who could rival the dealers and booksellers for learning, who possess and sell so many books? But if you

care to look into the matter, you will see that they are not much superior to you in that point; they are barbarous of speech and obtuse in mind like you.[4]

Both Lucian and Seneca contribute in these passages to a tradition of which Johnson was certainly aware and with which he had great sympathy.[5] His awareness of this tradition is part of the reason he absolutely could not bring himself to take over the family bookselling business, although his mother could certainly have used his help after the death of his father and brother in the early 1730s, and Johnson himself needed a way to make a living. However, our sense of Johnson's sympathy with the age-old derision of book collecting may be exaggerated by the celebrity of the anecdotes supporting it, by the desire of Johnson's early biographers, especially Boswell, to see Johnson as exceedingly serious and nonmaterialistic in his intellectual life, and by the aspects of Johnson's roughness with books that were a result of his physical and neurological problems rather than of his attitude to books.

Boswell provided one of the most famous glimpses of Johnson among his books when he reported, "On Wednesday, April 3, [1776] in the morning I found him very busy putting his books in order, and as they were generally very old ones, clouds of dust were flying around him. He had on a pair of large gloves, such as hedgers use. His present appearance put me in mind of my uncle, Dr. Boswell's description of him, 'A robust genius, born to grapple with whole libraries.' "[6] According to Boswell's notebook, his uncle had made Johnson "herculean" rather than "robust," and the biographer's version further emphasizes Johnson's merely physical, rather than supernaturally physical, treatment of the merely physical books. A *hedge,* according to Johnson's *Dictionary,* is "a fence made round grounds with prickly bushes," and a *hedger* is one who constructs such a fence, but "hedge, prefixed to any word, notes something mean, vile, of the lowest class, perhaps from a *hedge,* or *hedge-born* man, a man without any known place of birth." Hedgers' gloves were evidently meant to protect the hands from thorny branches, but they are implicitly mean things, intended for a low kind of employment; it is a sign almost of distaste for the physical aspect of books that Johnson would wear such gloves to reorganize his library. These workers' gloves are the opposite of the tight-fitting, formalwear white gloves required of readers using some rare-book collections, and they suggest an opposing attitude towards the book. Books handled with hedgers' gloves are low objects that get their value from the skill with which they are employed. Rural Ireland had its hedge-schools and Johnson was a hedge-bibliophile, or so Boswell's account might lead us to believe. The adulatory biographer was eager to make Johnson an "eye-reader" for much the same reason: by describing his reading as nonphysical (above both vocalization and other physical sensations), he implied that it was interior and intellectual in the highest degree.

David Garrick found a similar rudeness in Johnson's handling of books, although he was less inclined to attribute it to anything admirable in Johnson. The Shakespearean actor and book collector was so appalled by Johnson's way with books that he jeopardized his longstanding friendship with his grammar school teacher and fellow townsperson by refusing to ship Johnson some of his rare quartos and folios for his work on the edition of Shakespeare. Boswell suggests that Garrick opened his library to Johnson, rather than sending him the books, and that, moreover, he had good reason to be worried: "Considering the slovenly and careless manner in which books were treated by Johnson, it could not be expected that scarce and valuable editions should have been lent to him."[7] Frances Burney reported that Garrick had in his repertoire a little performance in which he imitated Johnson first stamping insanely at an invisible spot on the floor (to identify him for the audience, I presume) and then calling out "David!—Will you lend me your Petrarca?" Garrick meekly complied in the skit and then narrated the ensuing events:

> The book—stupendously bound—I sent to him that very evening. But scarcely had he taken the noble quarto in his

hands, when, as Boswell tells me, he poured forth a Greek ejaculation and a couplet or two from Horace; and then, in one of those fits of enthusiasm which always seem to require that he should spread his arms aloft in the air, he suddenly pounces my poor Petrarca over his head upon the floor! And then, standing for several minutes lost in abstraction, he forgot, probably, that he had ever seen it.[8]

Garrick's story sounds too entertaining to be true, but there is corroborating evidence of a sort in a note from George Steevens, Johnson's collaborator on his revised, variorum edition of the works of Shakespeare, to Isaac Reed. Steevens reveals to his friend his unscrupulous plan to improve his first folio of Shakespeare, which Johnson had marred, by buying another marred one from a Mr. Edwards of Pall Mall: "As soon as I have been cheated in my bargain (as I certainly shall be) I must think myself at liberty to cheat someone else in the purchase of my rejected volume. My plan nevertheless is, to retain, if possible, my own copy, exchanging only such leaves in it as had been blotted, greased, or scribbled on, by Dr. Johnson."[9]

Johnson both acknowledges and excuses his roughness with books in a letter accompanying a gift of a morocco-bound copy of Demosthenes to Mrs. Thrale, saying it was "too fine for a Scholar's talons."[10] The implication is that scholars, like Johnson, follow in the tradition of Lucian and cannot be bothered about the outsides of books as they pursue their research into the solid matters of learning. Booksellers even now call shabby books in their catalogues "working copies."

As he well knew, Johnson did not have to go back as far as Lucian to vindicate his roughness with books and his carelessness, if that is what it was, about their physical condition. Recommendations about a serious attention to the meaning rather than the surfaces of reading are given in Isaac Watts's works in the field of education in the early eighteenth century. Watts urged students, for example, to mark up their books so that they could review the important parts at any time, and not to worry about marring the objects, because true students are not book collectors. Johnson declared his admiration for Watts in *Lives of the Poets,* and he transmitted Watts's advice on reading in his *Dictionary,* in letters, and in conversation with young friends. But whether he quotes Watts or not, much of what Johnson says about books agrees with Watts's perpetual emphasis on the matter of books over the mere form.

This is an extension of a preference for the matter of books over the language or the style, which is prominent in Johnson's life of reading. For example, he said he "loved . . . the old Black Letter books; they were rich in matter, though their style was inelegant."[11] He said he could not read the Presbyterian John Macpherson's *Dissertation on Scottish Antiquity* because "you might read for half an hour, and ask yourself what you had been reading: there were so many words to so little matter, that there was no getting through the book."[12] Johnson had the same criticism of Carte's *History of the Life of James Duke of Ormonde*: "The matter is diffused in too many words; there is no animation, no compression, no vigour."[13] These remarks suggest that Johnson required his reading periodically to provide a semantic payoff, and that if it were too long delayed, he literally could not keep going. He could not read for style or language alone, even though he was a lexicographer and one of the most acute observers of style in the history of literary criticism.

The demand for matter and meaning in Johnson's approach to reading can be traced back at least as far as Plutarch, the historian of the first century A.D. Plutarch, whose native tongue was Greek, says he learned the Latin language from the meaning of the Latin works he read, rather than the other way around.[14] He expects his readers to doubt him on this point and calls it amazing but true. Often, especially as Boswell describes him and as he describes himself in his critical essays, Johnson was a Plutarch or a Watts in his reading, but this was not always the case.

Johnson liked reading some books for their style and—even more incriminating—he liked some of the truly superficial aspects of books, including paper, ink, and binding, as well as backs, title pages, and colophons. These attractions led to some famous instances in which Johnson was revealed as someone other than Watts's ideal reader. In *On the Improvement of the Human Mind* Watts says, "There is many a young student that is fond of enlarging his knowledge of books, and he contents himself with the Notice he has of their Title page, which is the attainment of a bookseller rather than a scholar."[15] In this respect especially, Johnson was, at times, just the sort of reader Watts discouraged. Boswell reported on a visit he and Johnson made to a gentleman in 1775: "No sooner had we made our bow to Mr. Cambridge, in his library, than Johnson ran eagerly to one side of the room, intent on poring over the backs of books. Sir Joshua [Reynolds] observed, (aside,) 'He runs to the books, as I do to the pictures: but I have the advantage. I can see much more of the pictures than he can of the books.'" Mr. Cambridge was evidently aware of the kind of criticism that Lucian or Watts might direct towards such an activity:

> "Dr. Johnson, I am going, with your pardon, to accuse myself, for I have the same custom which I perceive you have. But it seems odd that one should have such a desire to look at the backs of books." Johnson, ever ready for contest, instantly started from his reverie, wheeled about and answered, "Sir, the reason is very plain. Knowledge is of two kinds. We know a subject ourselves, or we know where we can find information upon it. When we enquire into any subject, the first thing we have to do is to know what books have treated of it. This leads us to look at catalogues, and at the backs of books in libraries."

Johnson extricated himself neatly from the accusation here, prompting Boswell's description of his argumentation in terms of dueling: "No formal preparation, no flourishing with his sword; he is through your body in an instant."[16]

Although Boswell's is the most famous of them, there are other stories about Johnson and the backs of books. Charles Burney describes how Johnson "was shewn into my book-room, and instantly pored over the lettering of each volume within his reach." His daughter Frances concurs in her report: "He pored over them, shelf by shelf, almost brushing them with his eye-lashes from near examination." Like most of those that have been recorded, this tale reflects well on Johnson's seriousness as a reader because in the end he hits on something he wants (a volume of the French *Encyclopédie*): "He took it down, and, standing aloof from the company, which he seemed clean and clear to forget, he began, . . . very composedly, to read to himself; and as intently as if he had been alone in his own study. We were all excessively provoked: for we were languishing, fretting, expiring to hear him talk."[17] As in those cases when he took reading matter with him to the dining table of his hosts, wrapped up in the tablecloth or on his lap, reading was on this occasion a defense against talking.[18] The book served him as a kind of party mask, and he took advantage of its physical qualities as well as of its intellectual stimulation.

The attention Johnson paid to such superficial elements of books as their backs and their bindings was not always for the intellectual reason that these would help him organize the field of knowledge, nor even for the social reason that they could excuse him from speaking. Sometimes his interests were unredeemably material. When he wrote to the bookseller Thomas Cadell, saying "I was bred a Bookseller, and have not forgotten my trade," Johnson was not simply being chummy with a colleague; he was complaining about the bindings that Cadell had put on some pieces that Johnson wished to give as presents. The letter begins, "The Duty of Man [by Richard Allestree] is not the right [binding]. Nelson [*Companion for the Festivals and Fasts of the Church of England*] is bound in Sheepskin, a thing I never saw before."[19] When he catalogued the great Harleian Library with William Oldys from about 1742 to 1745, Johnson made a good many notes about binding and a remarkable number about ink, along with his descriptions of authors and works. In addition, he seems to have inserted a short essay on vellum into the catalogue as a preface to a group of works printed on tanned skin rather than on paper. It is true that the little essay focuses on the weightier subject of the economics of book production, but it also reveals some concerns of the bibliographer and the bibliophile.[20]

It is clear that Johnson noticed the physical aspects of books and cared about them. He bound several books himself, although only one seems to be extant; he told several people of his ability to bind and apparently took pride in the accomplishment.[21] Further evidence of Johnson's sensitivity to the physical aspect of books may be found in his curious observation that an acquaintance had shown "a want of concern about veracity," not merely "inattention," as Boswell courteously said, when he claimed to have seen folios of Johnson's collected conversations in Boswell's possession. Boswell's collections were quarto and octavo sized, and it is possible that these were what had been seen. Even though the man who claimed he saw them was probably the dull-witted Paris banker Charles Selwyn, Johnson says that "he does not know that he saw any volumes. If he had seen them he could have remembered their size."[22] The physical appearance of a book was for Johnson a part of its existence, one that he could not ignore, even if his main interest was in texts and meanings and even if he was incapable of handling the physical objects adroitly. Buffeting his books, perpetually failing to keep them in order, fumbling and thumbing them, Johnson was nevertheless an appreciator of their superficial aesthetic qualities.

Johnson's attention to the superficial qualities of books turns up more frequently in letters and conversations with old friends than in his published works or, apparently, in his conversations with young and impressionable friends such as Boswell. Johnson's love of books was not a part of his teachings; it belonged rather to a less public life of conversation with his peers. It was therefore part of his private life of reading, whereas the focus on meaning was more dominant in his life as a critic and public interpreter of literature. In one of his personal letters Johnson calls Brian Walton's *Biblia sacra polyglotta* (1657) "undoubtedly the greatest performance of English typography, perhaps of all typography"; he proudly mentions his copy (which he bequeathed to Bennet Langton); and he approves of the acquisition of a large-paper edition for the royal collection.[23] In a much earlier letter Johnson gave advice to the king's librarian, F. A. Barnard, as he was about to depart on a book-buying mission to the Continent. Johnson's focus is mainly on intellectual history, or book history, but he converts it to the uses of the bibliophile, and he also talks about the desirability of "splendid" editions: "Of those books which have been often published and diver[si]fied by various modes of impression, a royal Library should have at least the most curious [i.e., elegant, finished] Edition, the most splendid, and the most useful. The most curious Edition is commonly the first and the most useful may be expected among the last. . . . The most splendid the eye will discover."[24] Here the eye is not so much an intellectual substitute for the voice as it is an organ of aesthetic appreciation in reading; this is a use of the eye that Boswell generally denied to Johnson and that Johnson himself tended to ignore in his published works. But it was part of his life as an "eye-reader."

The particular way in which Boswell wished to portray Johnson's attitude to books is revealed in a juxtaposition of the letter to Barnard with Boswell's account of a short discussion on book collecting that he had with Johnson on 19 May 1784:

> When I mentioned that I had seen in the King's library sixty-three editions of my favourite Thomas à Kempis, amongst which it was in eight languages, Latin, German, French, Italian, Spanish, English, Arabick, and Armenian, he said, he thought it unnecessary to collect many editions of a book, which were all the same, except as to paper and print; he would have the original, and all the translations, and all the editions which had any variations in the text.

This suggests the attitude of the scholar over that of the mere collector. However, Boswell goes on to note that Johnson approved of a very large collection of editions of Horace by one Douglas, which undoubtedly included some "unnecessary" editions.[25]

Moreover, Boswell's account contradicts the spirit and the

telling detail of Johnson's advice to the man who did much of the collecting for the king's library. In his letter to Barnard, Johnson reveals both the knowledge and the attitude of a bibliophile. Although he regards the history of printing rightly as an important part of intellectual history, he also shows that he has been curious in more purely antiquarian matters, such as printers' devices: "One hint more may deserve to be added," he tells the departing Barnard,

> though it is not likely that you will have an opportunity of turning it to profit. It is recorded by those that have with the greatest diligence examined the first essays of typography, and particularly by Naudaeus the Librarian of Cardinal Mazarine, that the stamp or insigne by which Fust marked his editions were Horns, and I have read an advertisement of a Book offered to Sale in Holland that was so stamped. For these horns I have looked to no purpose in the books printed by Fust which are commonly known.

Finally, in the same letter, Johnson provides a rare glimpse of himself in the auction room where, remarkably, he is concerned about at least one aspect of the condition of books: "In the purchase of old books let me recommend to you to examine with great caution whether they are perfect. In the first editions the loss of a leaf is not easily observed. You remember how near we both were to purchasing a mutilated Missal at a high price."[26] This might be seen as a concern for the matter of the book, but the missing leaf was not necessarily one bearing text, and besides, the text of a missal could always be supplied from a similar book. Johnson was worried about the physical condition of the work he almost bought either for himself or for the library of George III.

Despite this splendid letter from one book collector to another, in many respects Johnson did maintain the severe, Lucian-like attitude towards books, the attitude that Boswell emphasizes. Johnson's view of the physical aspects of books was not usually that of a connoisseur or collector. His own library had few examples of fine binding. On the other hand, not only was Johnson sensitive to such matters as binding, paper, and ink, he valued them. For example, when he gave books as presents, he often gave finely bound copies (which also shows that he had more of them than the 1785 catalogue of his library indicates). One of the few other fine morocco-bound books in his collection, for example, became a present for a gentleman named John Paradise, just as the Demosthenes had for Mrs. Thrale, and the books Johnson bequeathed to William Windham of Felbrigg Hall are fine volumes (though later owners further enhanced some of them with truly lavish bindings).[27] Johnson may have felt that fine books belonged in the hands of gentlemen and ladies (rather than in his own), but he easily recognized the qualities that made books fine. Although some of his own fine books arrived as gifts, Johnson may have acquired others himself: he enjoyed superior things, even some gaudy things—the red suit he wore to the performance of *Irene* and the extravagantly expensive gold watch he had inscribed with the biblical reminder of death and judgment νὺξ γὰρ ἔρχεται (night cometh), which ended up in the hands of the Shakespearean collector George Steevens, for example.[28] For all the Lacedaemonian strictness he could urge on some occasions, Johnson also loved pleasure and sought luxury—occasionally even luxury in books.

If Johnson feared the lashes of Lucian and Seneca for his book collecting, he could take refuge in an equally venerable tradition of book loving. In adolescence he undoubtedly found in the works of Catullus, Propertius, and especially Martial a sensibility, opposed to Lucian's, that treated the various parts of books with affection and invested the physical material of reading with a kind of tenderness. In scores of his epigrams Martial brings the technical terms of "book" production into the language of poetry. Of course the "books" or *biblia* he speaks of are usually rolls of papyrus, and sometimes the inferior rolls or piles (not bound into codices) of parchment or vellum. The pumice stone with which the ends are smoothed, the core or *umbilicus* of the roll with its ornamented ends or *cornua*, the flourish or *coronis* at the end, and the regal purple wrapper are all part of the reading experience that Martial envisioned for his books. Like his eighteenth-century poetic progeny, he dreaded the possibility that his books would become wrappers for fish or victims of the sponge or eraser. Clearly, the physical book was inseparable for Martial from the intellectual production; he expressed his hopes for it, for example, at the beginning of his third book of epigrams:

> For whom, my little book, would you become a present? Haste to get to yourself a protector, lest, hurried off to a sooty kitchen, you wrap tunny-fry in your sodden papyrus, or be a cornet for incense or pepper. Fly you to Faustinus' bosom? You are wise. Now may you strut abroad anointed with cedar-oil, and, spruce with the twin deckings of your brow, wax insolent with painted bosses, and a delicate purple clothe you, and your title proudly blush with scarlet.[29]

Elsewhere Martial fretted about the condition to which his books would be reduced after they had been rubbed by greasy chins, which might be employed in the process of rewinding the roll. The fresh, white "page" was preferred to the rubbed and ragged one, and the soft bosom of an appreciative reader was much better than the rough or rapid hands of one who would cause the book to be unrolled (*explicatum*) without reading it at all.

Martial's language is partly metaphorical, of course. The physical book stands for the intellectual experience, but it is a true symbol in the sense that it cannot be separated from what it signifies. Perhaps most concisely representative of this attitude towards books are the epigrams that Martial evidently wrote as gift cards or epigraphs for presentation copies. For example, on *The Battle of the Frogs and Mice,* attributed to Homer, Martial wrote: "Read through the story of the frogs sung in Homer's lay, and learn to smooth your brow by means of my trifles."[30] Indicating the capacity of tanned skins to hold in small print books that would occupy many rolls of papyrus, Martial declares of the works of Vergil, "How short a parchment has comprised the mighty Maro! The features of the man himself the first leaf bears."[31] These epigraphs seem to enact and enliven the metaphor in which we call a book by the name of its author. Martial often makes the book speak as an object that contains the author, and occasionally his verses seem to offer the reader an introduction to the genius within. Perhaps the best of these is the one Martial wrote for Cicero on parchment: "If this parchment shall be your travelling companion, imagine you are taking a long journey with Cicero."[32] Johnson could easily have thought of this epigram as he stuffed his pockets with books, as he always did when traveling.

The same conflation of the material book with the immaterial substance or spirit it contains appears in one of the first books entirely devoted to the love of books, Richard de Bury's *Philobiblion*. Written in the early fourteenth century, in the age of manuscripts, this work nevertheless became a favorite of print-age collectors and contains a great part of the credo of both earlier and later book lovers. It is important to the historical context of Johnson's attitude towards books because it fleshes out the view intimated in Martial and opposed in the satire of Lucian and Seneca. Richard de Bury also has his books speak, and several times they complain about the treatment they have received: "No healing drug is bound around our cruel wounds, which are so atrociously inflicted upon the innocent, and there is none to put a plaster upon our ulcers; but ragged and shivering we are flung away into dark corners, or in tears take our place with holy Job upon his dunghill, or—too horrible to relate—are buried in the depths of common sewers."[33] Assaults in the Grub Street wars of the Restoration and the eighteenth century often involved hurling an adversary's books into the jakes or shops where, in Dryden's phrase, they might become "Martyrs of Pies, and Reliques of the Bum."[34] Such derision was aimed at authors rather than at books, but it rested on a well-established tradition of connecting the two that was still alive for Johnson. When, for example, he received a book on loan from George Steevens, Johnson wrote, "I thank you for Neander, but wish he were not so fine. I will take care of him."[35] Johnson was evidently as good as his word in this case because the book, gilt edges and morocco binding intact, made its way back to Steevens's library, where it remained until his death.

I I

Johnson was probably speaking somewhat loosely to Steevens and perhaps adopting the language of collectors when he thanked him for Neander. Partly because he spoke and wrote differently in different circles of his acquaintance, it is difficult to assess the precise extent of Johnson's love of books or his related conflation of the physical work with the immaterial experience. Moreover, it would be unlike Johnson to have a single, unvarying position on any important matter. However, there is some hard evidence of how Johnson handled books; this is supplied by the many books once owned by him that have survived. One of the best writers on the history of books, Robert Darnton, suggests that Johnson's books, many of which are in the Hyde Collection at Four Oaks Farm, New Jersey, are in fact battered.[36] This fits Darnton's view that Johnson is an example of the kind of reader that Rolf Engelsing found arising in the eighteenth century, the first period of "extensive" reading. In this new kind of reading, radically different from the "intensive," studious reading that was predominant in earlier times, books were consumed rather than revered. There is plenty of evidence that Johnson participated in what Engelsing calls the reading revolution, or *leserevolt*. However, having looked at many of Johnson's books from Four Oaks Farm and elsewhere, I find they are not in very poor shape. The volumes are far from lavish, but John Hawkins seems excessive in describing Johnson's "own collection" of books as "a copious but miserably ragged one."[37]

One can tell by examining these books and the catalogue of the sale of Johnson's library the year after his death that his was not a precious collection, not a gentleman's collection, like Horace Walpole's at Strawberry Hill, and quite unlike the lady's library he laughed at in Paris with its dummy books and its volumes of fairy tales.[38] Yet most of the evidence does not

support the notion that Johnson's books were in terrible condition. It is true that some of the thirteen extant books that
Johnson marked up when he was searching for illustrative quotations for the *Dictionary* are fairly battered, but they must have
been handled by several people and kept open for copying, and
even they are not destroyed. The two-volume Bible that Johnson had bound in seven volumes for easier study (now in the
Hyde Collection) is in fairly good shape, despite extensive
marking. In fact, most of Johnson's extant books are in decent
shape, but it is generally the weightier, more serious tomes that
have been preserved. Johnson studied such volumes, but he did
not devour them; the particular kind of reading Johnson practiced on a book may be reflected in the condition of the relic,
but this does not tell us everything about his various ways of
reading.

When Johnson studied, he treated his books more respectfully, and such treatment is part of what defines the kind of
reading I call "study" or "hard reading." As pictures of Johnson
show, he could tear at a book physically as well as intellectually,
but he also practiced a more reverential, more studious, old-
world habit of reading in which he honored the physical object
as best he could. His tearing and bending belonged to the
newer age of extensive reading and in particular to the kinds of
reading I call "perusal," "mere reading," and "curious reading."
The books that survive are a small portion of those that passed
through Johnson's hands, and they are, by and large, books of
the heavier, better-bound, more important sort that he used for
study rather than for newer kinds of reading.

There are some survivors among Johnson's more frivolous
books, including, probably, his copies of the romances *The
Famous History of the Seven Champions of Christendom* and *The
Adventures of Gil Blas* and John Newbery's instructive collection
of travel accounts, *The World Displayed*.[39] These books are also
in decent condition, but then they are the sparse survivors of
what was a long file, if not a whole army, of popular books that
passed through Johnson's hands. The famous pictures of John-

son reading suggest that he may have destroyed many of these more ephemeral works, but such a conclusion would be rash: Johnson may have given many of his less important books casually to others during his life, and the executors of his estate, who were instructed to sell the books, may have given them to charity or to Francis Barber, who was named as a beneficiary of the sale.

Johnson was more careful with his more important books: he was interested in them as physical objects and (perhaps) as ritual tokens. He ceremoniously distributed some of them just before his death, and in a codicil to his will he named certain friends as recipients of some volumes and gave to others the privilege of a selecting a book of their choice.[40] Johnson cared about the disposition of his books—at least on second thought—and his donation of them to friends bespeaks the same feeling that led him to link friends and books in the note to Dr. Brocklesby in which he agreed to return to London to die: "There are my friends, there are my books to which I have not yet bidden farewell." In saying this, as in thanking Steevens for Neander, Johnson may not have been entering fully into the spirit of Richard de Bury's *Philobiblion,* but the metaphor he used was not dead for him, at least when it came to certain kinds of books.

It is especially striking that Johnson should have intimated even this much animistic fondness for the materials of reading because he had practically none of it for the material aspects of writing. One of the reasons that Johnson did not write down the verses of *The Vanity of Human Wishes* as he composed them is that he was somewhat uncomfortable with pen and paper. When his neurological and psychological problems were bothering him, his capacity to write was impaired, although his capacity to read, which he found soothing, was not. Lying in bed in Birmingham in 1731, when his neurological and emotional problems were at their worst, Johnson dictated to the publisher Thomas Warren much of his translation of *A Voyage to Abyssinia.* But throughout his life, even when he was well, Johnson took every opportunity to dictate his compositions. He dictated many of the vast number of works he wrote for others, beginning with the homework assignments he did for schoolmates in Lichfield, who would repay him by carrying him to school. He dictated sermons and dedications for friends, periodical essays that he wrote for them and contributed to their publications, and large pieces of the second Vinerian Law lectures, which he composed with and for his good friend Robert Chambers.[41] It may not prove much, but it is striking that a friend visiting Johnson in Temple Lane around 1760 and intending to post a note from that sanctified place found the great author without paper and ink.

The point should not be stretched too far; holograph manuscripts of many of his letters and some of his works testify to Johnson's capacity to deal with pen and paper, but there is also enough evidence to suggest a reluctance, what one friend called a "laziness," about writing. Johnson's handwriting varies immensely from the neat and legible to the sloppy and illegible. The breadth of his strokes has been taken as a sign of his weak eyesight, and perhaps this made him somewhat reluctant to write. But there may be a little more to it. The absence of pen and paper from his apartment suggests that they did not have the fetishistic attraction for him that such implements have for some writers. He evidently did not always have them with him on his Hebridean journey (although he stuffed his pockets with books), because he says he found them lacking on Skye. He kept his journal, and he wrote long letters to Mrs. Thrale, but there was little of fond ritual connected with writing for Johnson. To the extent that he had them at all, Johnson reserved such feelings for reading, and perhaps mainly for one kind of reading—study or hard reading—that, being reverent, was somewhat removed from the business of writing. Books such as Steevens's Shakespeare or the so-called copy-texts for the *Dictionary* that became part of Johnson's equipment for writing passed thereby out of the reverent realm of study and into the more practical sphere of perusal, where Johnson felt free and even obliged to mark them up and handle them as roughly as any other tools of the trade.

III

Overall, the record of Johnson's extant books shows a mixed attitude towards the physical objects—an unintegrated combination of Lucian's satire and Martial's reverence. This mixture of attitudes imprinted in the record of his extant books may reveal something about the contour of Johnson's life of reading, but the record is incomplete. A better-documented, similar, but more extreme mixture of the same view of books occurred in the reading life of John Locke. Although Johnson's feelings about books have deeper roots, it is possible that he inherited them, as he inherited so much of his intellectual life, directly from Locke.

A couple of generations before Johnson, Locke wrote the following condemnation of books as objects to his friend Anthony Collins:

> Your packet . . . I received and have reason to thank you for all the particulars in it. However you thought fit to prepare me for being disappointed in the bindings of my Greek Testament, there is nothing in it that offends me but the running of his paring knife too deep into the margin, a knavish and intolerable fault in all our English bookbinders. Books seem to me to be pestilent things, and infect all that trade in them, i.e. all but one sort of men, with something very perverse and brutal. Printers, binders, sellers and others that make a trade and gain out of them have universally so odd a turn and corruption of mind that they have a way of dealing peculiar to themselves, and not conformed to the good of society, and that general fairness that cements mankind. Whether it be that those instruments of truth and knowledge will not bear being subjected to any thing but those noble ends, without revenging themselves on those who meddle with them to any other purpose, and prostitute them to mean and misbecoming designs, I will

not enquire. The matter of fact I think you will find true, and there we will leave it to those who sully themselves with printers' ink till they wholly expunge all the candour that nature gives and become the worst sort of black cattle.[42]

As the editors of Locke's library catalogue point out, however, this may be "a confession of disappointed love" written by "one so enslaved to the bibliophile's passion that nothing in the everyday world of bookmaking and book preserving could be anything but unsatisfactory."[43] A substantial portion of Locke's library remains intact. It was given to the Bodleian Library by Paul Mellon, and Locke's notations have made it possible for the librarians to assemble the books in a room in much the same way Locke kept them during his life. The evidence suggests that Locke was nearly reverential about his books. He catalogued them carefully with very discreet marks that signified his ownership as well as their placement in the library. He wrote his own catalogue very neatly in an interleaved copy of a contemporary Bodleian Library catalogue, which provided him with an alphabetical framework and descriptions of many of his books. He added further notes in a code that has not yet been entirely deciphered. He kept careful accounts of books lent and given, and in his will Locke carefully disposed of his library. His reverence for books, however, did not keep Locke from believing the tirade against the materialistic world of book production that he unleashed in his letter to Collins. In his ambivalence about books, as in many other ways, Johnson was like Locke, but he was also more various, more changeable, and less extreme.

One sign of Locke's reverence for his books is that he rarely wrote anything in the margins, although he perpetually studied and read intensively. (The rare exceptions are his copious notes in several volumes of the New Testament, which he used in preparation for his *Paraphrase and Notes on the Epistles of St. Paul.*) Locke carried to an extreme the dictum of Richard de Bury that "the handling of books is specially to be forbidden to those shameless youths, who as soon as they have learned to

form the shapes of letters, straightway, if they have the opportunity, become unhappy commentators, and wherever they
find an extra margin about the text, furnish it with monstrous
alphabets, or if any other frivolity strikes their fancy, at once
their pen begins to write it."[44] Never approaching such defile-
ment, Locke filled notebooks and commonplace books with
carefully organized comments and excerpts, and on occasion he
had books bound with interleaved pages on which he wrote
copious notes in response to the text. Johnson had his own
Dictionary interleaved when he was preparing his revision of it
for the fourth edition of 1773, and he had some Bibles rebound
for easier study, but generally he took his books as he found
them and left them that way.

Not many of Johnson's notebooks survive; his marginalia are
few; and it is safe to conclude that Johnson was less organized
than Locke both in arranging his books and in cataloguing
his responses to them. Although in studious moods Johnson
planned commonplace books according to Locke's directions
and may have made entries in them, he kept his responses to
books, and even his extracts from them, in his memory to a
greater degree than Locke (and to a greater degree than many
readers of his time). He surprised his friends and acquaintances
by openly admitting that he did not read books through and
that he liked to look at their backs or titles. He may have
shocked them mildly by other forms of apparent disrespect—
reading only every other line of James Thomson's *Seasons* aloud
to his Scottish amanuensis, for example, and announcing that
he had read only the cut pages of a travel book he recommended to his table at a tavern. In giving advice on reading,
Johnson's emphasis is always on fostering attention, and it is
consistent with his editorial credo that notes may be necessary,
but they are necessary evils. His educational advice is always
to let students pursue their interests in reading, even to the
point of letting them begin books in the middle or read them
backwards.[45]

At times Johnson used and attempted to instill conventional
study habits, but he felt that the most important aspect of

reading was curiosity, which alone can lead to continued, un-
forced effort. This feeling had a deep intellectual background,
but it played into the so-called reading revolution that was
taking place in Johnson's time. This was a movement downward from study and perusal towards the mere reading of newspapers and journals and the curious reading of novels. Notes
suggest study, and some kinds of marginalia are incident to perusal, but mere reading and curious reading are defined partly
by their being unaccompanied by note taking of any kind.
However, Johnson's varied life of reading tends to show that the
old, studious habits of reading and newer, more desultory approaches are not incompatible, even if they differ and even if
they are antagonistic competitors for reading time and reading
markets.

Despite his laziness about writing and despite his tendency
to slide from study into rapid, traceless, curious reading, Johnson did make interesting marks in a few of his books. Some of
these rare jottings provide insight into what the act of reading
occasionally was like for him, but most of Johnson's marks
in books are uninteresting. With the exception of the books in
which he underlined words and bracketed passages for use in
the *Dictionary,* most of Johnson's marked books are ones he
acquired and probably read early in life when he was being
studious. Unlike most books that he obtained later in life, some
of his early acquisitions have signatures and accession dates.
His copy of Pliny's letters, for example, bears an inscription
commemorating the day of acquisition: "March 30 1726 ac-
cedit." Johnson was sixteen, and in another act of somewhat
self-conscious recording, he signed his name and wrote his date
of birth on the endleaf.[46] The other notes in this volume are
negligible, however, and there is not much to go on if we want
to reconstruct Johnson's teenage reading of Pliny. Perhaps, like
Locke at this stage of his reading life, Johnson transferred extracts to notebooks now lost.

In some of Johnson's other books there are squiggles next to
passages that Johnson evidently found worthy of note. In a
copy of Milton's *Paradise Regained,* with his essay on education

(London, 1725), there is a squiggle beside the famous remark that "the end of learning is to repair the Ruins of our first parents." There is another such mark beside the sentence "I call therefore a compleat and generous Education that which fits a man to perform justly, skilfully and magnanimously, all the offices both private and publick of Peace and War."[47] These are passages that eventually made their way into the *Dictionary*, but it is not clear that Johnson was calling on his earlier reading when he entered them in his great book. There are numerous *x*s next to important passages in Johnson's copy of the academic exercises of Famianus Strada, a Roman Jesuit who wrote elaborate parodies of several classical poets. Johnson noted Strada's astute remarks on Latin style as part of his preparation for writing neo-Latin poetry while he was at Pembroke College, where the book remains.

There are similarly emphatic underlinings in a copy of Philipp Melanchthon's letters that Johnson acquired in 1735.[48] It is impossible to be sure that Johnson made the marks in Melanchthon, Milton, or Strada because there were other owners of the books, and such marks are common. It is foolish to make more of the squiggles than the evidence warrants, but one more example is irresistible. A copy of the letters of Paolo Sarpi once in the Harleian Library has underlining and squiggling in places that suggest Johnson may have owned the book. (The presence in Johnson's library of many books also listed in the Harleian Library catalogue suggests that he was paid, at least partly, in books for that bibliographical job.) One passage picked out with lines and an "N.B." is "No man ought to write in his own time, and think to have the Praise and thanks of it too." Is this the source of the question Johnson poses with some melancholy towards the end of his preface to the *Dictionary*— "whether I shall add any thing by my own writings to the reputation of *English* literature, must be left to time"—or any of the other remarks he makes in the preface to his edition of Shakespeare and in *Lives of the Poets* about the importance of time in literary reputations? Perhaps, but it is hard to be sure if the few squiggles and marks in Johnson's relics tell us anything more about his reading than that, by and large, he did not, in his own words, "break the current of narration or the chain of reason" by writing in his books.

The paucity of marginalia in Johnson's books suggests that he tended towards kinds of reading less austere than study, but it does not prove it. There is, in fact, some evidence to the contrary. For example, Johnson did have notebooks in which he outlined *Ramblers*. Both Hawkins and Boswell saw these books and preserved bits of them. Johnson's rough draft of *Irene* reads in places like a chain of quotations; perhaps these came from lost notebooks, but even if they did not, the draft itself provides evidence that Johnson could and did read, at times, with the object of extracting and storing up elements of what he was reading for recombination. That is studious reading, but the more it is done with practical application in mind the more it belongs to the category of reading that I have identified as perusal.

There is more evidence of perusal in Johnson's books than of hard reading and true study. The most extensive evidence of Johnson's perusal is in the thirteen extant books that bear the marks he made when he was seeking illustrative quotations for the *Dictionary*. The particular power of reading shown in these marks is Johnson's ability to pull out key passages that sum up the gist of a writer's work. Sometimes Johnson extends this power of reading by editing the chosen passages down to statements more manageable and more pointed than the originals. I have said a great deal about this in *Johnson's Dictionary and the Language of Learning*,[49] so I will add just a little more here.

In the Sneyd-Gimbel copy of Johnson's *Dictionary*, an interleaved set of three volumes that Johnson wrote in and pasted up as a copy-text for the revised edition of 1773, there is a fine example of Johnson pointing and abridging Locke. Under the word *cementer* there is pasted a slip of paper with the following quotation from Locke, copied by an amanuensis: "God having designed man for a sociable creature, made him not only with an inclination to have fellowship with those of his own kind, but furnish'd him with language which was to be the great cementer of society." Coming to this passage, and looking for opportunities to reduce the size of his work, Johnson drew a line through all the words from "made" to "but." This excision makes Locke grant more to the role of language in human society than he really did, and Johnson may have enjoyed the boost he implicitly gave to his own profession. Johnson was thinking of editorial cuts like this when he worried in the preface to his *Dictionary* that he had often made the "philosopher desert his system" for lexicographical purposes. Locke may not "desert his system" here, but the effect of Johnson's penciling is to channel the passage into a single topic, a topic particularly germane to a dictionary. This is a practical, rather than purely philosophical, way to read Locke, and it is evidence of a certain frame of mind in reading, or a kind of reading, which I call perusal. True study, such as Johnson applied to his Greek Testament on Good Friday, would not seek to reduce a text; it might expand it, but it would not have an eye to application so much as to comprehension and, in the extreme heights of study, especially with sacred texts, memorization.

Under the verb forms *to do* and *to read* in his *Dictionary* Johnson printed an exhortation from his scantily marked copy of Bryan Duppa's *Holy Rules and Helps to Devotion Both in Prayer and Practice* that recommends a more serious kind of reading than he was doing at the time: "Go on to the reading of some part of the New-Testament, not carelessly or in haste, as if you had a mind to have done, but so attentively, as to be able to give some account of what you have read, or to single at least some one passage or more out of it, to be laid up in your memory, and to be made use of in the practice of an holy life."[50] This kind of reading is one degree less than pure study, but it is clearly different from and "higher" than the way in which Johnson was reading when he abridged Locke. Duppa urges readers to single things out, whereas Johnson was cutting and pasting. Johnson did not recommend this kind of reading, but in doing it so well (both in his *Dictionary* and in his many other works that use extracts) he implicitly authorized it for future generations of readers. In fact, Johnson defended the reader's

right to extract and abridge books in the thirty-one "Considerations" he wrote in order to help prepare a legal brief in defense
of Edward Cave. Joseph Trapp was planning to sue Cave for
unauthorized abridged publication of parts of his sermons in
the *Gentleman's Magazine.* Johnson's memo, which was not
published until 1787, acknowledges the author's right to his
literary property, but it is also a kind of bill of rights for readers,
supporting their freedom to handle books in any way that is
beneficial to them and others, including abridgment. Books, he
consistently asserts, are produced for the propagation of knowledge, and therefore primarily for the benefit of readers rather
than for that of publishers or writers.[51]

A few of the extant books that Johnson perused for illustrative quotations to fill his *Dictionary* reveal that he could on
some occasions be more personal and less practical in his life of
reading. In his copy of Duppa's *Holy Rules and Helps,* for example, Johnson wrote a couple of exhortations or confessions concerning his own level of attention in reading. He confesses on
page 134, "Non possum legere" (I am unable to read), and
elsewhere he says, "Preces quidam videtur diligenter tractasse;
spero non inauditus" (These prayers seem to be diligently performed; I hope I have not been inattentive). If he made them as
he was reading for the *Dictionary,* such notes suggest that Johnson fell out of the practical frame of mind that guided his
perusal for quotations and began thinking more seriously about
his own spiritual rather than authorial life. In other words, he
shifted his mode of reading from one that was largely public
and concerned with publication to one that was more personal
and inward looking.

Perhaps the most personal marks Johnson ever entered in a
margin appear next to the following passage in John Norris's
Collection of Miscellanies, another book that Johnson mined for
quotations: "It is supposed by the Ancient Fathers, that the
Sufferings which our Blessed Saviour underwent in his body
were more Afflictive to him than the same would have been to
another man, upon the account of the excellency and quickness
of his sense of Feeling."[52] In the margin Johnson wrote "my

brother." There is no telling when Johnson made this note because we do not know when he acquired and began reading Norris. It was at least ten years after his brother's death in 1737 that Johnson marked up Norris for use in the *Dictionary*. Nathaniel had been involved in some shameful business venture, probably involving bad debts of both a personal and a financial nature, and he was contemplating the terrible prospect of emigration to America when he died. Suicide was suspected but never proved. Evidence in Johnson's letters and in Nathaniel's suggest that the two did not get along and that Nathaniel was noisy and jovial in contrast to the more saturnine and studious Johnson. It looks as if Johnson wrote "my brother" as an example of "another man," one of ordinary feeling.

This highly unusual notation might be a gloss Johnson made to help him understand the text, but his choice of Nathaniel suggests that he was, at least for the moment, engaged in a less studious kind of reading. Did Johnson think his brother had endured some kind of persecution before death, like Christ? Did he then palliate his grief or guilt, and at the same time vent his continuing hostility, by assuring himself that Nathaniel could not have felt much in his suffering? These are questions that cannot be answered with any confidence, but it seems clear that in the course of reading Johnson could melt into contemplation of his inner life of unresolved feelings or memories. I am inclined to place this piece of marginalia (as well as those in his Duppa) early in Johnson's life of reading, perhaps while Nathaniel was still alive and the competition between the brothers was still vital and adolescent. Yet a notebook entry written at about the time of his mother's death in 1759 shows that Johnson continued to think about his brother, at least at times when family matters pressed him: "The dream of my Brother I shall remember."[53] Johnson definitely read Norris while preparing the *Dictionary* in the late 1740s, years after his brother's death, and he may at that time have slipped into a personal frame of mind that resulted in the unusual notation.

There seems to be a similar personal note in the copy of Matthew Hale's *Primitive Origination of Mankind* that Johnson marked up for use in his *Dictionary*. As part of his discussion of human perception Hale speaks of our awareness of our own active powers: "We feel our selves to understand in our Head, and that we will, and resolve, and love, and hate, and pity in our Heart, almost as plainly as we find our selves see with our Eyes, or hear with our Ears: I feel the propensions and inclinations of my Mind as really as I feel my Body to be cold or warm."[54] A place near the word "Heart" is marked with an *x*, and in the left-hand margin, on the same line with "Heart," there is another *x* and the words "Ego nihil" (I am nothing). Johnson may have marked the last clause of the passage for inclusion in the *Dictionary*; his procedure is not completely true to form, but he bracketed the clause and underlined "propensions." His regular procedure was to put the first letter of the marked word in the margin and to use vertical lines instead of hooked lines for brackets. What most distinguishes his procedure here from his usual one, however, is that Johnson commented on the bracketed passage in the margin. He wrote "tale Sentio" (such things I feel—in other words, "I agree with this"). Whatever "Ego nihil" means, it seems clear that Johnson was reading differently when he jotted this down than he was when he was searching for illustrative quotations. If he made the comments during the same reading, around 1747, when he was looking for quotations, he may have forsaken his task for the moment as emotion or recognition welled up inside him.

The passage in Hale, like the one Johnson marked in Norris, is about feeling or sensibility, and Johnson overflowed with sensibility. Hale's philosophical treatise is not particularly evocative, but Johnson's emotions were often close to the surface, and while he was reading they could evidently come forth and even issue in "a flood of tears." Given the great scarcity of his marginalia, it seems reasonable to assume that Johnson's emotions rose on many other occasions of reading when he noted nothing down. What kind of reading is this? It seems most appropriate for a personal letter, when there is an assumption that the text is meant for the reader alone and written by someone who knows the reader's heart. But crying over books or movies (even in crowded theaters) is not uncommon. As at weddings, it seems to involve a concourse of the public, cere- monial moment with some reference to oneself. Such reading can occur at certain moments of study or perusal when atten- tion to the task lapses or is unnecessary, and a consciousness of a reference to oneself and one's own life suddenly breaches the formality of the text. One of the recorded instances of Johnson crying over a text was, according to Hester Thrale, when he "would try to repeat the celebrated [traditional hymn] *Prosa Ecclesiastica pro Mortuis,* as it is called, beginning *Dies irae, Dies illa,* he could never pass the stanza ending thus *Tantus labor non sit cassus* [So great an effort should not be for nought] without bursting into a flood of tears."[55] In this case, "reading" was mere ceremony (an extreme form of study), and Johnson's mind was free to turn on its most melancholy preoccupations. This is what I conjecture occurred also in his reading of Hale, where his attention may have wandered through fatigue during the collecting of quotations (or for some other reason).

I could be wrong, and the apparent effusion in Johnson's copy of Hale might express something more rational and argu- mentative than I imagine; Johnson's reading at this point might be a more practical, less emotional kind of perusal. Johnson may be, in this instance, a student reader not altogether dif- ferent from the undergraduate who feels compelled to argue bluntly in indelible ballpoint ink with the authors of library books. There is one place in the copy of Hale where Johnson clearly does argue with the text, or at least qualify it by writing a sharper recapitulation in the margin. There are also some cryp- tic characters in the margin that look like *M*s, which may stand for *monitum* (be advised), the eighteenth-century equivalent of the modern student's checkmark. But the Latin comment seems different from these to me and evidence, although not proof, that the vicissitudes of his reading experience included occasional descents into personal, melancholic reflection.

Johnson argued with his books in their margins on occasion but not often, and less and less often as he grew older. A manu- script of the *Chancellor's Court of the University of Oxford,* copied from Johnson's own, perhaps crumbling, undergraduate copy, includes notes that Johnson may have made early on and that were preserved by an amanuensis. One of them comments on the text in obviously argumentative terms: "This I own is a Distinction I don't comprehend."[56] It is easy to imagine the angry young man of Pembroke College, as Donald Greene styled Johnson, folding back his copy of the university statutes and making this remark. As an older reader Johnson would not have bothered to comment, nor would he have been so exercised by the rules.

Even in Johnson's studentlike marginalia, however, added scraps of information are more common than arguments. He did not argue with his books so often as he improved them. His copy of William Camden's *Remains concerning Britaine,* for example, identifies George Buchanan, a favorite of Johnson's, as the author of certain verses, some of which are attributed by Camden to Queen Mary of Scotland.[57] In his copy of Inocui Sales's *Collection of New Epigrams,* Johnson identifies "P." as Parker in the following epigram:

> Milton and Marvel joyn'd, 'gainst [P.] did thunder
> But poor Jack Marvel was alone no wonder.

In another he supplies "John Dryden" for "J. D.":

> Wou'dst skill, what th'ast good or bad? T' J. D. go.
> All men judge: But he, how to judge does know.[58]

Johnson provides fuller information in a few other marginal notes. In his copy of Sir Thomas Browne's *Pseudodoxia Epidemica,* for example, he filled in the titles of three of Martial's epigrams, referred to only as "famous" by Browne.[59] In his copy of Camden's *Remains concerning Britaine* he provides cross-references to John Freind's *History of Physic* (a book he knew from his work on Robert James's *Medicinal Dictionary*); to Henry Peacham's *Compleat Gentleman;* and to *Menagiana* (the sayings of Gilles Ménage, edited by Antoine Galland), an example of perhaps his favorite kind of book, a collection of short, pithy remarks and anecdotes.[60] Elsewhere, in the most

elaborate attempt to correct an error in all his extant marginalia, Johnson comments on some commendatory verses pur-
ported to have been written by Ambrose Waters to John Heydon, author of *The Rosie Crucian Infallible Axiomata* (1660):
"These Latin verses were written to Hobbes by Bathurst, upon
his Treatise on Human Nature, and have no relation to the
book.—an odd fraud."[61] There is more than information here;
"an odd fraud" sounds like an aside, and this suggests that
Johnson's reading had become, for the moment, less studious,
more conversational, and somewhat more personal.

Improving one of his books without musing on it, Johnson
changed a comma in an epitaph he found in Camden. But the
adjustment here may be aesthetic; his change makes a difference in the tone of the epitaph, which reads:

> Quae pia, quae prudens, quae provida, pulchra fuisti,
> Uxor in aeternum, chara Maria, vale.
>
> (You were pious, prudent, and beautiful,
> Ever my wife, dear Maria, farewell.)

Johnson took the comma after "aeternum" and placed it after
"chara," so the line says "Ever my dear wife, Maria, farewell."
Johnson may have remembered this epitaph and turned his
reading to more personal uses when he wrote some courtly,
witty lines to his charming Whiggish friend, Molly Aston:

> Liber ut esse velim, suasisti, pulchra Maria:
> Ut maneam liber, pulchra Maria, vale.[62]
>
> (You have persuaded me to be free, lovely Maria:
> So that I may remain free, lovely Maria, farewell.)

Combining the reading of this passage with its rewriting suggests that Johnson was in this instance also having a conversation in the act of reading. This sort of reading resembles what
he did when reviewing Latin manuscripts for friends. In those
cases too he was likely at first to concentrate exclusively on
technical details, if he could get himself to read the unpub-
lished work at all. There is a fine example of this in Johnson's

comments on a Latin elegy written by the young Jeremy Bentham in the early 1760s, when Bentham was a teenage student at Queen's College, Oxford. Almost every remark concerns improprieties in the Latin, as judged by the absence of a classical precedent for the spelling or the declension. But at the end Johnson eases up and becomes conversational: "When these errors are removed, the copy will, I believe, be received, for it is a very pretty performance by a young man."[63]

A few other pieces of marginalia can be adduced to provide evidence of Johnson's style of conversation in reading. In 1735, for example, in the year of his marriage to Elizabeth Jarvis Porter, a widow twenty years his senior, Johnson read the letters of Philipp Melanchthon, one of the learned Protestant humanists he most admired. There are, as usual, very few marks in the book. Johnson made an interesting reconstruction of Melanchthon's aphoristic remark "patiendum esse ubi opus est" by underlining it and writing "patientes ubi opus est" at the foot of the page. He changed the meaning from "where it is hard that one must be patient" to "where being patient is hard." The change is largely technical, but it is telling that Johnson singled out this remark in light of his own struggles with patience, which were great enough that he was forced in college to write an essay on the theme *festina lente* (make haste slowly).

In the year of his marriage Johnson wrote a little comment on a letter from Melanchthon to a friend who was about to marry. His note, in Latin, states only that Melanchthon's correspondent appears to be a priest.[64] Obviously this was surprising to Johnson, but since he notes so little in his books, why this? He had studied the growth of Protestant reform in the sixteenth century, but it seems likely that his own impending or recent marriage sensitized him to literature on that subject. Here his consciousness of his own personal circumstances crossed over into his studious reading.

Johnson was suddenly moved to put pencil to paper as he read his Melanchthon and stumbled on a subject of immediate personal interest, but to whom were Johnson's notes written? To himself or to someone else? They were surely not written to

Melanchthon. Johnson did not enter into the kind of heated debates that Swift started in his reading of Thomas Burnet, for example. Swift not only argued with Burnet's statements but also felt compelled to fill his margins with such ejaculations as "A damnable lie," "partial dog," "Dog, Dog, Dog," and the blanket condemnation "All coffee-house chat."[65] Johnson behaved differently; his notation in Melanchthon registers personal surprise about a public matter and makes a public note of something that touched him personally. He was, as it were, on the fringes of a conversation, not entirely engaged in it, but not simply on the outside, analyzing, extracting, and epitomizing in a professional way. Johnson could be highly personal or highly professional in his reading, but he could also be in between. In fact, I suspect that is where he was much of the time. The informal but not private condition of reading was part of Johnson's contribution to the construction of literature in the modern world. Johnson took such a position himself and helped make it possible for others. This achievement is less explicit than it is implicit in his literary criticism: it is attributable less to his concept of the "common reader" than to the distinction he perpetually makes between himself—his own sensibility as a reader—and any critical construct.

As part of the movement that Jürgen Habermas calls the "structural transformation of the public sphere," Johnson's life of reading was later than that of Swift. In reading as he did and commenting aloud, as it were, Swift was clearly participating in the "public sphere of private persons," which Habermas and his followers describe as a political development of the republic of letters. The coffeehouses of London provided a venue for the new forum, but in reading and arguing with widely available, printed books one could participate without walking out. Habermas correctly perceives that in the world of print, as it is described in greater historical detail by Elizabeth Eisenstein,[66] readers were conscious of joining an extended community of people absorbing the same information or reacting to the same poetry in other places in their own country, and to a degree, throughout Europe, at roughly the same time. This community of readers, like the community of coffeehouse politicians (and overlapping with it), gave rise to a public sphere different from the court—and a more democratic one, even radically so, in Michael Warner's view.[67]

The problem is that almost as soon as it is formed, the public sphere begins to break up into a variety of public spheres, and the reader who might have spoken up in the assembly of citizens finds that he is addressing only his friends or even talking to himself, like Coleridge addressing his pocketbooks. Johnson accepts the isolation and privacy of other readers, but he elevates their privacy to a kind of universality in his "common reader," while maintaining a separateness for himself (which any other individual reader may claim for himself or herself). Johnson says, in effect, we are not all speaking to each other in this coffeehouse of the *respublica literarum,* but there is a common response that we all understand despite our individual differences. Swift stands up in the assembly of readers to speak his piece; Johnson usually stays at home, but he hears the voice of the people, and he positions himself in relation to it.

In my survey of Johnson's marginalia I have only two more instances to offer in which Johnson is speaking to an audience in his response to books. One comes from the last years of Johnson's life. In his copy of Francis Blackburne's *Remarks on Johnson's Life of Milton,* Johnson wrote a few notes in which he tried to clear up the record of his involvement with William Lauder, the Scottish Jacobite who claimed that Milton had plagiarized *Paradise Lost* and supported his claim by forging Milton's putative sources. Johnson had, in fact, furthered Lauder's efforts for a while, before the forgery was discovered. Johnson wrote in his copy of Blackburne, "In the business of Lauder I was deceived, partly by thinking the man too frantick to be fraudulent."[68] This is a public statement; it tries to set the record straight. However, it is also personal, both in the nature of its explanation and in that it represents Johnson's feeling that he needed to explain himself. The remark does not seem to be addressed to Blackburne or even to the public, although a broad public is Johnson's audience in much of his writing. The message is there to be seen, however; it is more than silence and less than rhetoric. It is perhaps a statement meant to be overheard, like the comment "an odd fraud" that he muttered, as it were, after correcting the attribution of the commendatory verses in his copy of Heydon on the Rosicrucians.

The last instance of Johnson's marginalia that I offer as characteristic of his quietly vocal performance as a reader is unfortunately lost and can only be inferred from a letter he wrote to his "Sweet Angel," Hill Boothby, the woman he considered as a possible second wife before complications in her private life interfered. On 31 December 1755 Johnson wrote:

> My Sweet Angel,
>
> I have read your book, I am afraid you will think without any great improvement, whether you can read my notes I know not. You ought not to be offended, I am perhaps as sincere as the writer. In all things that terminate here I shall be much guided by your influence, and should take or leave by your direction, but I cannot receive my religion from any human hand. . . .
>
> I beg you to return the book when you have looked into it. I should not have written what is in the margin, had I not had it from you, or had I not intended to show it you.[69]

In this case Johnson was reading and responding to his reading in marginalia with a strictly limited intended audience, but with an audience nevertheless. He wants the book back because he does not want his reading to be public, but he would not have written anything at all if he had not had an audience in mind. Johnson was not entering the public sphere in his reading of this devotional book, whatever it was, nor was he being entirely private. This in-between state, I think, is a model for the kind of modern reading that emerged after the short-lived utopia of Habermas's public sphere of private individuals.

Johnson's close friend Hester Thrale, a generation younger than he, filled her margins with remarks meant to be overheard—personal, yet intended for the public record. She kept journals of her life and her reading, as Johnson directed, but she could not help also writing in her books: "I have a Trick of writing in the Margins of my books," she noted, "it is not a good Trick, but one longs to say something & cannot stop to take out the Thraliana [her notebooks]."[70] The most famous of Thrale's marginalia are those in her copies of Boswell's *Life of Johnson*; they set the record straight for the public, yet they are personal. Johnson could evidently resist "saying something" while reading more easily than Thrale, but he could not always resist. He was perhaps as slow to write in his books as he was slow to speak in public. When he did speak in public, however, he tended to do so with great volubility and even with astonishing grammatical completeness and rhetorical periodicity. The marginal remark was not Johnson's métier, as it was of some romantic writers, such as Coleridge. Notebooks would seem to suit him better, and the record of those, although slender, must be examined. However, neither marginalia nor notes suited Johnson. As a private reader in the public sphere, he either hung back, for the most part, or became fully public by writing and publishing himself. For this reason Johnson's writing provides the fullest, although not the clearest, record of his reading.

In his writing Johnson often acted as a professional reader, almost like a secretary in the days when patronage rather than publication supported literary men. Sir Gabriel Harvey in the sixteenth century acted as a reader for the noblemen of action and power whom he served; Johnson acted as a reader for the public. Lisa Jardine and Anthony Grafton have carefully studied Harvey's annotations in his Livy, which he was reading in order to pass its wisdom on to the earl of Leicester and his associates. Harvey described himself as a "facilitator" in doing this work, and Johnson sometimes acted in a similar capacity for the reading public by editing, abridging, translating, collecting, and redacting literary materials in his *Dictionary,* in his book reviews, in essays, and even in his more original literary works.

There was another tendency even in such a thoroughly professional reader as Harvey, however, a tendency Grafton and Jardine call "modern," and Johnson exhibits this to a much greater extent than Harvey did. Grafton and Jardine find Harvey's modern mode of reading epitomized in an ironic note to himself that he jotted in his Livy amidst all his professional notations: "This vulgar bad habit of writing often makes readers dilatory and usually makes actors cowardly. The followers of Socrates were wiser: they preferred teachings that were unwritten, spoken, preserved by memorization. 'Take your hand from the picture,' runs the old saying. 'Take the pen from your hand,' so runs my saying now."[71] The example of Socrates makes labeling this remark "modern" problematic, but no matter what it implies about Socrates, Jardine and Grafton's notion about the modernity of Harvey is attractive, and I think Johnson's attitude towards reading tends to confirm and extend it.

Johnson wrote what sounds like an exposition of Harvey's remark when he ridiculed

> the practice of many readers, to note in the margin of their books, the most important passages, the strongest arguments, or the brightest sentiments. Thus they load their minds with superfluous attention, repress the vehemence of curiosity by useless deliberation, and by frequent interruption break the current of narration or the chain of reason, and at last close the volume, and forget the passages and the marks together.[72]

Unimpeded, attentive, and (if possible) vehement reading is the kind that Johnson usually recommends, and the sparseness of his marginalia suggest that it was the kind in which he most often engaged himself. It is modern reading because it calls for greater immersion in the text and a more personal relationship with the text than participating simultaneously in the public sphere permits.

No kind of reading (and no kind of communication) is ever completely replaced by another, and the more private sort of reading had not for Johnson, and has not yet for us, fully replaced the older kind of reading Harvey did for his employers. The older, professional aspect of reading persists in the way all readers from Harvey's time to our own have conceptualized and performed their task. Readers always read partly for others, or at least for themselves in their alternate roles as actors in the world. Johnson, often read for the purpose of transmitting information and advice to others. Even today, readers feel, on occasion, a kind of public role as they read: some cannot restrain themselves from passing on what they read, even if the person to whom they pass it is trying to read another book; readers of library books often feel compelled to pass their condemnation or approval of a passage on to the next reader in writing; more subtly, there is a certain mode of reading most people and all academics assume from time to time that compels them to note their reading so diligently that it becomes difficult to keep reading. Moreover, the modern—more private and personal—kind of reading has probably been possible from the beginning: Paolo and Francesca in the *Divine Comedy* misreading their way to hell is the most famous early example, but a recent commentary situates the eroticization of reading at the beginning of literacy.[73]

The history of reading is a story of changing emphases rather than origins. Johnson's sparse marginalia show that he emphasized personal kinds of reading, although he maintained his own affinities with older, more studious, and more public styles of reading. Johnson's innovations can be considered forms of perusal, but, whether he meant them to or not, his liberated modes of reading tended to promote the more casual and less intense "mere reading" that has become increasingly prevalent in the two centuries since Johnson's death. Johnson's life of reading shows, however, that the forms of reading now most prominent are not incompatible with study of the most intense and serious sort, or with any other kind of reading.

IV

For readers like Locke, who want to keep records of their reading but do not wish to mark up their precious books, the notebook or commonplace book is the best recourse. Johnson did not use notebooks to anything like the extent that Locke did, but he believed in and recommended Locke's directions for reading and for compiling commonplace books that would organize and preserve what one read. Both Boswell and Johnson's earlier biographer, Sir John Hawkins, saw notebooks and commonplace books on which Johnson had evidently drawn when composing periodical essays: one of them ran to six volumes in folio and contained an ambitious outline of prospective learning. Both Boswell and Hawkins quoted bits of these "adversaria" in their biographies of Johnson, but their short excerpts are all that now remains of them. There also existed at one time a "pocket book," dated on the first leaf "14 April 1752," which contained an index to a commonplace book. Such an index must have been of the kind that Locke recommended: a list of the letters of the alphabet with subentries for each of the letters that might follow the first letter in forming words—Latin or English—that could be topics, such as "riches," "beauty," "truth," and so on. Johnson's *Dictionary* provides a full understanding of what these topics would have been, if Johnson had been diligent enough to transfer his reading to a Lockean commonplace book. Another blank book from approximately the same period, now also lost, contained, according to Sotheby's, a "Scheme of Johnson's Works and the marks he used in the margin of his books."[74] There are so few marks in Johnson's books that this auction catalogue description strains credibility. Other notebooks have been cited by booksellers or friends of Johnson, but there is no solid evidence that Johnson actually kept notebooks of his reading, even though he obviously intended to do so and recommended on many occasions that others do so.

The characteristic Johnsonian commonplace book may be the apparatus he attached to a 1743 edition of the Book of Common Prayer now in the Hyde Collection. Johnson numbered the pages and lettered the verses for easy reference. In his notebook of "Designs," which contained his projected works, Johnson listed a "Dictionary of the Book of Common Prayer."[75] Perhaps this was the edition on which Johnson planned to construct his new reference work. He took the trouble to appropriate or tip in some blank pages at the back of the book for "observations," but he wrote nothing on the blank pages, and he never produced this particular dictionary. The only substantial piece of writing in the book is a prayer written on page 31 after the collect: "Grant, we beseech thee, merciful Lord, to thy faithful people pardon and peace, that they may be cleansed from all their sins, and serve thee with a quiet mind, through Jesus Christ our Lord. Amen." Then there is the cryptic mark "MM 54." It seems to me that what happens in this book is that the private life of reading vies with the effort to bring the book further into the public sphere, as a reference work. In his reading of this work Johnson again ends up between public and private. The rather conventional prayer is a fit representation of that middle state. The cryptic mark is probably a cross-reference and shows that Johnson was hanging on to his public, professional approach to the book as he was responding to it personally.

Johnson's empty commonplace books may also be further proof that he was lazy about writing. Johnson's hesitation about putting pen to paper while he read and even while he composed his writings was related to his memory. He probably found both that he did not have to write things down to remember them and that by relying on his memory he improved it. Johnson had many reference books in his collection, but he wrote most of his works without doing much careful research and without taking notes. He did not have a habit of research. He preferred to retrieve things from memory or from conversation. When writing *Lives of the Poets,* Johnson sent Mrs. Thrale to the British Library, but he himself spoke with old Ben Victor, a Grub Street insider with lots of stories to tell. He sometimes requested information in letters, but he was happier to acquire it casually, even though his standards of credulity were high. *Lives of the Poets* provides the most extended example, but in the *Rambler* and the *Dictionary* there are also many inaccurately remembered phrases. Johnson's memory was just faulty enough to show that he was using it rather than reference works, and it was accurate enough to show how extraordinarily large and faithful it was. Earlier in life Johnson was somewhat more reliant on "research techniques"; he appears to have used memory aids either of a written or nonwritten, oratorical sort. If Johnson was not drawing on notebooks and commonplace books in the draft manuscript of *Irene,* for example, he was using a mind organized as such books were supposed to be. (As I will show when I discuss Johnson's "study" or "hard reading," he used his mental or written collections of Claudian and Martial to compose certain passages of *Irene* just as if they had been written down.) Later, he eschewed this practice—out of laziness, perhaps, but perhaps also because he had integrated his studious and his conversational habits both of reading and of writing.

Whether Johnson used written or merely remembered collections, he was ambivalent about all kinds of notes on reading and became more opposed to them as he grew into middle age. His feeling that readers who took notes would "repress the vehemence of curiosity by useless deliberation" unites him with a reactionary approach to reading that Swift expressed but did not always adopt. Although Swift compiled commonplace books himself, he satirized writers who used them as intellectually barren and mechanical: "What tho' his *Head* be empty," he says in *A Tale of a Tub,* "provided his *Common-place-Book* be full."[76] Performing literary operations by means of notes and even reacting by means of notes probably also struck Johnson as mechanical, although his problems in assembling the *Dictionary* led him to use prototypes of the 3-by-5 card and thus to blaze a trail for the mechanical operation of the scholar.

Like that of Swift, Johnson's own practice sometimes was inconsistent with his views on literary reception and production. Unlike Swift, however, Johnson also preached a view apparently at odds with his derision of note taking: "Every man," he says, "should keep minutes of whatever he reads. . . . Such an account would much illustrate the history of his mind."[77] It sounds as if Johnson is here recommending precisely what he detracted in the *Idler* when he talked about breaking "the current of narration or the chain of reason." But there is a difference. The purpose of the notes that Johnson recommends is personal rather than professional. These notes serve the cause of self-knowledge and spiritual or psychological improvement. Accordingly, most of Johnson's records of his reading provide less an intellectual than a spiritual and emotional history of his mind.

Johnson's "minutes" are accounts of how much he read or how much he could read if he kept up at a certain pace for a certain amount of time. Especially early in his reading life, but to a degree throughout it, Johnson kept private accounts of his reading or reading plans. These records look on the page almost exactly like the financial accounts that he also sometimes entered. The two may have been closely related for him, as they were for Samuel Pepys and many other diarists.[78] For example, on 21 November 1729, about a month before completing his thirteen-month stay at Pembroke College, Johnson entered the accompanying chart in his diary.

Die	Hebdom:	Mense	Anno
10	60	240	2880
30	180	720	8640
50	300	1200	14400
60	360	1440	17280
150	900	3600	
300	1800	7200	
400	2400	9600	
600	3600	14400[79]	

Johnson also noted in Latin that a week (*Hebdomadis*) equaled six days, a month (*mensis*) four weeks, and a year (*annum*) twelve months. His chart calculates how many verses he could read in weeks, months, and years, if he read ten, twenty, or six hundred verses a day. Obviously this is meant to be hortatory, and it suggests a view of reading in which the activity is indistinguishable from other quantifiable activities, such as miles walked, or charitable donations made. There was a sense in which Johnson looked on reading as indistinct from these other activities, although it was one that he was more interested in recording than his mileage because he believed it had more to do with his particular life's work and his salvation. His often-quoted prayers on beginning a new study, on beginning the second volume of the *Dictionary*, or on the *Rambler* show how much he conflated his work as a reader and writer with his work of salvation. When it is looked at in this way, reading is barely intellectual; it is just one of the many kinds of work a person might do to earn salvation. Many of Johnson's notes about his reading strip the activity of intellectual meaning in order to give it religious significance. This is characteristic of a movement in the history of reading most explicit in Wesleyan tracts, but widespread and deeply rooted. In this movement, reading is a form of activity like sewing (and is often done along with sewing), one that keeps idle hands from doing the devil's work and occupies the mind with the harmless, easy activity of making sense out of black marks on the page. This may be a form of study, but the easiness of the activity gives its practitioners an aptitude for pursuing more promiscuous, curious reading.

Other records of Johnson's reading found in his diaries tend to be only a bit more specific than his raw numerical accounts. In July 1773, for example, a month before setting out for Scotland, he entered the following account in Latin in his diary: "I began reading the Pentateuch—I finished reading [Scaliger's] Conf[utio] Fab[ulae] Burdonum.—I read the first act of [Euripides'] Troades.—I read [Samuel] Clarke's last dissertation on the Pentateuch—two of Clarke's Sermons.—I read the battle with the Bebryces in Apollonius.—I read a hundred lines of Homer."[80] This and the many notes like it in Johnson's diaries tell us little about how he responded to his reading, or how he read at all. They are valuable for telling us what books he read, however, and they show how varied Johnson's reading was each day, or during whatever short period this note records.

Judging by similar notes, it seems likely that Johnson was always picking books up and reading them for a relatively brief time before moving on to something else. He probably did this even with books that he eventually read through, and even with those that he read many times. This is a style of reading utterly different from that of a great contemporary reader, Eudora Welty, who has told interviewers that she has read through to the end of every one of the books she ever opened. Welty is probably more unusual among modern readers than Johnson, who claims to have read through very few.

In his need for frequent changes in his reading Johnson is again identifiable as Victor Nell's "type A" reader who must have a book at all times but has difficulty being immersed in reading. The promiscuity of Johnson's reading also suggests that he was always deviating from study and even from perusal into more-cursory "mere reading." This seems to be the case in Boswell's description of Johnson's reading in the Hebrides. When he was stranded in a storm on the Island of Col, for example, Johnson frequently turned to reading to pass the time. Boswell reported of one particularly stormy day:

> We were in a strange state of abstraction from the world: we could neither hear from our friends, nor write to them. Col had brought Daille *on the Fathers,* Lucas *on Happiness,* and More's *Dialogues,* from the Reverend Mr. M'Lean's, and Burnet's *History of his own Times,* from Captain M'Lean's; and he had of his own some books of farming, and Gregory's *Geometry.* Dr. Johnson read a good deal of Burnet, and of Gregory, and I observed he made some geometrical notes in the end of his pocket-book. I read a little of Young's Six Weeks Tour through the Southern Counties; and Ovid's Epistles, which I had bought at Inverness, and which helped to solace many a weary hour.[81]

Boswell's account of their reading comes right after his remark about their "abstraction" and their inaccessibility. It is as though the books were meant to supply the place of society and to provide an entrance into the public sphere. But in this instance they were inadequate. As the storm continued, Johnson grew impatient. "He said, 'I want to be on the main land, and go on with existence. This is a waste of life.'"[82] A bit later he found some obscure, early-seventeenth-century treatises by Thomas Gataker, which he read on a walk while Boswell and the laird of Col examined the geology of the place. Sheltered from the wind, with his hat tied down around his ears, Boswell says, Johnson "had a most eremetical appearance; and on our return [from looking at one particular rock] told us, he had been so much engaged by Gataker, that he had never missed us."[83] But this solace did not last long, and in the next sentence Boswell says "his avidity for a variety of books, while we were in Col, was frequently expressed; and he often complained that so few were within his reach." Full engagement in his reading could provide Johnson with a substitute for the pleasures of society, but to maintain that engagement he required variety. He could become a curious or a studious reader only for brief spells. The desultory quality of mere reading was part of the attraction of reading for Johnson. In addition, this kind of reading left him free to drift back and forth between real society and the society of books—between one kind of conversation and another.

Johnson's notebooks do not tell us all we would like to know about how he read. Far from it. Part of what I have said about them is conjectural, but the notebooks do give us many of the titles of the books over which Johnson's eye traveled as he moved in and out of the engagement he sought. Johnson's notes help us piece together not merely a day's or a week's reading but the reading of a lifetime. In Johnson's lifetime of reading, as in anyone's, the particular titles mean a great deal, even though they do not in themselves define the kind of reading practiced on them. For all its variety, even Johnson's reading resided within certain boundaries and took a certain shape. In the succeeding four chapters I try to describe his life of reading in terms of the four kinds of reading I have outlined. I begin with "hard reading" or study, a kind of reading that Johnson did throughout middle and old age but which he did most assiduously at the beginning of his adult life, when he was a young man preparing to go off to Oxford in the late 1720s.

3

STUDY

*A*s his diaries indicate, Johnson perpetually berated himself for not reading enough. On Good Friday in 1779, for example, he reported on his reading of the New Testament:

> Having eaten nothing I went to church with Boswel. We came late, I was able to attend the litany with little perturbation. When we came home I began the first to the Thess[alonians] having prayed by the collect for the right use of the Scriptures. I gave Boswel Les Pensées de Pascal that he might not interrupt me. I did not, I believe, read very diligently, and before I had read far we went to Church again, I was again inattentive. At home I read again, then drank tea with a bun and an half, thinking myself less able to fast, than at former times; and then concluded the Epistle.[1]

Later he continued his confession: "In this last year I have made little acquisition, I have read scarcely anything." During that year Johnson had written a good deal of *Lives of the Poets*, including his long critical biography of Milton. It is possible, but unlikely, that he wrote *Lives* without doing much reading. Moreover, the diaries are filled with similar complaints, although it is clear that Johnson was reading. Part of the answer to this paradox is that in his confessions Johnson often means "reading" in a special sense. "Reading" in this Good Friday memorandum and many others in his diary means primarily, although not exclusively, Bible reading.

Bible reading is a privileged sort of "study"; it occupies a place at the top of my scheme of reading, but it is not unrelated to other kinds of reading. Even by the end of Johnson's entry for Good Friday the meaning of the word "reading" has fanned out to mean reading other important books, and, even more broadly, the acquisition of knowledge. However, it does not mean reading for pleasure or amusement; it can mean any kind of reading for self-improvement, but ideally it means reading in an ancient language and reading texts that one would not abridge or scan but to which one must humbly submit.

Study or hard reading includes a range of different practices, but for Johnson, reading the New Testament in Greek was the root or defining example. Johnson's impulse to record religious reading pervades the records of much of his other reading, so there is a reciprocal exchange of meaning in the kinds of reading Johnson chronicles: "reading" means reading the Bible and reading the Bible means studious reading in general. In all these cases, "reading" carries a special but not a highly specific sense, and it is always related to Bible reading. If it were possible—if we knew more about it—an enumeration of the ways in which Johnson read the Bible would provide a key to his life of study, if not to all the other aspects of his life of reading.

Bible reading provides the best evidence that the nature of reading is not determined by the text on which it is practiced: each individual reads the Bible differently, and the same person reads it differently at one time than at another. Johnson certainly read the Bible in a variety of ways, but most of them fit into the category of hard reading. At one extreme, Johnson approached a limit of reading in which the activity was uncritical, almost uncomprehending, and nearly incantatory. The furthest extreme of this kind of reading may be found in the recitation of Qur'anic verses by the many Muslims worldwide who do not understand Arabic. This is not pure incantation, which is a totally oral process distinct from reading, but it is at the limit of reading that approaches incantation.[2] Sanskrit pundits who "read" without ever looking at the books open on their laps may be practicing another version of this limitary kind of reading.

Although, like the Hindu pundit who turns from reading to commentary, Johnson could be an extremely critical and careful reader, his range extended almost to the incantatory limit. One of the most famous depictions of Johnson reading may have caught him approximating this mode: in Holy Week of 1772, Boswell recorded: "I paid him short visits both on Friday and Saturday, and seeing his large Folio Greek Testament before him, beheld with a reverential awe, and would not intrude upon his time."[3] Johnson's diary entry for that Saturday colors in the image of holy reading: "I resolved, last Easter to read within the year the whole Bible, a very great part of which I had never looked upon. I read the Greek Testament without construing and this day concluded the Apocalypse. I think that no part was missed."[4] That he read the Greek "without construing" is evidence that Johnson was reading in a less critical way than usual. This means not that he failed to understand what he read, but that he did not put it together (or pull it apart) grammatically, and perhaps even that he did not translate it, but left it in its own "decent obscurity." Johnson's Greek was good enough (though nothing like his Latin) and the Testament familiar and easy enough for him to do this with comprehension but not with critical comprehension. To appreciate this reading experience more fully, it would be helpful to inspect the "large Folio Greek Testament" in which Boswell found him buried on Good Friday.

If Boswell was literally accurate in his description, there are only a few identifiable candidates for the particular book Johnson was reading that day. Not many folios devoted to the Greek New Testament were available. Many of the works containing the Greek New Testament also included the Old Testament or Latin versions of one or the other. In the massive Harleian Library there was only one folio Greek New Testament without Latin. This was the edition by Robert Estienne, *Novum Testamentum Graecè ex bibliothequè regiâ* (Paris, 1550). In the Harleian Library catalogue, Johnson (or his collaborator, William Oldys) described this edition as follows: "Hac est omnium R. Stephani Editionum Nov. Testamenti optima, in qua quid praestitum fuerit docet Millius. . . . Hanc sequuntur Polyglotta Londinensia" (This is the best of all of Robert Estienne's editions of the New Testament. [John] Mill [1645–1707] explains how it excels. . . . The London Polyglot [ed. Brian Walton, 1657] follows this edition). The reference to the London polyglot edition, which Johnson owned, admired, and bequeathed to Bennet Langton, adds to the likelihood that Johnson wrote this adulatory note. Whether he wrote it or not, however, the volume is ideally suited for the kind of reading Johnson was doing on the Good Friday and Holy Saturday when Boswell came upon him.

In that volume there is no Latin translation of the Greek and no commentary, either of which would encourage "construing." The only distractions for the mind or eye are coded synoptic cross-references in the margins, and these are clearly recessive in relation to the beautiful, large but finely drawn Greek typeface of the text. This font, with exquisite ligatures connecting the letters and making new and exciting forms of them, may have facilitated the speedy reading that left Johnson slightly tentative about whether he had read or scanned it all: "I think that no part was missed." The 9-by-13-inch format, especially if it were open on a bookstand, would have allowed him to be physically immersed and protected from Boswell's intrusion. It is not clear that Johnson owned this particular edition, but he did have the 1620 Geneva edition, which follows it; he also had some edition of Estienne's publication of Theodore Beza's Greek Testament (1st ed., Geneva, 1565), which builds on Robert Estienne's edition of 1550. He owned it from his college days until his death, when he left it to George Strahan.[5] There are other possibilities, although none of them has quite the "simplicity of grandeur," to use a Johnsonian phrase, of Robert Estienne's edition of 1550.[6] It is before such a book as this, if not before this very book, that I wish to place Johnson for his Good

Friday reading. The format of this book and the kind of reading Johnson describes are perfectly compatible.

Many of Johnson's other Bibles were smaller books, and many were accompanied by Latin translations and commentary (Erasmus's 1527 edition, for example). In these Bibles Johnson did different kinds of reading. Translation, commentary, and apparatus discourage swift, incantatory reading and promote slower, more assiduous and critical kinds of study. It is likely that Johnson read his 1556 folio of the Bible in Latin with the commentary of Sébastian Chateillon, which he also took with him to Pembroke College, differently than he read Beza's Greek Testament. Commentary and translation invite one to argue and converse rather than intone and recite. Walton's polyglot Bible obviously stimulated philological and typographical interest, which also require a state of mind different from the one needed for devout reading.

Johnson had two or three editions of the Bible rebound in multiple volumes for the purpose of systematic study. He had a 1743, three-volume octavo bound in eight volumes, and a 1769, two-volume quarto bound in seven volumes. A note from a later owner of the 1769 edition suggests that Johnson had the books rebound to make "more convenient reading."[7] Throughout the book Johnson has written the last names of divines, such as Patrick Delany, Seth Ward, and Samuel Clarke, who used a particular chapter and verse in their sermons. In many places too Johnson wrote an *m* to indicate that the passage was omitted in daily lessons written by the named divines or elsewhere. Predictably, there are a great many *m*s in Leviticus. In this Bible and the 1743 edition, which contains similar marks, Johnson read with more-specific purposes in mind than he did in his "Folio Greek Testament." He was using the book for practical religious instruction, like the kind offered in the daily lessons of the divines he names. In these books, too, Johnson wrote dates at the ends of certain books and chapters, evidently indicating when he had finished a particular section, so these Bibles also became diaries of a kind, in the way that "family

Bibles," on a grander scale, often did through the nineteenth century and into the twentieth.

Johnson also owned more-compact editions of the Bible, which he used for impromptu sessions of study. John Jebb, the bishop of Limerick, visited Lichfield in 1826, and on Good Friday Canon Bailye gave him a tour of the cathedral. Jebb was delighted to find that Bailye had met Johnson and also retained several relics of the great man, including a Bible. He reported:

> The Bible is a pocket one, bound in red leather, with a clasp: the London edition of 1650, printed for the Stationers' Company; and (what one could not have expected to find with Dr. Johnson), consequently *a republican copy.* It bears marks of close and constant study, being folded down, according to his custom, at numerous passages. The present owner religiously preserves the folds as Johnson left them.

He concludes, "I hope it was with no unprofitable emotion that I held in my hand this little volume, the well worn manual of our great English moralist."[8] Reading this duodecimo Bible as a "manual" or handbook of morality, Johnson was operating in a different mode than he was when reading his folio Testament or even his "conveniently" bound quarto and octavo volumes. He had no pencil in hand, but dog-eared the expendable pocketbook for future handy reference to useful passages. This kind of reading really belongs more to perusal than it does to study. But because the book is the Bible, the reading of it retains an association with the highest forms of reading, in which the book is nearly talismanic. Such an association is implicit in the way Bishop Jebb and Canon Bailye felt about the "relic," religiously preserving the folds and with great emotion holding it in their hands.

Many of the books Johnson gave as gifts and bequests were Bibles. He gave them in all sizes, but even those that he may have given as manuals, such as the sixteenmo edition he gave to a young friend of the Thrales, carry a reminder of devotion and devout reading.[9] The gift signifies a measure of respect for the recipient as well as bearing the wishes or admonitions of the giver. One of the few times in later life that Johnson inscribed a book upon receiving it was when William Strahan, Johnson's printer and the king's, gave him a Bible. It is an octavo edition, solid but not splendid, yet Johnson wrote in it "Dedit Strahan Oct. 26. 1771," with the kind of pride with which he recorded the acquisition of books early in his life, when each one marked a new level of achievement or, at least, of added personal potential.

I I

Part of the reason Johnson always lamented the inadequacy of his achievements in reading is that he never fully detached reading from its associations with religious reading, and about everything concerning his religious attainments he was humble to the point of self-laceration. But another part of Johnson's diffidence about his progress as a reader later in life is that he looked back to a period in youth when, as he told Boswell, he had read "very hard," and he reflected sadly that he knew almost as much at eighteen as he did at fifty-four.[10] Here Johnson was talking primarily about reading classical literature, rather than the Bible, but classical reading was the part of study that occupied Johnson more than any other throughout his life, and it is the part of secular reading that he was most likely to conflate with reading in general.

Johnson told Bennet Langton that his great period of study lasted from the age of twelve to that of eighteen.[11] The most intense part of this period seems to have begun in August 1726, shortly before Johnson's seventeenth birthday, when he acquired a copy of Adam Littleton's *Latin Dictionary* and set seriously to work. Although he referred to his "idleness" during this period, he also described it as the time of his heaviest reading. He told Boswell he then read, "not voyages and travels, but all literature, Sir, all ancient writers, all manly: though but little Greek, only some Anacreon and Hesiod."[12] Anacreon and Hesiod may not have been quite so serious as the other authors he was reading, but these texts are adaptable, as I will show, for inclusion in Johnson's hard, "manly" reading. "In this irregular manner (added he) I had looked into a great many books, which were not commonly known at the Universities, where they seldom read any books but what are put into their hands by their tutors; so that when I came to Oxford [in 1728], Dr. Adams, now master of Pembroke College, told me, I was the best qualified for the University that he had ever known come there."[13]

Johnson certainly continued his reading at Oxford, but he was a somewhat dilatory college student. He told Boswell that "what he read solidly at Oxford was Greek; not the Grecian historians, but Homer and Euripides, and now and then a little Epigram; that the study of which he was most fond was Metaphysicks, but that he had not read much, even in that way."[14] John Hawkins said the course of Johnson's studies was "irregular," which only suggests that Johnson was following his habitual mode of desultory reading. Putting Boswell and Hawkins together, however, we might surmise that at Oxford Johnson was no longer reading with the intensity with which he had read in Lichfield before his matriculation. His period of heaviest reading was gradually coming to a close, perhaps curtailed by his complex feelings of social anxiety at Oxford and the onset of the melancholy that probably, along with financial problems, drove him from college in late 1729. Johnson's standards for hard reading or study were high; he said he "never knew a man who studied hard," although he was willing to infer from their works that Samuel Clarke and Richard Bentley had studied hard.[15] Consequently, his own identification of a period of "hard reading" is especially significant.

From twelve to twenty was probably the time of Johnson's heaviest and most influential reading, but what about his earlier reading experiences? Before "manly" reading there was reading of a softer, less businesslike kind that Johnson associated with women. It is a point of some interest that in the seventeenth and eighteenth centuries it was often the mother, or another woman, who taught children to read, although men usually taught writing. In his life of William Shenstone, Johnson suggests the way in which the teaching of reading could be involved in nurturing of a more strictly maternal kind:

> He learned to read of an old dame, whom his poem of *The School-Mistress* has delivered to posterity; and soon received such delight from books that he was always calling for fresh entertainment, and expected that when any of the family went to market a new book should be brought him, which when it came was in fondness carried to bed and laid by him. It is said that when his request had been neglected, his mother wrapped up a piece of wood of the same form, and pacified him for the night.[16]

The instruction given by eighteenth-century nursery school mistresses and mothers varied a good deal, no doubt, but it was likely to have been mostly elementary teaching only, because the schoolmasters, ushers, and tutors were men. The early-nineteenth-century biographer of Richard Bentley observes with some astonishment how much the great scholar had learned from his mother: "It is a circumstance not unworthy of record, that the most celebrated scholar of modern times received the first rudiments of his classical education from a female: it was his mother, who is represented to have been a woman of exceedingly good understanding, by whom Bentley was taught the Latin Accidence."[17] Neither Johnson's mother nor his instructor Dame Oliver, the widow of a shoemaker, was so learned, and Johnson's early reading was not so scholarly as Bentley's, but it had an enduring effect. As I suggested in the introduction, the story of Johnson's early reading of romances on his mother's knee represents a competing myth of the origin of Johnson's life of reading, which vies with the famous story of Petrarch and the apple, and explains Johnson's lifelong penchant for "curious" or "nonmanly" reading.

Johnson told Hester Thrale about the female component of his origins as a reader, but to Boswell he told only a story of initiation into the world of "manly" reading and study. Boswell reported:

He used to mention one curious instance of his casual reading, when but a boy. Having imagined that his brother had
hid some apples behind a large folio upon an upper shelf in
his father's shop, he climbed up to search for them. There
were no apples; but the large folio proved to be Petrarch,
whom he had seen mentioned, in some preface, as one of
the restorers of learning. His curiosity having been thus
excited, he sat down with avidity, and read a great part of
the book.[18]

The story suggests an allegorical interpretation. An Adamic
reader, Johnson reached for immediate and simple gratification
but grasped instead the old, intensive European Latin culture,
in which he then labored throughout his life. Like the great humanists he most admired—the Scaligers, Hugo Grotius, Peter
Burman, and the Heinsiuses, for example—Johnson was a fol-
lower of Petrarch.

The story is too good to be true. Did Johnson plant it for
posterity? Did he wish, like Keats, that his had been a life of
allegory? Maybe not, but Johnson does suggest that this was the
moment that gave him his intellectual bent. In his life of Abra-
ham Cowley he describes the origins of the poet's vocation in
the accident that "in the window of his mother's apartment lay
Spenser's *Fairy Queen.*" He may have been thinking of his own
life when he continued:

> Such are the accidents, which, sometimes remembered, and
> perhaps sometimes forgotten, produce that particular des-
> ignation of mind and propensity for some certain science or
> employment, which is commonly called Genius. The true
> Genius is a mind of large general powers, accidentally deter-
> mined to some particular direction. Sir Joshua Reynolds,
> the great Painter of the present age, had the first fondness
> for his art excited by the perusal of [Jonathan] Richardson's
> treatise.[19]

Johnson "had the first fondness for his art excited" by an accidental perusal of Petrarch; at least this is what he suggested to

Boswell, but there were several formative moments in Johnson's life of reading, each relevant to one of the different ways in which he read.

Johnson's life of reading has both male and female myths of origin, corresponding, respectively, to its "manly" or studious strain and its "female" or curious aspect. On the one hand, there is the fall, happy though it might be, in his father's bookshop and an injunction to earn his bread by the sweat of his brow; on the other hand, there is a myth of pleasure and engagement, an unbroken innocence in which reading is pleasure. I think Johnson lived with this dichotomy in his life of reading for a great many years, but the whole pattern of that life tended gradually to reconcile the conflict. A third competing myth of Johnson's ur-reading, which I will treat in the next chapter, suggests a possible compromise; it centers on the origins of his religious life and his failed attempt to read Grotius's *De veritate religionis* before his Latin was up to it.

Johnson's initiation into the world of hard reading was probably more gradual than his story about Petrarch and the apples would lead one to believe. In his father's bookshop from an early age Johnson encountered all kinds of important and impressive books. A catalogue for Michael Johnson's sale at the Talbot Inn, Sidbury, Worcester, on 21 March 1718 described his traveling stock as "choice Books in all Faculties, Divinity, History, Travels, Law, Physick, Mathematicks, Philosophy, Poetry, &c. together with Bibles, Common Prayers, Shop Books."[20] It is likely that Michael Johnson's shop stock was even more impressive, and a series of extant letters from a customer in nearby Ashbourne shows that he sold a wide range of serious works. Sir William Boothby ordered numerous religious works from Michael Johnson, including Bishop Burnet's *Sacred History of the Earth* and a work by John Norris, both of which Johnson quotes in his *Dictionary*. Boothby also ordered scholarly works by Sir Francis Bacon, Ezechiel Spanheim, Gerard John Vossius, and others whom the bookseller's son later read.[21] Michael Johnson also sold many books to Johnson's dear friend Gilbert Walmesley, as some extant bills show, and he even purchased the splendid and serious library of Lord Derby. The financial consequences of this ill-advised purchase dogged him for years. Many of the books were too splendid or too serious to be disposed of among Johnson's clientele, and they remained on his shelves, providing an informal but intensive education for his eldest son.

Apart from the books in his father's shop, Johnson also had available to him those in Walmesley's rather grand house, known as the Bishop's Palace, and those in the truly impressive Lichfield Cathedral Library. As the home of the St. Chad's Gospels, a priceless early manuscript, and many heavy folios concerning the church fathers and church history, the Cathedral Library certainly presented itself as a scene of study or traditional intensive reading. We do not know just how Johnson availed himself of the Cathedral Library, but his presence there contributed to his confirmation in the world of studious reading.

Studious reading was probably less on Johnson's mind during his extended visit with his cousin Cornelius Ford at Pedmore in 1725–26. This worldly scene undoubtedly encouraged reading of a more pleasurable and looser kind; Johnson definitely read Ford's favorite English poets—Samuel Garth, William Congreve, Joseph Addison, and Matthew Prior—during this period, and he expanded his classical reading of somewhat licentious, although serious, classical poets such as Anacreon and Martial. It is hard to tell how he read these classical authors, but the sojourn in Pedmore and its environs was probably something of holiday from the path of truly studious reading Johnson was beginning. However, there are signs that even Johnson's holiday reading was intensive, because bits of reading from this period appear in the scholarly works he wrote during the rest of his life. He began at this stage to file material away for use, and that is a sign of study or serious perusal, but not of reading for pure pleasure. For example, Johnson had access to a collection of books now in the William Salt Library in Stafford that had been given to the Stourbridge School in 1665 by Henry Hickman, a relative of Johnson who was a friend of Bishop

Hall and a collector of Hall's works as well as of many other serious tomes: traces of Johnson's studious reading in Stourbridge appear when he quotes Hall's *Sussurium cum Deo* in his edition of Shakespeare.[22] Johnson also had access to Ford's books, including those in a bequest from Ford's father that contained the works of dissenting ministers. Johnson's knowledge of dissenters' writings is observable throughout his scholarly writings, but some of Johnson's more subtle uses of Ford's books are also recoverable. For example, when Johnson cited Richard Johnson's *Noctes Nottinghamicae* in the *Harleian Catalogue* (no. 15142), he was using a book by Ford's teacher. Ford gave Johnson a copy of his teacher's grammatical works, and Johnson still had it with him, in hand or head, in about 1742 when he was writing the catalogue description of Thomas Cooper's *Thesaurus.*

When Johnson returned from his year at Stourbridge, the holiday from studious habits was over, and the next two years before his matriculation at Oxford in 1728 were the most intense in his whole life of reading. A focus on this period is perhaps most likely to reveal the nature of Johnson's study. Unfortunately, the existing documentary evidence does not permit a careful isolation of the two years before Oxford. Moreover, Johnson's hard reading spread into his thirteen months at Oxford and into the period beginning around 1734 when he was composing *Irene,* and to some extent it continued all his life, picking up force again in his later life when he was no longer writing. By focusing softly on the period from 1726 to 1728 and bringing in chronologically and temperamentally related periods of Johnson's reading, I hope to suggest what study was for him and what it continues to be for us.

One of the surest signs of study is that it is accompanied by writing, and usually by reference to more than one book. Study, unlike some other kinds of reading, is therefore performed at a desk or table and usually in a sitting or standing position. A certain variety in posture is possible in study, but departure from the norm tends to depress the intensity of the experience. I think John Wesley, for example, was doing something a little less than true study in his special reading chair, although he made all the associations Johnson did between reading the Bible and reading in general. Wesley had a chair fitted up so that he could sit backwards on it and lean his hands out over a lectern attached to the back, which was cut down sufficiently for his head to see over the top to the book. He found this comfortable but not soporific, one imagines, and, the lectern enabled him to take a note, although he would have had to rise to consult other books. This arrangement allowed him to hold the book in the light from a window, and it may have been a little easier for him to rise when sitting backwards, but reference and writing must have been difficult.

Still, Wesley's posture allows for harder reading than that described by Lynne Sharon Schwartz in an article called "True Confessions of a Reader." Schwartz describes her father's manner of reading as the model for her own. He preferred the more "manly" world of newspapers and politics to the family sagas and historical romances favored by her mother, but his posture suggested that his reading was not entirely suited for study:

> He read as I do, slowly, absorbedly, the book at arm's length from his eyes, but as I cannot do, he read lying down, stretched diagonally on the bed, stockinged feet crossed. His right hand, which held a cigar, was behind his head, the right elbow sticking out at a sharp angle, while his left arm was extended, the hand supporting the book from the bottom and turning its pages at the lower spine with a right-to-left flick of the thumb.

His seriousness was, however, suggested by this detail: "He was still in his business clothes, white shirt unbuttoned at the neck and tie either hanging askew or removed."[23]

Johnson must have been sitting up in his days of hard reading because he probably took some notes, and he consulted other books, such as Littleton's *Latin Dictionary*. He may have seesawed over his book, full of tics and gesticulations, but he was certainly upright. Johnson's physical posture while reading is part of what made his reading an act of study and distinguished it, for example, from the reading of Robert Hill. Joseph Spence compared both Johnson and Hill to Antonio Magliabecchi, but, at least early in life, Johnson was capable of a kind of reading that was beyond either of those eccentric bookworms, despite their great feats of reading. Hill, says Spence, was "happy lying under his hedge reading all day," and he preferred Alexander Pope's *Odyssey* to that of Homer. Although he too owned a broken copy of Littleton's *Latin Dictionary,* Hill's posture and his refreshing but idiosyncratic views make him different from the sort of hard reader Johnson was, or at least aspired to be.[24]

The storied Magliabecchi was a quite different reader from Johnson too, despite outward similarities. He learned to read by staring at the print on the pages used as wastepaper in his master's fruit store, and he learned to find books before he could read them. He seems to have interpreted language as a nonverbal sort of code, like a map, rather than hearing it as discourse. He knew the whereabouts of all the books in Florence, and he knew what was in them, but he only read titles and chapter headings.[25] He was almost the opposite of Hill because he took no real pleasure in books, but what he did was a highly mechanical form of study in which the discourse has no effect on the reader. In true study, information is stored, but it changes the computer who stores it.

Nevertheless, study has some of the qualities that were the only aspects of reading for Magliabecchi, and they are visible in the effects of Johnson's early hard reading. One of the few extant documents providing a glimpse into Johnson's early life of study is the rough draft of his play *Irene.* In the final version of the play, Aspasia, the pious Greek maiden who rejects the sumptuous temptations of the infidel Mahomet, assures her companion Demetrius that she will be happy "To live obscure upon a foreign coast, / Content with science, innocence and love":

Nor Wealth, nor titles, make Aspasia's bliss.
O'erwhelm'd and lost amidst the publick ruins
Unmov'd I saw the glitt'ring trifles perish,
And thought the petty dross beneath a sigh.
Chearful I follow to the rural cell,
Love be my wealth, and my distinction virtue.[26]

In a note on the rough draft of *Irene* that editors have plausibly assigned to this passage, Johnson wrote:

She answers that she is in little care about the means of Subsistence. Providence will provide for her—at least suf-ficient—Let the Luxurious feel innumerable Wants—she knows that the demands of Nature are few—Nor is Provi-dence obliged to provide for desires it has not created—In-gratitude charges Providence as penurious though it satisfies their needs, because not their desires.—Petronius—candi-dus esse Deus—Claudian—Verona—Martial Vitam quae faciunt—she can exchange the pomp and luxury she was born to, for the magnificence of nature and chearful pov-erty, and having drunk of the river sleep with innocence upon its banks.[27]

The first of Johnson's references is to a verse fragment of Petronius printed at the back of most editions, after presenta-tion of the famous *Cena Trimalchionis* (sometimes translated as "The Millionaire's Dinner Party") and the other, more contin-uous pieces of narrative. The poem begins, "Omnia quae mis-eras possunt finire querellas, / in promptu voluit candidus esse deus" (Good God has ordained that everything which can put a stop to our sad complaints is ready to hand). Line 5 of the poem may have provided Johnson with his note about drinking from the river: "Flumine vicino stultus sitit" (Only a fool is thirsty with a river nearby). And a memory of line 8 may have inspired Johnson to let Aspasia lie down after drinking: "Nil metuit licito fusa puella toro" (The girl who relaxes on a lawful bed has nothing to fear). The sexual meaning of the line would have been no deterrent to Johnson in his use of it for more philosophical purposes. When he was studying, Johnson read Petronius and other classical writers for the moral and ethical wisdom that could be extracted from their writings—not so much for the usefulness of the wisdom as for its potential.

The classics could be read for pleasure or for instruction, but in the economy of study their value is more potential than active. When a reader knows what he or she is looking for, study becomes perusal. When Johnson turned to writing, he transformed his studies into materials for perusal. Although perhaps not quite so vast, Johnson's head, like Magliabecchi's in Spence's account, was "an universal Index both of titles and matter."[28] Unlike Magliabecchi, however, Johnson put his index to work in his writings; Magliabecchi, like some learned people in universities even today, wrote little. His reading took the form of study, but he was, in effect, never a peruser of his own studies. Johnson read others, and he read himself as a reader when he turned to writing. One of the reasons the pure reader—the one who does not write—is so rare in the modern world, as Italo Calvino perceives, is that that reader does not read himself or herself.

Johnson acquired his own copy of Petronius's works in 1727 when he was seventeen or eighteen. His was the 1669 Amsterdam edition. The editor's preface to the reader confesses Petronius's epicureanism, but quotes from Diogenes Laertes' biography a brief passage attributed to Petronius connecting true pleasure with virtue. With such a simple substitution much of Petronius and many other classical writers could be read profitably and safely. The copious notes in the edition Johnson read help the reader extract value from the text and connect it to other, usually more respectable, classical authors. Johnson's own copy of the edition, which still exists in the Hyde Collection, contains no penciling or marginalia of any kind. The book is signed and dated on the title page, but there are no other indications that Johnson read it. *Irene* is stitched together in such a deliberate way that it seems likely to me that Johnson was working from notes rather than from memory only. Moreover, the absence of marks in his Petronius suggests that Johnson was storing information from it somewhere else. It may have been in his capacious memory, but he owned notebooks, and one of them was probably open while he drafted *Irene* and drew on the stores of his greatest period of study.

The reference to Claudian in the draft of *Irene* identifies a short poem by Claudian Claudianus called, in the edition Johnson used, "De sene Veronenso qui suburbium numquam egressus est" (The old man of Verona who never left the city limits). The poem begins, "Felix, qui patriis aevum transegit in agris, / Ipsa domus puerum quem videt, ipsa senem" (Happy is the man who passes his life on home ground, whom the same home shelters when he is young and when old). The poem celebrates the retired, simple life that Aspasia welcomes in *Irene*. Nicolaas Heinsius, the editor of the edition Johnson used, appends the note of an earlier editor, Caspar von Barth, to these opening lines, explaining that living in an inherited home is one of the things that makes for a happy life and citing Martial 10.47, "Vitam quae faciunt," precisely the epigram Johnson referred to in his note:

> Vitam quae faciunt beatiorem,
> Jucundissime Martialis, hac sunt:
> Res non parta labore, sed relicta;
> Non ingratus ager, focus perennis.[29]

(The things that make life better, most happy Martial, are these: some wealth inherited, not gained by labor; a garden that is not too stubborn and a fire always in the hearth.)

Barth went on to cite Hesiod on the desirability of χρήματα θεόσδοτα, god-given wealth. Johnson's chain of association, at least insofar as he wrote it down, ended with Martial. But the point is simply that Johnson made such chains of learned reference in his writing, and his written works are the outgrowth of the kind of reading Johnson did, in which fragments of writing can be distributed under preexisting topics and brought together in chains or groups by these means. Other jottings on

Johnson's draft of *Irene* use fragments of Homer or of a poem by Thomas Tickell to stand for other topics. Johnson's own copy of Claudianus, also in the Hyde Collection, contains a few penciled notes, but nothing on the poem he refers to here, so again the presumption must be that he either kept such things in his head or wrote them down in commonplace books now regrettably lost.

Johnson's notes were probably highly fragmentary; he could bear to write down only half lines of *The Vanity of Human Wishes* as he composed it in his head at up to seventy lines at a time, so his notes were also probably half lines at best. His jottings, however fragmentary, stood nonetheless for whole thoughts. In fact, one has the sense that Johnson's notes stand for thoughts that are more complete and aphoristic than the contexts in which he employs them. One use of his commonplaces was to supply mottoes for his own and for others' periodical essays. Johnson's adeptness in providing epigraphs suggests something about how he read and filed away crystals of literature that could be made to stand as titles or summary statements for pieces of writing that were more heterogeneous and less compact. He used mottoes to advertise forthcoming issues of the *Rambler* before he had written them, thereby setting himself a topic for composition out of his stores of aphorisms.

Johnson's edition of Shakespeare and many illustrative quotations in the *Dictionary* also show that Johnson read with an eye to the extractable, complete thought. In his Shakespeare, as has often been shown, he dilates these crystals, making them into small *Ramblers*, thus completing the work of instruction that Shakespeare, according to Johnson, had left undone. In the *Dictionary* the aphoristic quality of many writers comes out in Johnson's selections. This is especially true of George Herbert, for example, whom Johnson quotes more than a hundred times. Although the aphoristic quality of Herbert's verse has always been there, we have learned to read him more dramatically than earlier readers did; we hear him as a voice in conflict, working towards resolution.

Sweet day, so cool, so calm so bright
The bridal of the earth and sky
Sweet dews shall weep thy fall tonight
For thou must die

is the opening gambit in "Virtue," a poem about the durability
of the soul, but in Johnson's studious reading it is also a true
statement in itself, one that reminds us of death without assuring us of resurrection. The dramatic dependence of the statement on what follows is absent, and scores of similar examples
suggest that Johnson could in his studious mode read even the
most obviously dramatic works as though they were collections
of aphoristic truths. Extracting the still points in a dramatic
movement is a quality of study; storing them up and using
them in other contexts requires perusal. The rough draft of
Irene provides some of the best evidence of how Johnson performed both these kinds of reading.

In an important respect, Johnson's style of study is simply an
imitation of the humanistic mode of reading, most brilliantly
and stupendously visible in Erasmus, who collected thousands
of aphorisms in a nearly comprehensive reading of the classics.
Although he did not preserve his collections, Johnson's notes
for Shakespeare, his poetry, and his fictional works are based
on his collections of aphorisms out of Juvenal, Euripides, and
Horace. However, not all humanists are the same, and it should
be possible to distinguish Johnson's own particular manner of
study from the tradition to which it belongs. Let me first try to
show the difference between Johnson's method of study and an
act of hard reading of a later date, that represented by George
Eliot's notebooks and proved in her fiction.

Eliot transcribed passages from Greek tragedy, Goethe, and
Dante with an eye for the aphoristic statement. Inevitably, she
extracted at times the same passages noted by Johnson, or passages with similar aphorisms in them. Such similarities of reading matter allow one to see that Eliot's use of her collections was
less abstract than Johnson's, and her method of reading probably less abstracting. She wove the *materia literaria* into her tales

more often than she used it to summarize them. She did employ the summarizing, titular power of aphorisms, especially in her epigraphs to chapters of her novels, but not to the degree Johnson did. She used and sometimes invented epigraphs that stand in complex relation to the chapters that follow. They work as hints to the reader about interpretation as well as pieces of wisdom on their own.[30]

Johnson's practice is more conventionally humanistic than that of Eliot. For example, Johnson took from Euripides the following epigraph for *Rambler* 67:

Αἱ δ᾽ ἐλπίδες Βόσκουσι φυγάδας, ὡς λόγος,
Καλῶς Βλέπουσιν ὄμμασι, μέλλουσι δέ.
Euripides, Phoenissae, ll. 396–97

Exiles, the proverb says, subsist on hope.
Delusive hope still points to distant good,
To good that mocks approach.[31]

Johnson's translation itself is a reading that pushes the proverb into the more abstract and allegorical realm of *The Vanity of Human Wishes,* but the essay that follows turns completely into allegory, and it is entirely about the nature of hope. Eliot also copied the motto into her commonplace book, although she took it from Aeschylus's version: οἶδ᾽ ἔγω φεύγοντας ἄνδρας ἐλπιδας σιτοῦμενους.[32] At the time, Eliot was beginning *Felix Holt.* She took from Aeschylus an epigram for the whole novel, but she also wove into it a complex use of various themes in the *Agamemnon* and other Greek tragedies. Her thinking about the aphorism in question, for example, focused not only on hope, as Johnson's did, but also on exiles. In fact she wrote "exiles" over the quotation in her commonplace book and undoubtedly thought of it when writing her novel, which includes several characters separated from their homes. The difference between Eliot and Johnson is partly one of outlook: Eliot was more sensitive to place than Johnson was in his writing; Johnson liked to stress the Horatian, stoic sense that place has little effect on the important part of life ("caelum non animum mutant qui trans mare currunt"), even if he felt differently at times. But there is also a shade of difference in method between the use of the aphorism for a title and Eliot's sense of it as partial only—a part of the complex web she wove.

Also characteristic of Eliot and not of Johnson is her use of a quotation from Sophocles' *Antigone*: Οὔτοι συνεχθεῖν, ἄλλα συμφιλεῖν ἔφυν (Not for hatred but for mutual love was I by nature made). As the editor of Eliot's notebook tells us, "this passage appears slightly transformed in *Daniel Deronda,* chapter 32, when Mirah tells Deronda, 'It is so much easier to me to share in love than in hatred. I remember a play I read in German . . . where the heroine says something like that."[33] Here, Eliot keeps the thought almost entirely within its original literary garb so that it is distinct from her fiction, although obviously an influence on it. This tends to make the relationship between her fiction and the aphorism ironic; the two are at odds and separated from each other even as the aphorism appears within Eliot's text. Johnson characteristically made his fiction an embodiment of the thoughts he found in the wisdom of the past, abstracting both the thoughts and his own fiction.

Johnson and Eliot clearly belong to the same reading tradition, but there are differences between them. Although she could do certain reading for specific purposes, as she looked into books on John Wesley and Wesleyanism to write about Dinah in *Adam Bede,* Eliot still had the humanist's faith that general reading, especially of the classics and the Bible, is the best preparation for writing literature, no matter what the particular subject turns out to be. Hard reading in the humanistic mode is a preparation for writing anything. Eliot is different from Johnson, however, in the extent to which she subordinated the wisdom of the past to the demands of her settings and her more modern ideas of representation. Johnson was closer to the earlier, pure humanist ideal than Eliot, but he too mingled with it a greater attention to experience than his learned predecessors, and he too let irony creep into the relation between old text and new.

For Johnson, the world of literature still supplied the guideposts for life, but even when he was most abstract, Johnson gave greater admittance to the world of contemporary facts than the founders of his intellectual tradition or earlier humanists such as Erasmus. Johnson was a late humanist, not so late as Eliot, but late enough to find the world of aphoristic knowledge breaking up rather than still abuilding. Even in the allegory of the Garden of Hope in *Rambler 67*, which begins with the epigraph about the food of exiles, Johnson shows an awareness that he is dealing merely with *materia literaria* rather than with truth. There is a parodic quality to his treatment of the conventions that is signaled in one way by excessive abstraction and compression and in another by references to contemporary follies. Among the votaries of hope in this unhappy valley, for example, are a person about to discover a method for determining longitude at sea and another about to invent a diving bell to go to the bottom of the ocean: these were both contemporary, historical instances of the search for the philosopher's stone. Johnson's excessive, parodic abstraction is evident throughout, but most of all when he quickly wraps up the episode and rather obviously, in journalistic terms, puts the number to bed: "Among this gay race I was wandering, and found them ready to answer all my questions, and willing to communicate their mirth: but turning round I saw two dreadful monsters entring the vale, one of whom I knew to be Age, and the other Want. Sport and revelling were now at an end, and an universal shriek of affright and distress burst out and awaked me."[34]

An important aspect of study is the sort of reading that finds the nuggets of wisdom locked in the literature of the past, whether or not the reader, who is usually going to be a writer after this kind of reading, believes in the system of wisdom he or she might gather from that source. Study lends itself better to nondramatic uses because it puts knowledge above character and particular situations. *Irene* is not dramatic, but then Johnson probably did not read Euripides, for example, primarily as a dramatic writer. In the preface to his edition of Shakespeare, Johnson recalls that it was said of Euripides that every line was an aphorism, and it is a commonplace of Greek scholarship that Euripides is closely related to the rhetorical tradition that stresses the uses of aphoristic remarks. It is difficult for a modern reader to understand Euripides in this way, however, because we are accustomed to mimetic and often more fully dramatic forms of fiction, such as that found in many novels. We see greatness in dramatic terms, and Johnson's play will never seem so great to us as many of Dryden's, who, for all his learning, was not a hard reader. Johnson noted Dryden's limited range of reading in his life of Dryden, and Johnson's editor corroborates the perception with Dryden's own testimony: "I must confess it to my shame that I never read anything but for pleasure."[35]

Johnson probably describes Dryden's life of reading correctly when he says:

> Of him that knows much it is natural to suppose that he has read with diligence; yet I rather believe that the knowledge of Dryden was gleaned from accidental intelligence and various conversation; by a quick apprehension, a judicious selection, and a happy memory, a keen appetite of knowledge, and a powerful digestion; by vigilance that permitted nothing to pass without notice, and a habit of reflection that suffered nothing useful to be lost. A mind like Dryden's, always curious, always active, to which every understanding was proud to be associated, and of which every one solicited the regard by an ambitious display of himself, had a more pleasant, perhaps a nearer way to knowledge than by the silent progress of solitary reading. I do not suppose that he despised books or intentionally neglected them; but that he was carried out by the impetuosity of his genius to more vivid and speedy instructors, and that his studies were rather desultory and fortuitous than constant and systematical.[36]

In his note on this passage, G. B. Hill says Johnson is describing himself here, and the precision of his description suggests that this is so. Johnson clearly experienced the life and the life of reading he describes. But this was only part of Johnson's life. When Johnson grew older he became more thoroughly like the

Dryden he describes, but he was a hard reader in his youth, and he retained some of those studious habits forever. Johnson never stopped pursuing "the silent progress of solitary reading," although his capacity for it ebbed and flowed, and was largely interrupted during the busiest years of his career. Moreover, his capacity to combine his inclination to desultoriness with his earlier habit of study grew gradually throughout his life, and his synthesis of the two modes of reading was an intellectual achievement beyond Dryden's reach.

III

The value of a notebook to a student or hard reader is that it provides an easy way of going over one's reading. Some books, however, resemble notebooks already, and when a student en-counters these, he or she is likely to experience another class of study. This kind of study is a little softer than the hardest read-ing because the work of breaking up the text into thematically organized pieces has already been accomplished by the author. The *materia literaria* is disentangled from its original places in histories and fables and set out in a new, looser scheme. This type of hard reading falls between the standard humanistic study of primary texts on the one hand and the use of reference books on the other. It may be the kind of reading to which Johnson was most attracted; the attraction evidently began early in his life of reading, and the effects were long-lasting.

When he made his first trip to Pembroke College with his father, Johnson surprised his prospective tutor with a citation of Macrobius, an author well suited to studious reference read-ing. The principal works of Macrobius, a fifth-century Latin author, are *Saturnalia* and the *Dream of Scipio*. The *Dream* is a commentary on Cicero's response to Plato's notion of the after-life as a fact that supports the essential love of justice in a repub-lic. The work contains all sorts of odds and ends of knowledge as well as more-concentrated material on the immortality of the soul. Some of the bits on the soul, such as the contention that the soul knows no rest, show up eventually in *Rasselas,* in the penultimate chapter. Other fragments in Macrobius's collection show up elsewhere in Johnson's work. For example, the myth that the cataracts of the Nile deafen inhabitants in their vicinity appears in Johnson's preface to Father Jerónimo Lobo's *Voyage to Abyssinia*.[37]

Other thoughts in Macrobius seem diffused throughout Johnson's work as part of his general approach to moral questions and human psychology. Hope and fear, for example, are linked in Macrobius, as they often are in Johnson, and there are in the works of both writers similar expressions of the sense that life is a trial, an opportunity to prove or purify oneself. Johnson read at an early age and took to heart this sentence of Macrobius: "Ideo ergo concessis utendum vitae spatiis: ut sit perfectae purgationis maior facultas" (The time of life allowed to us must be used so that the mind may become more perfect through purification).[38] The young Johnson, wishing to distinguish himself by his learning, and proud of his somewhat obscure studies, may have taken some of his deepest convictions from Macrobius, even though nearly everything he found there was available in more-conventional sources. This kind of farrago suited Johnson's desires in reading, as did Burton's *Anatomy of Melancholy*, which he also started reading early, and many collections of ana and bits and pieces of *materia literaria*, such as Aulus Gellius's *Attic Nights* and the collected sayings of Gilles Ménage, *Menagiana*.

The other work of Macrobius included in all the editions of his *Opera* is even more miscellaneous than the *Dream of Scipio*. Macrobius addressed the preface of *Saturnalia* to his son, Eusthachius. The book was meant to supplement the boy's education by making available to him his father's reading. Moreover, Macrobius says, his collections are not heaped together in confusion but digested and arranged to form a coherent body of material that will be easier to remember—a softened form of studious reading. Macrobius says we should all be gatherers and digesters, like bees,

> so I too shall put into writing all that I have acquired in the varied course of my reading, to reduce it thereby to order

and to give it coherence. For not only does arrangement help the memory, but the actual process of arrangement, accompanied by a kind of mental fermentation which serves to season the whole, blends the diverse extracts to make a single flavor; with the result that, even if the sources are evident, what we get in the end is still something clearly different from those known sources.[39]

As a student, later as a teacher, and then as a writer of educational texts such as the *Dictionary,* Johnson was perpetually interested in educational works. He took several with him to Oxford in 1728, and it seems likely to me that he was reading *Saturnalia* shortly before his departure for college. He did not take Macrobius with him, perhaps because it was an expensive and fairly heavy book, but he quoted Macrobius to his tutor on their first meeting. No one knows what passage or even what work Johnson quoted. It is rash, I know, but I would like to believe that Johnson quoted from *Saturnalia* and furthermore that he said, "Non ergo fortuna homines aestimabo: sed moribus" (I do not judge men by their fortune but by their habits or accomplishments).[40] It is possible that Johnson was exhibiting the same point of view that caused John Hawkins to pause in his biography to rebuke the young man for thinking that "the scholar's, like the christian life, levelled all distinctions of rank and worldly pre-eminence."[41] It is clear that Johnson felt rebellious at Oxford and uncomfortable socially. On his first meeting in the splendid precincts of the university, what better remark to make? It at once asserts his independence from the social ranking evident around him, which was heightened by his father's presence and his Staffordshire accent, and it simultaneously demonstrates his learning. Later in his college career Johnson refused to write a certain stated exercise and substituted a piece called "Somnium," modeled on Macrobius's *Dream of Scipio,* but it may have been with a quotation from *Saturnalia* that he made his first, somewhat defiant entrance into the world of Oxford. With the same gesture, I think, he displayed himself as a hard reader of the Macrobian variety.

The best evidence we have of what Johnson was reading shortly before and during college is a list of books he wrote on the back of a letter to Gilbert Repington, a friend of the friend with whom Johnson left his books when he departed from Oxford in December 1729. The list of nearly a hundred books suggests the kind of study in which Johnson was engaged and that he planned to continue at this point in his life. He had editions of classical authors, which was certainly to be expected, but he also had some slightly out-of-the-way poets. Some of the editions Johnson took with him to college were the work of the humanist scholars he most admired. He had Nicolaus Heinsius's Claudian, Silius Italicus (a historian of the Punic Wars), Vergil, and Valerius Flaccus (the author of *Argonauta*). He had Ovid, Velleius Paterculus, and Phaedrus (*Aesop's Fables*) in editions by Peter Burman, whose life he later wrote. Johnson was as interested in the work of his favorite humanist scholars as he was in the classical writers they edited. He expressed his interest in the list of books by being careful about naming editors in most cases. He also took with him independent works by some of the editors he most admired. He had William Baxter's Anacreon, and perhaps his Horace, but certainly his commentary on the Latin language, *De analogia*. Although he may not have had any editions by either of the Scaligers, he had the famous critical work *Poetice* by the elder (Julius Caesar) and the collected poems of the younger (Joseph). He had other important critical treatises, such as Marco Girolamo Vida's *Ars poetica* and Longinus's *On the Sublime*. It seems clear that Johnson cared not only about the classical texts but also about the commentary that they accrued in the footnotes of editors, and he cared about the editors themselves. The kind of hard reading displayed by these scholars inspired Johnson; in addition, their learned notes, like the Macrobian collections, offered parboiled hard reading for their audience of students.

Johnson continued to read in scholarly editions throughout his life, and he clearly became increasingly sophisticated about scholarship as he got older, acquiring more editions of his favorites and forming opinions about their quality. Johnson's advance in sophistication as a student is particularly evident in his changing collection of dictionaries. The *Latin Dictionary* he bought in 1726 to aid his reading was a work by Adam Littleton. This English-Latin, Latin-English dictionary was important in its time, although it was partially superseded by the *Cambridge Dictionary* late in the seventeenth century and completely outdone in 1736 by Robert Ainsworth's work in the bilingual field. Littleton's work was never a match for the Latin-Latin dictionaries of Basilius Faber or Robert Estienne (Stephanus) produced on the Continent, but it provided the right degree of erudition for Johnson's life of reading at the time he acquired it. Littleton entered both Greek and Hebrew translations of the Latin words, perhaps imagining that these constituted etymologies, before giving the definitions in English. He cited authorities by name but seldom provided quotations. There is an air of somewhat strained erudition about the book, even though there is plenty of solid learning in it too. Littleton was a fine scholar who was invited to take the place of the famous Richard Busby as headmaster at the Westminster School. His work was excellent for students (much better than Elisha Coles's Latin-English dictionary, for instance), but it had only a pretense to being much more than a student's dictionary and a schoolmaster's book. Later in life Johnson would have Stephanus and Faber at hand for his researches, but early on Littleton was his guide. (The very book, signed "Sam. Johnson / Sept 7th 1726," is part of the library at the Lichfield Birthplace Museum. A sum is near the inscription: "1726–1709 = 17." But none of the other sparse notes in the book seems to be Johnson's work.)

His contemporaries' or students' sense that Littleton's work was minor league is most amusingly enshrined in a funny though apocryphal story. A recent bookseller's catalogue retells the story thus: "When Littleton was compiling the work, he announced the word 'concurro' to his scribe, who, imagining the translation, blurted 'concur' [which is not the primary meaning]. To which Littleton replied peevishly: 'Concur? Con-dog!' And the loyal scribe, whose job it was to copy down exactly what his master said, did his duty, and 'condog' was thus entered as a meaning for the word."[42] In fact, as the *Oxford English Dictionary* testifies, *condog* is an English word meaning "concur" that was in use as early as 1592. Moreover, the sixth sense of *concurro* in the *Oxford Latin Dictionary* supports the sense "concur" insofar as it means "to be in agreement, to harmonize."

Littleton undoubtedly made mistakes, but one reason for the derisive joke has nothing to do with the defects of his diction-ary in particular. Johnson was not merely pleading for sympa-thy when he talked in the preface to his own *Dictionary* about the reputation of lexicographers for drudgery. Dictionaries and their makers were derided throughout the seventeenth and eighteenth centuries as participants in a world of reference reading and indexical knowledge that was divorced from the true, more "gentlemanly" ends of reading. Studious reference reading, such as one might do in dictionaries and some com-mentaries, was seen as a shortcut to the goals of true study. A defender might argue that such works permit a higher level of achievement than most people could attain without them, but it is impossible to deny that they abridge part of the activity of study. The same is true of such databases as *Ibychus, Perseus,* or the *Oxford English Dictionary* on CD-ROM today, and as such instruments become more widely available, there will be more debates about the "true" nature of study.[43]

In the eighteenth century no "high-tech" scholar was sati-rized more heavily or frequently than Richard Bentley, the per-son Johnson most often acknowledged as a truly hard reader. In contention with the "gentlemanly" William Temple and then with Christ Church College as a whole, Bentley was a defender of the moderns against the ancients in the so-called Battle of the Books. He was in favor of modern, historical textual schol-arship and commentary, as opposed to the more topical and often more tendentious scholarship of the past. His oppo-nents cast him as also opposed to reading in the "gentlemanly" sense—reading for the purposes of self-improvement, courtesy, pleasure, and virtue, and not for the trade of writing or the compulsion of compiling.[44]

In the economy of reading implicit in the derision of Bentley, the scholar's highly organized kind of study was seen as a modern barbarism. The more "gentlemanly" readers often tended also to be High Church readers, closer to the Roman religious economy in which reading was not encouraged. For all his love of Pope, who castigated Bentley mercilessly, and despite his High Church affiliations, Johnson was certainly on Bentley's side, and Littleton's, in the debate about the nature of reading implicit in the Battle of the Books and the contest between the ancients and the moderns. With his Graevius (Johann Georg Graeve) edition of Cicero's works, James Upton's Dionysius, and his Didymus on Homer, Johnson was doing hard reading of the most serious and, to some, the most laughable sort. As Littleton himself acknowledged in his preface to the learned reader, "Neque deerunt forte, qui me pipilo difflent . . . ad Grammaticorum rursus subsellia provocem, & in Dictionariis conscribillandis operam abutar" (Nor do they err very widely who ridicule me [because] I recall the grammarians to their seats of judgment and misspend pains in scribbling dictionaries). Johnson is like Littleton here both in his scholarly reading and writing and in his awareness of their susceptibility to derision from a more conservative class of readers. Conservative readers such as Swift wished, at least in principle, to keep study closer to its roots in less-critical, more-recitative, and perhaps even holy reading. Such conservatism is always returning to the critical scene, because it is fundamental to reading; it might be called, in fact, fundamentalism in reading, and it is as likely to keep reappearing as fundamentalism in religion. It has had modern reembodiments in Susan Sontag's *Against Interpretation,* in Reuben Brower's seminal essay "Reading in Slow Motion," and even in Jacques Derrida's *Grammatology.* Each of these works tries to isolate the text and reader from the interpretations of other commentators. Early in his life, at least, Johnson was not interested in that kind of isolation; he wished to enter the society of commentators and become one of them.

IV

Bibles and classical texts are not all that Johnson took with him to Oxford. He had the great English writers of the present and previous generations: Pope and Dryden and a good deal of Milton, including some of his prose, which is surprising in light of Johnson's general antipathy to Milton's political views. He also had some books aimed at the instruction of youths like himself, but perhaps the most interesting group of his college books is his collection of neo-Latin poetry. Some of these works provided Johnson with material for the kind of studious reference reading discussed in the previous section. John Barclay's *Argenis,* for example, is a mixture of verse and prose, and another example of Johnson's favorite, Menippean satire. It is a measure of how invisible Johnson's scholarly and studious life became to posterity that in annotating his own copy of Barclay, Coleridge issued his most contemptuous remark about Johnson. Coleridge deplored the idea that popular taste was such that it could ignore Barclay and pay heed to Boswell's collection of "Johnson's pilfered brutalities of wit."[45] Coleridge did not know that Johnson was himself a reader of Barclay—probably a more studious reader of him than Coleridge was. Johnson liked Barclay sufficiently to use an English work of his as a specimen in the "History of the English Language" that he included in his *Dictionary.* But Barclay was only one of the many neo-Latin poets Johnson carried to Pembroke College. Many of the others were not studious collectors of choice fragments in the *materia literaria,* which students might pilfer. Many were in fact lyric poets who maintained a close connection to the classics and in so doing sought to preserve a special, elite world of readers and writers in the midst of modern (and therefore crowded and ugly) literary life. Reading these poets and writing Latin poetry himself, Johnson participated in a fourth kind of study, which, because of its size and social attitude, I call coterie reading.

Despite Coleridge's lamentations about his neglect, Barclay

may have been fairly popular among young students like Johnson; also well known were the poems of the Scaligers and
two collegiate collections: *Carmina Quadragesimalia ad Aedis
Christi alumnis composita et ad ejusdem baccalaureis determinan-
tibus in schola naturalis philosophiae publice recitata* (Lenten
Poems for the students of Christ's Church College and publicly
recited at their graduation exercises in the school of natural
philosophy; Oxford, 1723) and *Musae Anglicanae* (2 volumes;
Oxford, 1692–99). These works may often have been acquired
as graduation and matriculation gifts. That there are so many
copies still extant in libraries shows that the books were popular
but also, perhaps, more revered than read. The same may be
true of another of Johnson's favorites, George Buchanan; his
works include Latin translations of Euripides, one of the Greek
authors Johnson said he read at college. Johnson took these
works with him to Pembroke College along with many other
volumes of neo-Latin verse, including a collection of Italian poems in Latin—*Anthologia, seu selecta quaedam poemata
Italorum qui Latine scripserunt* (London, 1684).

However others felt about these learned, elegant neo-Latin
poets, Johnson's interest in them was not perfunctory, and it
was not confined to his college days. From the second volume
of *Musae Anglicanae,* for example, Johnson took a quotation
and placed it under *to ganch* in the *Dictionary.*[46] He also used
the volume of Italian poets all his life, citing much later some
of the anthologized writers, including Giano Vitale, Baptistae
Mantuani Carmelitae, and Giovanni Battista Guarini.[47] In
fact, Johnson refers to his collegiate collection of Italian poets
in his life of Pope, his last major composition:

Pope had sought for images and sentiments in a region not
known to have been explored by many other of the English
writers; he had consulted the modern writers of Latin poetry, a class of authors whom Boileau endeavoured to bring
into contempt, and who are too generally neglected. Pope,
however, was not ashamed of their acquaintance, nor un-
grateful for the advantages which he might have derived

from it. A small selection from the Italians who wrote in Latin had been published at London, about the latter end of the last century, by a man who concealed his name, but whom his Preface shews to have been well qualified for his undertaking. This collection Pope amplified by more than half, and (1740) published it in two volumes, but injuriously omitted his predecessor's preface. To these books, which had nothing but the mere text, no regard was paid; the authors were still neglected, and the editor was neither praised nor censured.[48]

There is an element of self-regard in Johnson's remark, evident in his display of his knowledge of the volume on which Pope based his forgotten work. At the time that Johnson studied this volume and took it to college he was preparing himself for a career writing and editing Latin poetry. He issued proposals for an edition of the Latin poetry of Angelo Poliziano in 1734, but the paucity of response told him that the author would be "still neglected," and the editor "neither praised nor censured." In short, as in many of Johnson's best writings, there is a small piece of hidden, elegiac autobiography in this paragraph on Pope's interest in neo-Latin poetry. But this would not be clear without the knowledge that Johnson had this book with him at college and probably continued to have it by him throughout his life.

As the passage in the life of Pope suggests, Johnson identified himself with an interest in neo-Latin poetry, and that identification is the key to understanding the kind of reading that this part of his undergraduate collection of books stimulated. It was not the hardest kind of study because these were not classics; they were certainly not biblical; and reading them was not part of the required general preparation for a life of poetry or scholarship. On the other hand, the poems are modeled on classics in most instances, and they are often translations of Greek into Latin or even of Latin into Greek. Poliziano's Latin Homer, George Buchanan's Latin Euripides, and Joseph Scal-

iger's Greek Vergil made solid hard reading—study of the kind
that makes a student fit for literary labor. The same might be
said of Vida's loose imitation of Horace's famous epistle called
Ars poetica. These are all works that Johnson may have treated
largely as he treated the classics—gathering from them commonplaces, topics, and perhaps imagery for his own work.

There were other poems in Johnson's collection, however,
that were less serious and less susceptible to the kind of study at
which Johnson and other humanists excelled. These looser and
lighter poems were represented in Johnson's collegiate collection in several volumes: the works of Jean Bonnefons (1554–
1614), whose *Pancharis,* modeled on Catullus's *Baccia,* had been
translated into English in 1721 with the subtitle *Queen of love, or
Woman unveil'd . . . containing the whole art of kissing, in all its
varieties and the many different stratagems used in loves's-warfare*;
the *Poetae rusticantis literatum otium: Sive carmina* of Andreas
Franciscus Deslandes, a similar French writer who wrote a little
later than Bonnefons; and some of the works in the collection
Anthologia, seu selecta quaedam poemata Italorum. Some parts of
Scaliger's *Poemata* and much of the two collegiate collections of
Latin poetry also belong to this part of Johnson's reading. It
may have been in 1731 that Johnson acquired the works of
Andreas Naugerius, and in 1732 he acquired the works of Clem-
ent Marot, both of which added to his collection of neo-Latin,
mostly Continental verse. The classical love poetry and pastoral
in Johnson's collection is also related to his interest in these
modern Latinists. Given Johnson's famous strictures on pastoral poetry it is somewhat surprising that he went off to college
not only with his Landesius but also his Catullus and Tibullus,
his Ovid but also his Grattius (with other Latin poets on hunt-
ing), Anacreon, and Theocritus. To some extent, any classical
writer could be a suitable subject of study, but some were more
suitable than others, and Johnson was often doing a different
kind of hard reading in the raft of books I mention here. I call it
coterie study because in reading these authors Johnson joined
not the whole humanistic world of learning but a more select

and elite part of it. Another way to think of this reading is as a kind of learned holiday reading, but in any case, there are important differences between it and hard reading par excellence.

The most important difference is that the community of readers Johnson joined in his coterie reading was different than the community implicit in reading the Bible or universal classics such as Homer and Vergil. The nature of the society composed of neo-Latin poets is evident in the *Anthologia* that Johnson took to college. The preface is addressed "Benvolo Lectori" (To the kind reader), but right away the author changes the address to "erudite Lector" (the learned reader). In the late seventeenth century prefaces contained so many addresses to so many different kinds of readers in so many registers of sobriety and satire that it is dangerous to draw any conclusions from the nature of an address. However, in this case, the learned reader is the target audience, and the author seeks to appeal to coterie values.

According to the editor, the qualities that recommend these Italian Latin poems are purity, clarity, sweetness, terseness, tenderness, gracefulness, and successful emulation of the ancient models of Catullus and Tibullus. There are reassurances that care has been taken by the editor as well as the authors to avoid Italian dangers such as lasciviousness and, of course, popery, but subject matter is not so important to the poets or the editor as style. The great judges of style the editor invokes are poets and scholars with many of the same interests as those he selects. Julius Caesar Scaliger is the greatest authority, but overall it is "suffragiis doctiorum" (by the suffrage of the learned) that the case for these poets is decided. For all its deserved fame, however, the world of these poets is small. They refer to each other and to each other's poetry; they write poems to each other and for each other. This is implicitly so in most cases because of the allusive, intertextual nature of the verse, but it is also in many cases literally so. In Joseph Scaliger's *Poemata*, for example, there is a whole section of poems entitled "encomia librorum" (praises of books), and most of the other poets Johnson had with him are named. There are two poems of praise, for example, to Bonnefons's *Pancharis,* and several of the scholarly editions Johnson owned are lauded. Johnson's collection of Oxonian Latin verse (*Musarum Anglicanarum analecta,* also known as *Musae Anglicanae*) is not quite so closely cross-referenced, but it is concerned with asserting the glory of an English circle of greats in the intellectual as well as the political sphere: there are poems to scientists and scholars such as William Harvey and Thomas Sydenham as well as political figures such as William III and Charles II. There are also an attack on Hobbes, a dissertation on the art of flying that Johnson may have remembered when he wrote about the aeronautical mechanic in *Rasselas,* and a mock georgic about gaming called "Mensa lubrica." The holiday spirit of the works is evident, as is the insider quality of the jokes. It is significant that most of the works are signed, something that was relatively uncommon in the more-public verse of the day.

Displaying the names of the authors is a part of the social aspect of this neo-Latin poetry and part of what made it a coterie experience. Johnson's reading in these works is best compared to the reading that writers and aspiring writers do in the works of their heroes when they see them as senior members of the guild rather than as inaccessible spirits or stars. Coleridge may have complained about Johnson's preeminence over Barclay, but Coleridge was partly responsible for making authors such as Barclay and even Shakespeare more remote and numinous. Johnson could feel a kinship with Barclay and see Shakespeare as a fellow writer, with a fellow writer's understandable weaknesses, in a way Coleridge rejected. Coleridge liked reading numinous presences, but the public has generally preferred the more down-to-earth Johnsonian approach, although, in fact, the eminently accessible Boswell has often been the author through whom we have got our sense of Johnson's criticism. Boswell's Johnson invites a wide readership into a kind of coterie reading experience that only dimly resembles the much more elite society of neo-Latin readers to which Johnson himself subscribed.

Virginia Woolf may provide the best example of a modern

coterie hard reader; she reflected a life of such reading not only in *The Common Reader* but also in *A Room of One's Own* and even in her novels, with their artist heroes. Woolf was a "common reader" only in that she did not belong by gender or training to the old coterie world of readers to which Johnson aspired. She was a coterie reader nevertheless because she had the ability to take literature into a personal, socially narrow orbit. Like her hero/heroine Orlando, she traveled in the company of her favorite authors. She was not a professor, not a hard reader par excellence, but a participant in the society of authors. Johnson, who deserves credit for inventing the phrase "common reader" in its modern sense (which is certainly the sense Woolf inherited), recognized his own distinction from that abstract but reader-friendly personage.[49] He sometimes agreed with "the common reader," as he did in liking a certain passage of Gray's *Elegy,* and he acknowledged the common reader's preeminence as a judge of literature, but Johnson knew he was more learned and more specialized. Setting the type for the Hogarth Press edition of *The Wasteland,* the better to appreciate the beauties of its composition, surely Woolf also knew that her perspective was different from that of the common reader. She was in the guild, even at the center of it. Bloomsbury was a place of real coterie literary activity, like St. John's Gate in Clerkenwell, home of the *Gentleman's Magazine,* Dilly's Bookshop, or the Mitre Tavern. Even more than these Johnsonian haunts, Bloomsbury became an intangible scene of coterie literary activity in which outsiders could and still do participate. The participation of readers in the coterie world of Bloomsbury or the Strand is vicarious, but all reading provides vicarious participation in a social group. We join the fellow readers of our text, more or less, when we read, and the size and makeup of that intangible society is part of the reading experience.

The world of neo-Latin poets was Johnson's own Bloomsbury of the mind, and his vicarious participation in that world constituted the least disciplined of the four types into which I have divided his hard reading. In biblical, classical, Menippean

or Macrobian, and coterie reading Johnson was in varying degrees preparing for a life of writing (or even an afterlife) more
than he was taking immediate benefit or immediate pleasure.
In these four kinds of hard reading there is a successively con-
tracting, implicit community of other readers. In biblical reading Johnson joined all souls; at least this was the possibility he
pursued, especially when his reading was not meant to be critical so much as propaedeutic. Johnson's temperament may not
have allowed him to exclude critical attention from any of his
reading, but he was not a biblical scholar, and he was certainly
not doing biblical scholarship when he read his Greek Testament "without construing." For all his study of the Bible, Johnson quotes the work relatively infrequently in all of his writing
except his sermons.

The somewhat narrower and obviously more secular world
of the classics was Johnson's greatest source of *materia literaria.*
In reading the classics Johnson was preparing for a life of writing, and he was doing a round of reading that was required for
writers and for many of the people to whom he wished to
speak. He was also preparing to write when he was reading
books made out of classical quotations, such as Macrobius, but
he was then getting outside the regular round of reading. When
he mentions Sulpitius to Hester Thrale as "above" her reading
or satirizes a scholar, like himself, curling up with his Smigleus,
Johnson acknowledges his membership in a rarefied society of
readers.[50]

The true elite to which Johnson aspired early in life is represented by the best writers of neo-Latin poetry, who were also in
many cases the best editors of classical texts. It was not a broad
public sphere that Johnson sought to join in reading his Landesius and Bonnefons, but it was a public sphere nevertheless.
He was not reading works in manuscript or hearing them read
in private. These were printed works also being read by young
scholars like Johnson all over Europe, although the total number of readers was small and shrinking fast, especially in relation to the growing body of general readers.

When Johnson held his Landesius in his hands at Oxford in

1729, he was holding his membership card in the society of readers he most wished to join at that time.[51] When he went to work as a professional writer, he first saluted Edward Cave with a Latin poem based on an ode by Casimir Sarbiewski (1595–1640), an upstanding member of the guild when it was closer to its glory days. He then saluted members of Cave's staff at the *Gentleman's Magazine* with Latin and Greek poems. He was trying to turn the public sphere that read Cave's publication into something like the one he imagined joining when in college. Cave liked it, and he hired Johnson to upgrade his magazine. If he were a New York editor he would have called Johnson's contributions "classy," but the world of journalistic readers was not destined to be so elite or so learned as Johnson hoped, and when he finally went to London permanently, his life of hard reading suffered a decline. He was forced to yield to the necessity of reading for immediate and specific preparation rather than for general and long-range qualification.

The record shows, however, that Johnson continued his hard reading all his life and increased it whenever his duties relaxed their hold on his time. His biblical reading late in life is well attested in his diaries. A date and a signature on a copy of Horace that he might have taken with him to college show that he read it through again in 1780. *Lives of the Poets* shows that he probably kept up his study even in the more narrow, coterie branch of hard reading. Not only greats such as Buchanan and Scaliger turn up in his last writings, but also less famous figures, such as Wowerius (Jan van der Wouwer), Franciscus Floridus Sabinus, and Jean Passerat. Johnson kept part of himself in this elite world throughout his life, no matter how far his reading horizon spread in other directions. That expansiveness is an important part of Johnson's greatness.

4
∞

PERUSAL

*I*n a letter to his friend Richard West, Thomas Gray
described his life of reading as a Swiftian Battle of the
Books in which a novel, "Madame de Sévigné's sixth tome, is
squeezed to death by Aristotle. Her cousin Bussy Rabutin [an-
other author of a scandalous novel] would come to her rescue
but finds himself being murdered by Strabo." At last Gray's vade
mecum puts an end to the commotion by crying out, "Pshaw!
I and the Bible are enough for anyone's library."[1] The vade
mecum is a practical moral handbook that belongs to a kind of
reading that is clearly beneath Bible reading, but because of its
religious content it claims a moral superiority to the reading of
classical philosophy and certainly to the reading of the letters of
a high-society gossip such as Madame de Sévigné (née Marie de
Rabutin-Chantal, 1626–96). Despite its moral superiority, the
vade mecum is easy to read; in terms of Gray's dream, it is
voluble. Because of its volubility and morality, the handbook
resolves the dispute raging in Gray's imaginary library between
the hard reading of the classics and the light reading of contemporary journalistic letters and fiction. In Gray's real life of reading, as his dream suggests, this battle was won by the classics and
by the kind of study for which they are suited. Johnson, too,
experienced the conflict dramatized in Gray's dream, and religious handbooks also offered him a haven in profitable reading
that was not limited to religious handbooks but could be most
justifiably practiced on them. I call this kind of purposeful,
attentive, yet relatively easy reading "perusal."

The conflict that perusal resolves was strong in Johnson's life of reading. One sign of its strength was Johnson's skepticism about the storied reading feats of others. Thomas Gray's reading was famous enough that Johnson felt an obligation to discuss it in his life of the poet. Johnson may not have been thoroughly incredulous about Gray's achievements, but a distinct feeling of skepticism lurks in the background of his introductory remark and in his assignment of the discussion of it to a writer quoted by Gray's adulatory biographer, William Mason:

> His character I am willing to adopt, as Mr. Mason has done, from a letter written to my friend Mr. Boswell, by the Rev. Mr. Temple, a rector of St. Gluvias in Cornwall; and am as willing as his warmest well-wisher to believe it true.
>
> "Perhaps he was the most learned man in Europe. He was equally acquainted with the elegant and profound parts of science [i.e., knowledge], and that not superficially but thoroughly. He knew every branch of history, both natural and civil; had read all the original historians of England, France, and Italy; and was a great antiquarian. Criticism, metaphysicks, morals, politicks made a principal part of his study; voyages and travels of all sorts were his favourite amusements; and he had a fine taste in painting, prints, architecture, and gardening."[2]

Johnson says that he is "willing" to believe the account, not that he believes it.

Johnson's source goes on to discuss Gray's flaws: his fastidiousness, his contempt for those less learned than himself, and his affectation of upper-class status. Johnson was happy to distinguish himself from Gray in many ways, but he envied his hard reading. In a passage Johnson probably knew but did not repeat, Gray explained his great reading to his biographer: "He said he knew from experience how much might be done by a person who did not fling away his time on middling or inferior authors, and read with method."[3] Gray's dream indicates that he had flung away some time when he was young, but the first catalogue of his library suggests that his efforts were more concentrated than Johnson's even early on, and after 1742, when he was only twenty-six, he settled into a life of methodical study with more steadiness of purpose than Johnson ever achieved. Johnson may have ignored Gray's deposition because he found it invidious or because he could not believe it. In any case, Johnson's notebooks are full of complaints about the laxity of his reading, and he both wished he were more like Gray and found it hard to believe that anyone could be so undistracted by the temptations of desultory reading.

Johnson expressed skepticism about other famous lives of reading, and his doubts suggest not only that he was competitive as a scholar, which he was, but that he felt it was the nature of the consciousness one experiences in reading to change or wander. The enduring steadiness of attention required for heroic reading was not something Johnson experienced, so he could not easily believe it existed in others. He was willing on secondary evidence to infer (but not definitely to believe) that Richard Bentley and Samuel Clarke were great readers, but he dealt mercilessly with the pretensions of lesser lights. William King, says Johnson in his life of the poet, "is said to have prosecuted his studies with so much intenseness and activity that, before he was eight years standing, he had read over and made remarks upon twenty-two thousand odd hundred books and manuscripts." Johnson was incredulous and he did some arithmetic of the kind he used in projecting his own schemes of reading: "[King's] books were certainly not very long, the manuscripts not very difficult, nor the remarks very large; for the calculator will find that he dispatched seven a day, for every day of his eight years, with a remnant that more than satisfies most other students."[4] Johnson's arithmetic is persuasive, but it is also an expression of his own experiences as a reader and the conflict of attention that he felt and imagined others must feel in reading.

Gray's life of reading, like Bentley's and even King's, was more consistent and in some respects more heroic than that of Johnson. What kept Johnson from this level of achievement was, in part, his need to work for a living. Although Johnson's work required him to read, it caused him to give up the hardest kind of reading. In his journalistic work, and even in writing biographies, he read for immediate rather than long-term purposes. He read to discover the facts he needed for writing biographies or book reviews. This kind of perusal was something to which Gray rarely stooped. Although Gray composed the outlines of many scholarly works in his notebooks, his reading was done for "gentlemanly" purposes in the end, and therefore did not lead to publication.

The complete reverse of Gray, who read for projects he never wrote, Johnson often wrote what he had barely researched. For many of his writing projects Johnson relied on the stocks of reading he had gathered earlier; for some he did no new reading at all. In fact, this was how he did an immense amount of his writing, even when his subject required research. His memory helped him enormously, but he also had the trick of reading quickly and picking out what he needed. He cultivated an ability to peruse books and find what he was looking for. He liked to read in dictionaries, encyclopedias, and reference works of all kinds, and he made a great many of his books out of these sources, the books most suitable for perusal.

I I

In addition to the obvious and immense category of reference books, the texts on which perusal can be practiced are numerous: the Bible and even classical texts can be used, as can moral philosophy, sermons (an enormous and varied category), handbooks, manuals, enchiridia designed to offer specific advice on moral behavior, and the still lower realm of how-to books addressing matters of diet, social behavior, and other areas for self-improvement.

The central focus of this kind of reading is the lower end of the scale, what contemporary American bookstores call "self-help," unconsciously referring to the greatest manual of them all, Samuel Smiles's *Self Help* (1859). Smiles's Industrial Age work, like many of its predecessors, stresses the importance of hard work and industry in the quest for salvation or for secular achievements. Johnson's most popular work, *Rasselas,* is in a sense a self-help book. The successful method of escape from the Happy Valley in *Rasselas* by means of persistent industry (digging), when shortcuts to the goal (flying) have failed, is the epitome of the message of many self-help books published before the late nineteenth and twentieth centuries. In more-recent works an increasing premium is put on relaxation and the individual's need to escape the rigors of modern work, modern science, and modern civilization.[5] Although the emphasis has shifted in the past hundred years, the concerns of recent books are certainly not new. Precedents for them can be found in earlier religious works, and the dangers of stress, business, and confusion to spiritual life have been acknowledged since ancient times. When George Beard wrote *American Nervousness* in 1881 he was repeating some of the concerns of George Cheyne's *English Malady* of 1733, and Cheyne in turn was repeating some of the themes of Stoics such as Celsus.

Until the genre has its own history, it will be difficult to say whether through the ages there has been more change or more stability in the self-help category of books. There are, however, observable trends at various times. In the eighteenth century, although there were many self-help books that stressed industry and secular goals, such as Benjamin Franklin's *Way to Wealth,* the genre was less secular than it was to become. It also had not entered so fully as today's market has into matters of sexual life.

But there were a few sex manuals available in the eighteenth century, including an old standby called *Aristotle's Masterpiece.* Delarivière Manley demonstrated the power of this book to evoke latent sexuality in a passage about the defloration of Stuarta Howard by her sophisticated stepfather, but she distinguished it from books about erotic passion.[6] There were other, somewhat more sober books of advice on marriage and breeding. Johnson had with him at college both Latin and English versions of a curious, extremely elegant poem on the subject, *Callipaedia* by Claudius Quillet. This work is not so concerned with increasing pleasure as are modern manuals such as Alex Comfort's *Joy of Sex,* and it is much more concerned with fine writing, but it provided both information and titillation to young men and women of the seventeenth and eighteenth centuries. Here is an example of its gynecological information from book 2, which advises moderate repetitions of intercourse for the cultivation of the proper lustiness of seed and womb for the production of males:

> Beneath those Parts, where stretching to its Bound,
> The low Abdomen girds the Belly round,
> The Shop of Nature lies; a vacant Space
> Of small Circumference divides the Place,
> Pear-like the Shape; within a Membrane spreads
> Her various Texture of Mæandrous Threads;
> These draw the Vessels to a pursy State,
> And or contract their Substance, or dilate.
> Here Veins, Nerves, Arteries in Pairs declare
> How nobler Parts deserve a double Care;
> They from the Mass the Blood and Spirits drain,
> That irrigate profuse the thirsty Plain;
> The Bottom of the Womb 'tis call'd; the Sides are cleft,
> By Cells distinguish'd into Right and Left.
> 'Tis thought that Females in the Left prevail,
> And that the Right contains the sprightly Male.
> A Passage here in Form oblong extends,
> Where fast compress'd the stiffen'd Nerve ascends,
> And the warm Fluid with concurring Fluids blends.
> The Sages this the Womb's Neck justly name;
> Within the Hollow of its inward Frame,
> Join'd to the Parts, a small Protub'rance grows,
> Whose rising Lips the deep Recesses close.
> For while the Tiller all his Strength collects,
> While Hope anticipates the fair Effects,
> The lubricated Parts their Station leave,
> And closely to the working Engine cleave;
> Each Vessel stretches, and distending wide,

The greedy Womb attracts the glowing Tide,
And either Sex commix'd, the Streams united glide.
But now the Womb relax'd, with pleasing Pain
Gently subsides into it self again;
The Seed moves with it, and thus clos'd within
The tender Drops of Entity begin.[7]

In spite of its somewhat strained explicitness, Quillet's poem (especially in the Latin version) is a piece of fine writing, and it served Johnson in his coterie studies, in addition to providing sexual information. There is no evidence that Johnson was much interested in libertine literature or that he possessed other sex manuals. He surely was not immune to the titillation offered by Quillet, but he could study it as poetry also; in a similar way he may have perused material of a sexual nature in Latin classics such as Ovid and Petronius, while also studying them.

The lowest kind of self-help book in which Johnson took a demonstrable interest, and which cannot be easily related to study and higher reading habits, was the diet book. Among these, Johnson tended to select those that were mixed with philosophical or technical considerations, but it is clear in many cases that he was perusing these books for self-help rather than studying them. That is, he was scanning them for tips on daily life, rather than examining their structure or building up his stock of knowledge per se. Gleaning, accompanied by a relaxation of the critical faculty and a temporary extension of credulousness, is most characteristic of perusal.

Perusal is not all of one kind. For example, Johnson perused John Arbuthnot's work on diet when he read it for the *Diction-ary,* but in that reading his principal goal was to make the *Dictionary* a useful text for perusal rather than to improve himself personally. But the latter kind of perusal seems to me most central to this kind of reading and most distinct from study. Johnson took John Locke's *Essay of Education* to college with him, and at that time he probably perused its advice on diet with attention to his own situation; this was a more definitive and purer kind of perusal than he did later on when he read the work to find illustrative quotations for the *Dictionary*.

Much of the advice in Locke's book concerns children, but the philosopher argues for its application to adults as well. For example, in recommending that children not eat too much and stay away from meats before the work of the day is done, Locke said that he too enjoyed a moderate diet, concentrating on easily chewed and digested bread during most of the day. Johnson was concerned with his diet and probably took the advice seriously. Locke began his work with a quotation from Juvenal's tenth satire, *Mens sana in corpore sano* (mental health comes from a healthy body), and he also recommended physical exercise, a recommendation Johnson always passed along to friends and readers but only fitfully followed himself. By "education" Locke certainly meant, as his editor James Axtell points out, "the whole process by which culture transmits itself across the generations."[8] His *Essay of Education* cannot therefore be classified as mere self-help, but it has elements of that lesser genre, and it shares some of its assumptions. When Locke says, for instance, that "we are all a sort of Camelions" and lays stress on the malleability of human personality and human destiny, he asserts one of the principles on which all self-help books rest.[9] The point of reading such books is self-improvement, and that goal requires a suspension of the established, defensive, critical self.

With their combination of psychology, medicine, philosophy, and diet, the works of George Cheyne were also important to Johnson, and he perused them in hopes of finding a cure for his problems. *The English Malady* came out in 1733 when Johnson was still suffering through his worst bout of depression, and he must have felt that the work spoke directly to him. Cheyne discusses nervous disorders precisely like those from which Johnson suffered, and he attributes them to causes that Johnson either exhibited or worried about in himself. For example, Cheyne traces nervous tics to scrofula, which Johnson certainly had, to tenderness in the sensibility, to laziness, and to "other corruptions in the Habit." *Habit* is a key word in Johnson's morality, and he must have responded to a work that handled the word in a biological as well as a moral sense. *Habit* in Cheyne's works refers primarily to its semantic roots in the Greek word ἕξις, which means the state a body is in. Cheyne saw excessive salt as one of the major corruptions of the habit, and such corruptions, he believed, were the true cause of what we call disease:

> When, by *Food* of *ill* Qualities, or an immoderate Quantity of even wholesome *Food,* the *Humours* are vitiated, the Structure of the *Animal Machine* is such, that Nature (*i.e.* the *Mechanism of the Body*) is presently rouz'd to struggle with all its Might, to attenuate (or concoct, as we commonly say) the gross and vitious Humours, and so bring them to an healthy State. . . . This *Struggle* is the one only proper and real Disease of the Body, arising from the Habit . . . the vast Variety of particular Diseases, spoken of by *Physicians,* being only so many particular or various *Issues* of this general Struggle of Nature.[10]

In attributing medical and psychological disorders to matters of diet and internal "balance," Cheyne resembles such modern nutritionists as Victor Lindlahr, the author of *You Are What You Eat,* and Adelle Davis, who sold some five million copies of *Let's Eat Right to Keep Fit.* Cheyne had much less nutritional information available to him, but his prescriptions were not wildly different from those Lindlahr made. He recommended plenty of exercise and, especially for the sedentary and studious, a vegetarian diet with many helpings of milk. Cheyne made a fortune promulgating his diet at Bath, creating a fad like the Beverly Hills Diet, and he even reduced his own three hundred pounds of bulk to a manageable size as a demonstration of his scheme's effectiveness. Although the change was temporary, Cheyne did outlive the canonical three score and ten by two years.

Johnson could and did study the medical and philosophical authorities upon whom Cheyne drew, such as Thomas Sydenham and Seneca, but he perused Cheyne along with the many thousands of less learned readers who could not follow Latin medical books or classical texts. Such reading also threw him into the company of many, such as David Hume, with whom he had little contact for ideological rather than social reasons. The kind of perusal involved in self-help reading connects one to a larger and more varied community of readers than study. Self-help books provide a link between the studious world of learning and learned books, to which they are functionally closely related, and the world of the general reader.

Cheyne's mastery of the self-help form is manifest in his definition of the best diet in terms of the common people; his description bears a striking resemblance to Johnson's later definitions of the best reading in terms of the preferences of the common reader:

> It is in *Medicines* as in *Food*, (Medicines being only a more *rare* and less natural Kind of Food) that which is *common* to the middling Sort of every Country, and which has the Approbation of the Generality of the Inhabitants, and is suited to the Constitution of the Community, is generally the most *beneficial;* since it is the Experiences and Observation of the Generality that makes them common: and special or particular Things, or Rarities, are justly to be suspected.[11]

As Francis Bacon suggested in his famous distinction among works to be tasted, chewed, and thoroughly digested, there is a conventional analogy between reading and nutrition. Cheyne's work displays another side of the analogy; his is a book about nutrition that shares some of the principles of reading in the mid–eighteenth century and may have helped form them.

I I I

Johnson read plenty of other books that contain advice on diet, but many of these were either too technical or too learned to be perused as self-help books. Yet, interested as he was in the health of his body, like most of his contemporaries Johnson was even more concerned about the health of his soul. Accordingly, he did most of his self-help reading in the vast array of religious handbooks available in his time. Johnson was particularly drawn to works that combined religion with a psychological or protopsychological component. The progeny of these books are familiar to us because psychology began dominating the genre of self-help in the early twentieth century and is still supreme today. Despite the pope's rapprochement with Catholic psychiatrists in 1992, the history of the self-help genre shows that psychology competes strongly with religion as a means by which people undertake to know and improve themselves. Johnson was interested in the ancestors of popular psychology books, but he hardly approved of them all.

The great-grandfathers of feel-good or Me Generation books disgusted Johnson: he satirized their authors in chapter 22 of *Rasselas*, "The Happiness of a Life Led According to Nature." In his famous review of Soame Jenyns's insipid, feel-good theodicy, Johnson blasted facile schemes in which suffering is rationalized as part of a cosmic plan, the wisdom of which is inscrutable to human understanding.[12] What appealed to Johnson were works of religious self-help that recommended hard work, self-control, and a degree of self-laceration and that, in addition, combined these recommendations with some scheme of psychology that acknowledged the reality of pain and suffering. One such book was Thomas à Kempis's *Imitatio Christi*; Johnson read it throughout his life, and he was familiar enough with it to use a copy in Dutch, as many linguists use familiar parts of the Bible, to assist him in learning that language.

Another favorite was John Bunyan's *Pilgrim's Progress*; it was one of the three books Johnson said he wished were longer than it is. But Bunyan's work contained an added element that raises questions about the role of religious self-help reading in Johnson's whole life of reading. Bunyan's combination of allegorical psychology and practical theology certainly attracted Johnson, but the story was also an incentive to reading, and in providing adventures, the book satisfied Johnson's childhood love of romances. There are giants and castles in Bunyan as well as morality. Obviously Johnson took pleasure in reading Bunyan, but he took pleasure in perusing other self-help books too; comprehending Johnson's pleasure, as well as his profit, in these books is essential to understanding how he read. Given his penchant for reading romances, it is easy to understand how Johnson found Bunyan pleasurable, but how did the less fabulous self-help books attract him? How is it, for example, that he could say of Isaac Watts's *Improvement of the Mind,* "Few books have been perused by me with greater pleasure"?[13]

In the story I wish to tell of Johnson's life of reading, self-help books are crucial because they provided him with a way of reconciling two fundamentally different interests in reading; they gave him a means of integrating the pleasure-seeking reader who read about knights and monsters on his mother's lap with the serious scholar who plucked Petrarch from the top shelves of his father's bookshop and devoured humanistic hard reading. The perusal of religious manuals reconciled the male and female myths of origin in Johnson's life of reading. There is even some basis for proposing a third myth of Johnson's ur-reading life in his early experience with a work of practical religion. Mrs. Thrale reported in her *Anecdotes* a story she must have heard from Johnson:

> At the age of ten years his mind was disturbed by scruples of infidelity, which preyed upon his spirits, and made him very uneasy; the more so, as he revealed his uneasiness to no one, being naturally (as he said) "of a sullen temper, and reserved disposition." He searched, however, diligently, but fruitlessly, for evidences of the truth of revelation; and at length recollecting a book he had once seen in his father's shop, intitled *De Veritate Religionis, &c.* he began to think himself highly culpable for neglecting such a means of information, and took himself severely to task for this sin, adding many acts of voluntary, and to others, unknown penance. The first opportunity which offered (of course) he seized the book with avidity; but on examination, not finding himself scholar enough to peruse its contents, set his heart at rest. . . . He redoubled his diligence to learn the

language that contained the information he most wished for; but from the pain which guilt had given him, he now began to deduce the soul's immortality.[14]

The most striking aspect of Thrale's account is that religion was generated in Johnson without any reading of the desired text. The mere existence of Hugo Grotius's *De veritate religionis Christianae* and its alleged contents stimulated feelings in Johnson that led him to deduce one of the basic principles of his religion.

The foundation of Johnson's religion may indeed have been guilt. There is no question that he felt guilty about many things: his behavior towards his parents, his treatment of his brother, his relations with his wife, his outbursts at friends, his failure to rise early and discipline himself in other ways, and his laziness about his work, or rather his perceived laziness. But one of the things that soothed Johnson was reading, and the kind of reading that may have soothed him most of all was reading in plain and simple books of divinity such as Grotius's, which was written not for the great Latinist or the scholar but for the semieducated worker and in particular for the enlisted sailor. Johnson evidently read the book many times throughout his life, and it was the volume he pulled from his pocket and seesawed over in his fantastic, nervous way when Frances Burney observed him making a spectacle of himself in public.[15] It is hard to be sure, but it seems likely that he felt the fit coming on and soothed himself with reading. But why did he choose this book for the antidote? In what anodyne experience of reading did it permit him to immerse himself?

Grotius composed his first draft of *De veritate religionis Christianae* in Dutch verse while in prison for heresy (c. 1621). He completed a version in simple Latin in 1625, and the work was soon translated into all the languages of Europe. The work was later edited, corrected, and illustrated (with further examples) by Jean LeClerc and translated into English by the educator John Clarke. Which edition or editions Johnson owned it is impossible to say. The Elsevir Latin edition of 1662 would have been convenient for his pocket, but so would many others. The work tries to prove the most fundamental truths of Christianity by appeals to common sense, reason, and the testimony of the ages. For example, section 2 sets out to show simply that there is a God. The proof of this essential religious conviction is threefold: a first cause of the universe is required (it had to come from somewhere and start somehow); observation shows that the belief in a God is common in all places and at all times; and no other hypothesis adequately explains the obvious facts of nature.

In the next section Grotius asserts that the necessary existence of God implies God's singleness. The troubling problems raised in Johnson's lifetime by Hume do not even come into the margins of Grotius's work. His conviction, like that of Robert Boyle and those who lectured on the chair established by Boyle's bequest, is that in our analysis of nature, we rise from various natural causes to a contemplation of the first cause. There can be only one point at the top of the pyramid. Hume suggested that reasoning from the harmony of nature, if it really exists, might lead us to posit many gods. Grotius and his later augmenters do not consider this strange possibility, but rather enlist the world's great thinkers as allies in supporting the commonsense conviction. The divine creation and continued divine government of the world by Providence are supported by testimony from Tertullian, Lucretius, Vergil's *Eclogues* and *Georgics*, Horace, Lactantius, Seneca, Moses Maimonides, and others in opposition to Aristotle. The list of supporting documents grew with later editions, but the framework was there from the beginning; the point is obviously that those who were better, wiser, and more numerous than we concurred in affirming the basic tenets of our religion.

Clearly, the past is read tendentiously in Grotius's book, but this must have been part of the appeal for Johnson and others who made the book so popular. The voice of Grotius, himself one of the most learned men in European history, supported by a chorus of greats from the past, reaffirming Sunday school religious basics must have been comforting. This was especially so in a world that still relied on texts and documents as the primary evidence in matters of natural and civil history. Even those branches of science in which experimentation and observation had made inroads still observed some of the methods of textual learning: the natural world was a text, and it told us the truths of Christian religion in a standing revelation of God's wisdom, power, and glory. In this atmosphere of conviction and confidence, even the troubling problem of evil melts away. Evil is an inevitable outgrowth of the principle of freedom, without which human life and human action would be a mere charade: "When God made Man a free Agent, and at Liberty to do well or ill (reserving to himself alone a necessary and immutable Goodness) it was not fit that he should put such a restraint upon evil Actions."[16] "It was not fit" (just two words in Latin) and a quick parenthesis cover all the ground on which the doubts of unorthodox thinkers from the Manichees to Hobbes sported.

The first part of *De veritate religionis Christianae* covers all the basics of Christian religion. Part 2 addresses specific, somewhat disputed tenets of Christianity. The sticky question of the resurrection of the body is handled in less than two pages: if God created the universe out of nothing, how easy must it be for him to reassemble the dispersed atoms of our fleshly selves at the last trump. The Christian virtues are extolled in this section and referenced to places in the New Testament for further reading, but it is marvelous how skillfully Grotius also marshals such infidels as Democritus, Euripides, and Claudian, all in the cause of basic Christianity. The miraculous spread of Christianity finishes the chapter, and there is no hint of the heinous suggestions of the more rigorously historical Gibbon that there may have been social and secular reasons for the rise of Christianity. Part 3 asserts the authority of the received Christian canon. Part 4 confutes all religions but Judaism and Mohametanism. Part 5 confutes Judaism, and part 6 dispatches Mohametanism. In this chapter, Grotius treats the historical schism of the Christian church with frequent citation of Marcellinus Ammianus. The lesson here is nearly equivalent to the lesson of the whole book: "As of old, the preferring the Tree of Knowledge to the Tree of Life, was the Occasion of the greatest Evils; so then nice Enquiries were esteemed more than Piety."[17] Grotius has it both ways here because he is immensely learned and he is not "nice" or oversophisticated in his inquiries. He keeps it simple as he ranges over the great literature of the Western world. This is reassuring: we may study all we like without endangering faith; in fact, further study only strengthens faith, as long as we keep commonsensically to the basic tenets of Christianity.

In some of Grotius's precursors the basic facts of Christianity are much more antagonistic to learning. In Lactantius, in Nicholas of Cusa, and in Henry Cornelius Agrippa learning only proves our ignorance and the need to "pause awhile from Letters, to be wise."[18] There is an ironic relation between the vast learning in these writers' works and their assertion of inevitable human ignorance. According to them, the simplicity of Christian conviction embarrasses learning. In Grotius, too, Christian ways are superior to learning, but only excessively subtle inquiries will lead to trouble, and somehow in the end everything will be all right: "The Time will come, when all things shall be most certainly known. But this is required of every one, that they do not unprofitably keep by them the Talent committed to their charge; but use their utmost endeavours to gain others unto Christ; in order whereunto, we are not only to give them good and wholesome Advice, but to set before them an example of reformation of Life."[19] It would be hard to find a passage in all of Johnson's reading about which he felt more conviction. Much has been said about the importance of the parable of the talents to Johnson's religious and moral life and his perpetual uneasiness about whether or not he was using his gifts properly, and it is all true. It is clear that Johnson believed in the doctrine, and reading it in the works of such an awesome scholar as Grotius must have had a settling effect on him. In a way, this was both the counterpoint to and the completion of Johnson's life of hard reading. It displayed the simplicity of truth as distinct from the complexities of learning and showed that the greatest books and authors really were united in testifying to the basic truths of Christianity.

The tranquilizing effect he found in Grotius may be what Johnson was seeking from his reading on Easter Eve in 1775 when he noted in his diary that after a visit from an old Grub Street acquaintance, "I then read a little in the Testament, and tried Fiddes's B. of Divinity, but did not settle. I then went to Evening prayer, and was tolerably composed. At my return I sat awhile, then retired, but found reading uneasy."[20] Richard Fiddes's *Body of Divinity,* a work in two folio volumes, was suitably hard and pious reading for the solemnity of Easter Eve, but it did not offer the ready and comfortable access of simpler books. In the *Dictionary,* where I think Johnson valued accessibility in his choice of illustrative quotations and may also have been conscious of performing in the self-help genre, he quoted Fiddes occasionally, but not from his *Body of Divinity*; he chose instead his more readily perused sermons.

Although Grotius may have been breaking new ground in some respects when he first wrote *De veritate religionis Christianae,* most of it was received truth for Johnson, who was reading it one hundred years after its first appearance. Its presence in his pockets when he was an old man suggests that he was not troubled by the encouragement that Grotius's comparatively rational approach to religion had given to extreme rationalists, such as the deists John Toland and Anthony Collins, who sought to strip away most of the thirty-nine articles and the mysteries of Christianity, including the divinity of Christ. Johnson did not read Grotius in a highly critical way. He felt he was on comfortable ground; he perused expected truths and ignored collateral complications. Johnson also applied this soothing style of reading to many other books of the self-help kind; indeed, it is hard to imagine him reading them in any other way. Some of those that he took with him to college are much more simplistic than Grotius: William Sherlock's *Practical Discourse concerning Death* and Cardinal Giovanni Bona's *Manuductio ad Coelum,* translated as *A Guide to Eternity* by Roger L'Estrange. Much later in life, Johnson declared that Sherlock's style was "elegant," and in the last year of his life he recommended Sherlock's sermons to a minister who sought help with the plan of his studies.

However, Johnson was not uncritical in his reading of all self-help books. For example, he ridiculed the immensely popular *Meditations* by James Hervey. At Inveraray, Johnson read aloud from Dr. Samuel Ogden's sermon on prayer, which he liked, and then called for more books. The *Meditations* was brought forth, and Boswell reported with some discomfort:

> He treated it with ridicule, and would not allow even the scene of the dying Husband and Father to be pathetick. I am not an impartial judge; for *Hervey's Meditations* engaged my affections in my early years.—He read a passage concerning the moon, ludicrously, and shewed how easily he could, in the same style, make reflections on that planet, the very reverse of Hervey's, representing her as treacherous to mankind. He did this with much humour. . . . He then indulged a playful fancy, in making a *Meditation on a Pudding,* of which I hastily wrote down, in his presence, the following note. . . . "LET us seriously reflect of what a pudding is composed. It is composed of flour that once waved in the golden grain, and drank the dews of morning; of milk pressed from the swelling udder by the gentle hand of the beauteous milkmaid . . . who, while she stroked the udder, indulged no ambitious thoughts for the destruction of her fellow-creatures."[21]

Hervey may have been the Kahlil Gibran of his day, but Johnson's objections were to the style as much as to the message of the *Meditations.* His reaction to the artifice blocked his capacity to peruse the work with comfort, even though its doctrine was probably acceptable. Hervey is ingratiating and pseudopoetical, whereas Sherlock is more straightforwardly conversational.

Sherlock's theme was admittedly more attractive to Johnson than Hervey's, since it was a variation on the theme of the vanity of human wishes, but Johnson certainly could have mocked Sherlock's repetitiveness and predictability had he been in-

clined to do so. He was not so inclined, however, because
Sherlock transported him to a comfortable realm of meaning
and a comfortable activity of reading in which criticism rather
than engagement is blocked out. Sherlock says from the start
that he "shall not go about to prove" the basic assumptions of
his book: that we die, leave our earthly bodies, and enter into a
new, permanent state. However, the rest of the book merely re-
hearses the facts and the commonsense conclusions we should
draw from them. There is no development of the ideas and no
real questioning. The book operates reasonably but never in-
vestigates its assumptions. It is so highly repetitive that almost
any page offers a representative example of its contents:

> For let us thus reason with ourselves: I find I am mortal, and
> must shortly leave this world; and yet I believe that my soul
> cannot die as my body does, but shall only be translated to
> another state; whatever I take pleasure in, in this world, I
> must leave behind me, and know not what I shall find in the
> next: but surely the other world, where I must live for ever,
> is not worse furnished than this world, which I must so
> quickly leave. For has God made me immortal, and pro-
> vided no sorts of pleasures and entertainments for an im-
> mortal state, when he has so liberally furnished the short
> and changeable scene of this life? I know not indeed what
> the pleasures of the next world are, but no more did I know
> what the pleasures of this world were till I came into it; and
> therefore, that is no argument that there are no pleasures
> there, because I did not yet know them. And if there be any
> pleasures there, surely they must be greater than what are
> here, because it is a more lasting state.[22]

It would be dangerous and careless to slight this work; Joseph
Addison called it "one of the strongest Persuasives to a Religious Life that ever was written in any Language."[23] But from
an aesthetic or logical point of view one would have to say that
the book is closely and repetitiously woven to its starkly unex-
amined assumptions. Despite these failings, however, the ac-
ceptability of its doctrine and its unfailing good manners kept

Johnson and many of his contemporaries perusing, receiving confirmation of what they believed true, without being critical. If once Johnson had cast a critical eye on the work, if once his pleasure in the confirming doctrine had been spoiled by poor writing or thinking, he could have been devastating in his critique, just as he was in his attack on Hervey's *Meditations*.

Johnson's pleasure in Sherlock's *Practical Discourse concerning Death* and similar books is a version of the pleasure that all readers of self-help works take in perusal. In a recent sociological study, Wendy Simonds interviewed thirty female readers of self-help books. She reported that they "were unanimous in their recognition that self-help books were repetitive, and thus secure. Reading could be a ritual of self-reassurance where repetition was desired."[24] This is not a fundamentally different pleasure than that offered by self-help books on diet or sex. Much of what Johnson found in Cheyne about exercise and the need for moderation would have been as familiar as can be, and it is likely that he knew much of the rudimentary anatomy and folklore in the *Callipaedia*. Likewise, he knew everything Sherlock had to say before he read it, but reading it reassured him, strengthened an inner voice that he felt needed strengthening, and excluded from his mind, for a time, the disturbing vagaries of his imagination.

Johnson found similar relief in *Manuductio ad Coelum*, written by Cardinal Giovanni Bona (1609–74) and first published in Cologne in 1671. Its place of publication suggests that its doctrine may not have been agreeable to the pontiff, and, to a degree, all such manuals are inimical to Roman Catholicism in that they emphasize the power of the individual rather than the church in the work of salvation. Bona's book resembles Grotius's in the way it marshals the learning of the past in the service of fundamental religious and moral principles, but it is less learned and even more determined to be plain and simple. In his preface, as translated by Roger L'Estrange, Bona says:

> I have here drawn up a Compendium of moral Institutions and Counsels (the best I could) out of the Writings of the

Fathers, Seneca, Epictetus, Antoninus, and others of the Ancients, both Christian and Pagan. What I have found effectual in my own Case, I have here communicated for the Benefit of others; without so much as saying where I had it, without clogging my Paper with Citations, or playing the Orator. My Design is to work upon the Passions, not the Fancy; and if the Physic be proper, no matter for the plainness of it, or who mingled the potion.[25]

Like Cheyne's diet, Bona's spiritual advice provides food for the common taste. The notes added in later editions, however, show that he drew heavily on classical moralists associated with Stoicism, especially Epictetus and Seneca, and that the whole work is buttressed by a tradition like the one that Grotius made explicit in his more visibly learned work. Bona's work is directed at conduct rather than belief, and its practical recommendations often resemble Sherlock's, but Bona suggests cultivating a contempt for worldly pleasures that goes beyond Sherlock. Bona begins in the area that Sherlock explores so thoroughly: "The readiest way to master our Corruptions, is to propound to our selves, that every Day is to be our last." His recommendations on the control of particular passions and appetites often culminate in homely, highly conventional aphorisms that Johnson surely remembered: "He is a great master of himself that commands his belly"; "A tongue without a guard upon it, is like a city without a wall"; "To contemn pleasure is the greatest Pleasure"; and "He that hates himself as he ought shall be saved."[26] When Johnson wrote of the carefree needy traveler in *The Vanity of Human Wishes* "Increase his wealth and his peace destroy," he was thinking of Juvenal but perhaps also of his adolescent reading of Bona: "Look but the poor and the rich Man in the Face, and compare their countenances, and you shall see that the one, in the sourness of his Looks, betrays the anxiety and solicitude of his Thoughts: the other's Brow is clear and open, in testimony of an honest and chearful mind. . . . He spends the Day merrily, and sleeps soundly at night, whereas the other on the contrary is never at ease."[27]

Throughout his life, when he composed poetry or spoke to friends, Johnson had in mind not only the great works of the classical and modern world but also a number of books that used the thoughts in those works to fashion quasi-literary manuals and advice books. No theme is more central to Johnson's moral essays than the human tendency to ignore the present in favor of the uncertain, imagined benefits of the future. Bona could have been framing the question for much of Johnson's contemplation when he asked, "Why do we lose this instant which is our own, and pretend to dispose of the future which is out of our power?"[28] There are many instances in the *Dictionary* when Johnson added material to his book from memory, and often his memory ran to manuals like Bona's that he had absorbed in his youth. He did not forget to include the word *godward,* for example, which appears only in the stylistically homely phrase "to godward," which Bona and other writers of religious manuals regularly used.[29]

At the end of his "Grammar of the English Language," a part of the preliminary matter of his *Dictionary,* Johnson included a section on prosody in which he probably took all his examples from memory. Many of them are from popular ballads and religious or moral poetry. He remembered a poem by Samuel Wesley, an epitaph on an infant, for example, and a quatrain of this ballad, called "The Sailor's Rant" or "The Sailor's Ballad":

> When terrible tempests assail us,
> And mountainous billows affright,
> Nor power nor wealth can avail us,
> But skilful industry steers right.[30]

This is not deathless verse, but it was in Johnson's mind, along with the greats of English, Latin, and Greek literature; it may not be so illustrious as the greats, but it may have been as prominent for Johnson as they.

Similarly, as an example of the "*anapestic,* in which the accent rests upon every third syllable," Johnson selected the chorus of a popular song called "The Wish" by Walter Pope:

May I góvern my pássions with ábsolute swáy,
And grow wíser and bétter as lífe wears awáy.

This was also a favorite of that great reader and creator of popular handbooks Benjamin Franklin, who referred to it as "The Wishing Song." Walter Pope was circulating in his mind, as well as Bonnefons and Scaliger; thus Johnson was united to a popular community of readers that cut across national, political, and religious boundaries. Unlike the virtual community of readers whom he joined in study or coterie reading, this more popular group also transcended educational and class divisions. The experience of religious manuals, like that of great books, also cuts across the barriers of time, because, although the books change, the material in them often stays the same.

In 1982, in an aptly named essay, "The Company We Keep," Wayne Booth described his equally durable childhood experiences of reading in a set of gold-bound books and of perusing the loose sheet music of popular songs:

> And here I am, more than half a century later, able to remember more about the set of illustrated books and those popular songs than I can about anything my parents said or did at the time. . . . I can remember making up songs of my own, no doubt borrowed from favorites like "Hello, Central, Give Me Heaven," "You Can't Holler Down My Rain Barrel," and one about the ancient story of a sweet little "babe in the woods" who lay down and died, with her brother.[31]

Johnson quoted the same fable of the babes in the woods (and their sad, edifying end) in the *Dictionary* (s.v. "redbreast"). He probably did not read the often reprinted and versified ballad as part of his preparation for writing his great book. It was already in his mind, as it was two centuries later in the mind of Wayne Booth when he sat down to say something about his life of reading. Such simple works are every bit as much a part of many great lives of reading as the texts that represent the highest artistic and intellectual achievements of our culture.

Like many of the other manuals Johnson read, Bona's also contains advice on reading. Like Isaac Watts, who was probably Johnson's all-time favorite writer of practical handbooks, Bona recommends a life of reading in which study preponderates; he acknowledges, however, the golden rule of temperance, *nihil nimis* (nothing in extremes), and therefore allows that some variety in reading is beneficial. The reading he favors most is useful study or attentive perusal; the reading he fears, except for occasional relaxation, is desultory, extensive, "mere" reading:

> Wisdom does not consist in knowing much, but in knowing things that we are the better for; and those things, in the first place, that concern our Salvation: Not that I am against human Learning neither; provided, that a good Use be made of whatever we read toward the ordering of our Lives and manners. In the reading of many Books we are apt to take up a rambling Humour of skipping from one thing to another, and swallowing Abundance; but we digest Nothing. Whereas we should rather pitch upon some certain Authors, take what's good out of them; read them over and over, and study them, if we would have any thing stick by us. Variety of reading, may be pleasant; but it is the steady and certain Application of our Studies that improves us.
>
> III. And yet we are not to be so intent upon our studies neither, as never to give ourselves Breath and Respite: The Mind is to be sometimes unbent.[32]

Bona does not mention specific books or even specific kinds of books, but his own work is a compromise between the extremes he recommends. It is light reading because its doctrine is familiar, but its subject is serious. In his scheme of education for children, Milton recommended using the tired evening hours for instruction in the fundamentals of religion, and books like Sherlock's and Bona's make relaxation profitable. They reconcile the opposition between study and desultory reading that was as strong in Johnson as it was in any of the readers to whom Bona ministered.

No treatment of Johnson's reading in the realm of self-help

books would be complete without a discussion of William Law's *Serious Call to a Devout and Holy Life*. This work was published in 1729 while Johnson was at Pembroke College, and it is known that he read it there. Boswell prefaces his famous account of Johnson's momentous encounter with Law with an anecdote about Johnson's childhood rejection of Richard Allestree's *Whole Duty of Man* (1658), perhaps the most popular religious self-help book of the eighteenth century:

> Sunday (said he) was a heavy day to me when I was a boy. My mother confined me on that day, and made me read "The Whole Duty of Man," from a great part of which I could derive no instruction. When, for instance, I had read the chapter on theft, which from my infancy I had been taught was wrong, I was no more convinced that theft was wrong than before; so there was no accession of knowledge. A boy should be introduced to such books, by having his attention directed to the arrangement, to the style, and other excellencies of composition; that the mind being thus engaged by an amusing variety of objects, may not grow weary.[33]

Obviously Johnson felt that Allestree's work was not engaging for aesthetic reasons. He remarked with some hint of surprise or disdain that his stepdaughter Lucy during an illness would have nothing by her but *The Whole Duty of Man*. This is not because he disapproved of Allestree's doctrine. In the first edition of his *Dictionary* Johnson preferred to quote Allestree's slightly less well known works, *The Government of the Tongue* and *The Decay of Christian Piety*. He added numerous quotations from *The Whole Duty of Man* in the fourth edition, published in 1773, but even his implicit recommendation of the work does not necessarily indicate that Johnson had read it. On the day after Easter in 1781 in his diary Johnson reported reading "the first Sunday in the Duty of Man, in which I had till then only looked at by compulsion or by chance."[34] This suggests that Johnson's amanuenses actually did for him the reading in *The Whole Duty of Man* that is reflected in the fourth edition of the *Dictionary*. In any case, it is clear that this manual did not appeal to Johnson for reasons of style, whereas Law's *Serious Call* had great appeal, probably also for reasons of style, although Boswell and other Johnsonians have always stressed the importance to Johnson of the book's message.

According to Boswell, Law's *Serious Call* made "religion . . . the predominant object of his thoughts" for the rest of Johnson's life.[35] But is this because of its overpowering doctrine or argument? Probably not. Boswell's version of Johnson's religious history is really no more reliable than Hester Thrale's, in which Johnson's failed reading of Grotius is the crucial event. Boswell casts aspersions on the Grotius story at least partly out of jealousy of Thrale (and all of Johnson's other biographers), but he also had Johnson's now famous testimony on his side: "When at Oxford, I took up 'Law's Serious Call to a Holy Life,' expecting to find it a dull book, (as such books generally are,) and perhaps to laugh at it. But I found Law quite an overmatch for me; and this was the first occasion of my thinking in earnest of religion, after I became capable of rational inquiry." Still, there are other competing stories of Johnson's religious awakening. Late in life Johnson referred to his unreligious adolescence and attributed his spiritual rebirth most plausibly to a nonliterary cause: "It had dropped out of my mind. It was at an early part of my life. Sickness brought it back, and I hope I have never lost it since."[36] In his works and in person Johnson recommended Law's work to many people, and his story about its importance in his religious life might have been part of his way of recommending it to Boswell. In less paternal moods, Johnson recommended Law by reference to its style. He called it "the finest piece of hortatory theology in any language," and, more tellingly, he said "William Law, Sir, wrote the best piece of Parenetick [persuasive] Divinity; but William Law was no reasoner."[37]

Despite what he told Boswell, Johnson probably did not have quite the enthusiastic and unreserved response to Law experienced by his fellow Oxonian John Wesley, who talked about the light flowing in on his soul. In fact, with his awareness of the rhetorical life of the text, part of Johnson's response may have been like that of Gibbon. Gibbon knew Law as his father's former tutor and reported on the minister's literary and rhetorical qualities: "His satire is sharp, but it is drawn from human life; and many of his portraits are not unworthy of the pen of La Bruyère. If he finds a spark of piety in his reader's mind, he will soon kindle it to a flame."[38] Johnson's dozen or so quotations from Law in the first edition of the *Dictionary* are all slightly flawed, which shows that he was quoting from memory and had the writer in mind, much as he had in mind the ballads that he produced to exemplify several measures of verse in his prosody. Law's work was like a ballad to Johnson, memorable for its language, and moving, but not especially powerful in doctrine or argument. A closer look at Law's work confirms the likelihood that what Johnson responded to was its art rather than its religion.

One of the qualities of Law's rhetoric that Johnson obviously found attractive was his frequent use of characters, after the manner of La Bruyère, as Gibbon suggests. Law's characters have allegorical names such as Flatus and Feliciana; they resemble Bunyan's characters in their sparseness, and they are very like those of Isaac Watts, a near-coeval who used the same devices at approximately the same time. It is partly because of these characters that Johnson said he derived so much pleasure from Watts's *Improvement of the Mind.* Johnson himself employed characters in his *Rambler* and other periodical essays; his Pertinax, Quisquilius, and Minim are somewhat more classical, less religious relatives of Law's Flatus and Flavia. Law provides a nice apology for the use of such characters in a religious book: "Characters of this kind," he says,

> the more folly and ridicule they have in them, provided that
> they be but natural, are most useful to correct our minds;
> and therefore are no where more proper than in books of
> devotion, and practical piety. And as in several cases, we
> best learn the nature of things, by looking at that which is

contrary to them; so perhaps we best apprehend the excellency of wisdom, by contemplating the wild extravagancies of folly.[39]

How trenchant Johnson found Law's portraits of extravagance is suggested by the way he remembered the character of Feliciana when he wrote it into the *Dictionary* from memory in illustration of *gee-gaw*. At the end of his sketch of vanity Law wrote, "But turn your eyes now another way, and let the trifling joys, the gugaw-happiness of Feliciana, teach you how wise they are, what delusion they escape, whose hearts and hopes are fixed upon a happiness in God."[40] Johnson entered merely "Let him that would learn the happiness of religion, see the poor *gee-gaw* happiness of Feliciano." Hewing to the path of his pleasure in reading, Johnson kept the character (although he changed the sex) and skipped the explanation.

By making such a reduction Johnson trimmed Law's rhetoric back to its roots in the Renaissance emblem books. His pleasure and interest in Law were related to his interest in these earlier works and their progeny. Johnson had an edition of the works of Andrea Alciati, one of the most famous emblem writers, but he also admired the fundamentally emblematic tales of Aesop. He owned an edition by the great scholar Peter Burman, and in this work, which he probably acquired close to the publication date of 1727, he found and evidently translated a funeral oration on Burman, which he later used in his life of the scholar for the *Gentleman's Magazine*.[41] Burman's scholarly work was certainly fit for harder reading than the translation of Aesop by Hoole that Johnson read in primary school, but it surely also provided a way to link study with the easier perusal of the self-help book. The language of the fables is conscientiously simple even in their Sanskrit relatives, the *Hitopadesha* and *Pancatatra,* and the stories seem universal in their appeal. They induct young readers into learning, and they assist learned readers in recapturing the fundamental rules of morality.

Law's characters function in a similar way, successfully linking abstract study and useful morality, especially for the learned, who might be inclined to reject some moral treatises as merely simpleminded. The genius of Law's characters is evident in his portrait of a man wishing to fly as the archetype of a man with unnatural wishes. He concludes, "Where-ever you see an ambitious man, there you see this vain and senseless flyer."[42] Surely this image stayed in Johnson's mind when he wrote his "dissertation on the art of flying" in chapter 6 of *Rasselas*. In Law's work the allegory is simple but intense; it requires a concentration and compression of meaning in the image without overinstructing the reader how to interpret it. As in a fable in the *Hitopadesha* or Aesop, there is a surplus of meaning in the image that the moral or summation does not thoroughly explicate. The proof of this is in the wide applicability of some of the images: the dog in the manger, the leopard and his spots, the jackal who is dyed purple in the *Hitopadesha* and thinks he is therefore a Brahmin until his involuntary howling brings on recognition and destruction. This excess of meaning gives the character or the fable a literary quality that the overactive and overexplicit imagination in Hervey's *Meditations* or, to name a modern exemplar, the *New York Times* column "About Men," fail to achieve.

Another quality in Law that Johnson may have found stimulating is his paratactic multiplication of clauses or phrases, especially in the most hortatory passages. The astringent laceration of the following passage was not irrelevant to Johnson's attraction, but the style was certainly part of the appeal:

> Let us judge ourselves sincerely, let us not vainly content our selves with the common disorders of our lives, the vanity of our expences, the folly of our diversions, the pride of our habits, the idleness of our lives, and the wasting of our time, fancying that these are such imperfections as we fall into thro' the unavoidable weakness and frailty of our natures; but let us be assured, that these disorders of our common life are owing to this, that we have not so much Christianity as to intend to please God in all the actions of our life, as the best and happiest thing in the world.[43]

This direct coupling of clauses serving the same grammatical function is perhaps closer to the incendiary prose of Jeremy Taylor in *Holy Dying* (1651) than to Johnson's more measured parallels and antitheses, but Johnson admired both writers and, although his prose does not blaze in these ways, it sometimes burns in similar if slower patterns. I may not be able to prove that Law had a greater effect on Johnson as a stylist than as a theologian or philosopher, but I think Johnson could not have read Law for his morality if his style had not fired him up and kept him reading without engaging the cooler aesthetic critic who ridiculed Hervey and was bored by Allestree.

Johnson's breast certainly returned an echo of the sentiments in Law. I do not want to deny that. His journals and diaries show that he felt as Law did: "if we are to follow Christ, it must be in our common way of spending every day." His frequent self-condemnatory remarks in those diaries show that he too felt that "religion is a state of labour and striving" and "the salvation of our souls is set forth in Scripture as a thing of difficulty, that requires all our diligence, that is to be work'd out with fear and trembling." Johnson certainly felt, as Law puts it in his version of the parable of the talents, that he was one of "those, of whom much will be requir'd, because much is given unto them." Although he called Law "no reasoner," he could not avoid the logic of his pronouncement that "he that truly knows, why he should spend any time well, knows that it is never allowable to throw any time away."[44]

On the other hand, Law took many positions with which Johnson had little sympathy. Law campaigned against theatergoing, for example, and even warned about the dangers of reading poetry: "How much better would it be," he asks rhetorically, "to be furnished with hymns and anthems of the saints, and teach their souls to ascend to God; than to corrupt, bewilder, and confound their hearts, with the wild fancies, the lustful thoughts of lewd poets?" Johnson felt a sting from Law's invectives against sleeping late, and probably agreed that prayer "is the noblest exercise of the soul, the most exalted use of our best faculties, and the highest imitation of the blessed inhabit-

ants of heaven . . . [whereas] sleep is the poorest dullest refresh-
ment of the body." Yet he did not agree that all prayers should
be begun with a psalm chanted or sung or that "a psalm only
read is very much like a prayer that is only look'd over."[45]

It might have been Law's extreme absolutism that made
Johnson call him "no reasoner." Although his own sense of
guilt and failure may have made him receptive to Law's absolutism on personal matters, such as thrift with time, he must have
found Law's extrapolations to the social realm somewhat simplistic. I doubt he followed Law closely in reasoning thus:

> If we consider mankind in a higher view, as God's order or
> society of rational beings, that are to glorify him by the right
> use of their reason, and by acting conformably to the order
> of their nature, we shall find, that every temper that is
> equally contrary to reason and order, that opposes God's
> ends and designs, and disorders the beauty and glory of the
> rational world, is equally sinful in man, and equally odious
> to God.[46]

These are the kinds of moral harmonics that set Johnson off in
his review of the work of Soame Jenyns and made him always
dismissive of Alexander Pope's philosophy and contemptuous
of that of Lord Bolingbroke.

It is hard to know exactly how Johnson read Law, but it was
not in a consistently critical fashion. He found much with
which he was in sympathy; he took pleasure in the rhetoric; and
he allowed himself to feel Law's exhortation to be born again.
Such a suspension of the critical faculty is essential to perusal or
self-help reading, and it is a quality that links this kind of
reading with genres of reading that are still further removed
from study and hard reading—mere reading of newspapers, for
example, and curious reading in travel books and novels. The
suspension of critical faculties required differs in each of these
genres of reading, and those differences are part of what define
each genre, but suspension is required in all of them, and they
are all, therefore, different from study. The stance Johnson took
in reading Law was quite different, for example, than the one

he assumed in reading Law's challenging opponent Bernard Mandeville, whose *Fable of the Bees* (1714) is satirical and philosophical rather than pious and plain. Johnson said Mandeville "opened my views into real life very much."[47] He engaged a critical spirit in Johnson that made him question assumptions about the operation of society and its supposed foundation in ideals of honesty and cooperation. "Real life" is the underlying texture of human nature that a critical and sometimes jaundiced eye can discern. In Law Johnson did not seek an opening of his views into real life, but a remission from "observation with extensive view" so that he could focus on his own efforts to pass through the narrow gate and achieve salvation. Like Bunyan's Christian when doomsday approaches, Johnson reading Law was sometimes a penitent running to heaven with his fingers in his ears.

More than most other kinds of writing, self-help books often inscribe within themselves a kind of advertisement or apology for themselves. Mary Baker Eddy's books, for example, generally take a stand against excessive reading, but they make an exception for themselves. Likewise, Law suspends his absolutism and allows one of his characters an evidently lovable flaw. He contrasts Flavia, a hot-tempered seeker, with the more moderate and self-controlled Miranda. Flavia is condemned for spending money on books of poetry and many other items. However, Miranda is not quite perfect: "She is sometimes afraid that she lays out too much money in books, because she cannot forbear buying all practical books of any note."[48] One of these books could of course have been Law's *Serious Call,* which was more than six hundred pages long and, although not lavishly produced, expensive enough to keep Johnson's near-contemporary at Pembroke College, the important Methodist George Whitefield, from purchasing it.

The curious way in which the self-help book often makes an exception of itself in an otherwise restrictive view of the value of intellectual exploration is mirrored in the responses of its enthusiastic readers. For some self-help books Johnson makes an exception to his generally critical approach to reading. He does so because from this form of reading he received a comfort and satisfaction that he needed. Some readers get the same satisfaction from partisan reporting or even from propaganda. In these genres too the reader permits a suspension of his or her critical faculties for the sake of personal satisfaction and confirmation. Johnson did not easily permit himself such relaxation, and the book with which he could unbend had to beguile his sharp aesthetic censors. Law's *Serious Call*, like Dryden's poetry, "found the passes of his mind,"[49] and permitted Johnson to have the kind of soothing experience that he also found in Grotius, Bona, and Sherlock. This experience was important to Johnson's whole life of reading partly because it linked him with the common reader.

The common reader is Johnson's name for a sensibility that is not exceedingly critical but that does have standards of morality—durable though not strict standards—and a wish for pleasure in reading. As a popular genre that satisfies abstract and lasting standards of morality, the self-help book is well suited to the common reader. To the extent that Johnson accommodated himself to that constructed sensibility, his own reading became a form of self-help perusal. This accommodation grew gradually throughout Johnson's life, and it may be a sign of its near completion that at the age of seventy-one he was finally able to read Allestree's *Whole Duty of Man*. Johnson's accommodation to the sensibility of the common reader, however, was never total. Johnson makes such a good subject for a history of reading because he read in so many different ways and because he never abandoned any of them. He persisted in older modes of studious reading even as he experienced and helped construct newer, more curious, less critical kinds of reading.

MERE READING

*A*fter suffering in the Royalist cause throughout the Interregnum, at the Restoration Roger L'Estrange was rewarded with the title "Surveyor of the Imprimerie and Printing-presses." His charge on taking up the office shows how much of the printed material available in England in 1663 was devoted to works unsuitable for the kind of reading I call study, or intensive reading, to use Rolf Engelsing's influential term. Along with the duties implied in his title, L'Estrange was given

> the sole licensing of all ballads, charts, printed portraictures, printed pictures, books, and papers; except books concerning common law, affairs of state, heraldry, titles of honours and arms, the office of Earl Marshal, books of divinity, physick, philosophy, arts and sciences, and such as are granted to his Majesty's peculiar printer; and except such books as by a late act of parliament are otherwise appointed to be licensed.[1]

In addition, according to a manuscript cited by John Nichols in *Literary Anecdotes of the Eighteenth Century,* L'Estrange had

> all the sole privilege of writing, printing and publishing all Narratives, Advertisements, Mercuries, Intelligencers, Diurnals, and other books of public intelligence; and printing all Ballads, Plays, Maps, Charts, Portraictures, and Pictures, not previously printed; and all Briefs for Collections, Playbills, Quacksalvers Bills and Tickets in England and Wales;

with power to search for and seize unlicensed and treason-
able, schismatical and scandalous books and papers.[2]

The difference between what is excluded from L'Estrange's pur-
view and what is included suggests a division in reading material between the worlds of intensive and extensive reading. In
my scheme of reading, newspapers, narratives, advertisements,
and such ephemera as tickets and playbills are the material of
"mere reading" or "curious reading," whereas the works reserved for the king's printer generally belong to study and serious perusal.

The details of the charge given to L'Estrange indicate a new
period in the history of reading; in my scheme of reading, a
downward shift occurred, and reading became more frequently
a matter of mere reading and less often a matter of study. The
main vehicle of this change, as Rolf Engelsing has perceived,
was the newspaper. There may be psychological reasons for the
change: an acceleration of perceived time induced by the vast
increase in the availability of clocks and watches and by the
more rapid transmission of news may have contributed to a
change in reading tempo and reading style in general. Reading
is a form of perception that creates a time frame of its own, but
it is not independent from cultural assumptions about the
shape or signature of time. The temporal element in reading
can only be expressed partially on the page, but the changes in
reading that accompanied the spread of journalism are visible,
to a degree, in the formats that such works presented to the eyes
and minds of readers as well as in the content of the works.

Before pursuing this relation, however, I must spend a few
paragraphs on a caveat. Kinds of reading are precisely equivalent neither to spatial arrangements nor to literary forms of
writing, and they are never exhaustively defined by them. Even
the Bible, the preeminent text for the highest sort of study in
the West, has the potential to be read as self-help, fiction, or
even as news, as the etymology of "gospel" or the Greek εὐ-
αγγέλος implies: both mean literally "good news." Likewise, in
some unusual cases any scrap of print can be the subject of an

act of study. The "second narrator" in *Don Quixote,* sometimes identified with Cervantes, reveals in chapter nine that he searches through and reads intently scraps of all kinds of papers blown about the streets of Toledo. The storied hard reader Antonio Magliabecchi learned to read by intently studying the waste papers used to wrap fruit in his master's store.

On a pair of facing pages in André Kertész's collection of photographs *On Reading,*[3] there are a priest reading a religious tome and a man reading a newspaper. The juxtaposition shows how the two acts of reading are different and yet the same. The priest's book appears to be an antiphonal for the Mass. Its heavy double belts lie open on the massive wooden lectern that supports the book. The priest is in his robes and holds the book open in front of his large crucifix necklace. There is a slight smile on his face, despite his look of concentration, which is enhanced by the light striking the contours of his large forehead and also by his studious eyeglasses. It is as though he were experiencing the holy pleasure of the Mass itself or some kind of religious communion. This surely is a high form of reading, a form of biblical hard reading.

Opposite the priest in Kertész's book is a man on the street reading a newspaper that he has apparently just plucked from a public wastebasket. The reading materials and the scenes of reading in the two pictures could not be more unlike. Instead of being situated in a high-ceilinged chamber full of books, the newspaper reader is at the curbside near a lamppost. The background of pavement, dirty stone facing, and a brick building seems meaningless. In the foreground is the heavy right rear bumper of a 1950s Chevrolet. However, there are similarities between the two scenes. The base of the lamppost recalls a column in the Ionic mode, making an allusion to classical times and studious, classical reading. The wastebasket is a hideously modern lectern, but a lectern nonetheless. Most importantly, the reader himself displays the same kind of concentration as his counterpart on the facing page. Dressed in a long black coat and a black hat, with his full white beard, he looks somewhat rabbinical; the rag of a tie dangling only halfway down his shirt front faintly suggests a ceremonial article of clothing. This pair of pictures is silent. It is impossible to be sure what kinds of reading are being experienced in them, but the outward similarities, despite the obvious differences, graphically suggest that reading matter is only one element and not the defining element in kinds of reading. Even newspaper reading can be hard reading, and not only for transcendentalists in the midst of experiencing "something far more deeply interfused."

But this is not usually the case, and most newspaper reading is not hard reading. It is a kind of reading that in many respects bridges the differences between self-help reading and the reading of narrative fiction. Most of the pictures of people reading newspapers in Kertész's collection show newspaper reading in its "normal" state. The positions in which it is done and the settings are usually casual: the readers of newspapers are typically sitting, often with their feet up, frequently outside. The paper is often folded, as heavy books cannot be. Lighter books, pamphlets, and paperbacks can be peeled back, however, and this quality makes them closer to newspapers in content and in the kind of reading they encourage.

The most famous picture of Johnson reading shows him peeling back a pamphlet or coverless book, as though he were applying the techniques of newspaper reading to a book. This detail of the picture reveals a truth about Johnson's life of reading. He could and did apply newspaper-reading techniques to some books, even some that might have been meant for other kinds of reading. It was part of his achievement as a reader to be able to move up and down the scale of reading, almost no matter what sort of text was in his hand. The kind of reading appropriate to a newspaper spread to other kinds of texts during the eighteenth century, not only for great readers like Johnson, but for almost everyone. My favorite picture of newspaper reading in the Kertész book, the most "normative" picture in my view, shows a woman reading a folded paper while sitting down in a wooded place in the autumn. The fallen, loose leaves are all around her, and they seem to me to represent the loose, unbound leaves of the newspaper. It is an autumnal scene of reading, and newspaper reading is likewise late and likewise concerned with the harvest, or the leavings, of the literary world. But after the spread of newspapers, much reading became late, loose, and piecemeal.

Apart from its obvious fragmentary quality, one of the most important aspects of newspaper reading is the peculiar demand it makes on credulity. Like self-help books, newspapers cannot easily be read without credence. Yet they allow for a volatility and variability in credence that goes beyond what is allowed in self-help reading. Once we disbelieve the author who advises us, we stop reading. We are much more likely to keep reading a newspaper even if parts of it are unbelievable. There is often a kind of tantalization of credence in newspaper reading, as evidenced today in some of the tabloids where the line between the true and false is intentionally blurred, or the reader is invited to indulge in a degree of credence that is unusual and exciting. This uncertainty is imbedded in the history of the newspaper, which took advantage of an already existent kind of reading adapted to fabulous travel books, to certain kinds of histories, and to pamphlets and broadsheets.

The kinship of pamphlets and newspapers is a matter both of format and of content. Johnson's collaborator on the Harleian Library catalogue, William Oldys, got it right in his dissertation on the origin of pamphlets (1732). His third of four reasons for preserving pamphlets is that they are

> the liveliest pictures of their times. Pamphlets have this considerable advantage, that, springing usually from some immediate occasion, they are copied more directly from the life; so likelier to bear a resemblance, than any more extended draughts taken by a remoter light. But being therefore a kind of reading à la mode, and the events, their sources, so suddenly giving way to every fresh current of affairs, it is no wonder if these little maps of them are, in like manner, overborne, and become as transient as they.[4]

Newspapers are also "a kind of reading à la mode": both forms approximate direct, recent experience. For this reason, they must approximate the credibility of direct experience, but, like gossip and other forms of spreading the word, they can and probably should strain credibility a little in order to be most successful.

In his introduction to *The Harleian Miscellany,* an eight-volume collection of pamphlets, on which he did a little work before Oldys took over the job entirely, Johnson links the rise of pamphlet production to the spread of liberty (mainly from Roman Catholic repression) and the origins of the "Trade of Writing."[5] The growth of the "Trade" is inseparable from the spread of reading and the extension of printed concerns to the concerns of a wider public. The community of readers implicit in pamphlet reading is broader and more common in its concerns than the community implicit in hard reading or self-help reading. Pamphlets and, *a fortiori,* newspapers indicate a level of achievement in the democratization of reading and they encourage further democratization; in addition, they constitute a written form in which reading seems to approach participation in the events described, and such virtual participation would seem to have a democratizing effect on society.

Virtual participation, however, like today's virtual reality, is an artifice that tries to deny its artificiality, and the history of newspapers displays a continual concern with believability. Even a cursory look at the titles of the early "courants" listed by John Nichols in his *Anecdotes* shows how unsteadily the form fluctuated between the believable, or the historical, and the fictional: "Strange Newes out of diverse Countries, never discovered till of late, by a strange Pilgrim in those Parts, April 13, 1622"; "The certain newes of the present Week, August 21, [1622]"; "A Discourse of Newes from Prague in Bohemia, of an Husband who by Witchcraft had murthered eighteen Wives, and of a Wife who had likewise murthered nineteen Husbands."[6] Somewhat later and better-established papers continued to manifest an anxiety about credibility in their titles: "True Newes from our Navie now at Sea, Nov. 6–11, 1642"; "An Exact Diurnal"; "Mercurius Candidus"; "An Exact and True Collection of the most remarkable Proceedings of Parliament and Armies, Feb. 16–March 2, 1645–6"; "The Parliament Kite, or the Tell-tale Bird, No. 5, May 12–June 16, 1648"; "The True Domestick Intelligence; or, News both from City and Country, published to prevent false reports."[7] Like travel books, newspapers were suspected of being false because they so often concerned what was hidden from view; but, again like travel books, they could only flourish where inspection of the hidden world of news and newsmakers seemed suddenly possible and desirable for an increasingly informed public.

Recently in America we have witnessed many episodes of mass addiction to breaking news stories: during the Watergate investigation, the Gulf War, the presidential election of 1992, and the O. J. Simpson trial, many people watched an unusual amount of television over the long periods of time it took for these stories to unfold. The networks certainly wished to give viewers the sense that they were on the scene, and they succeeded, even though there was often a good deal of repetition in the reports, and even though it is impossible to be "on the scene" of events such as the shifts in public opinion that determined the outcome of the 1992 election.

A mania for the breaking story also existed in the eighteenth century, even though news reports were often weeks behind the events they were recording.[8] (In 1758, reports were about two weeks behind naval action in Europe and sometimes more than two months behind events in the Colonies.) One account written in 1712 speaks of "such a furious itch of novelty . . . and epidemical distemper, that . . . has proved fatal to many families; the meanest of shopkeepers and handicrafts spending whole days in coffee-houses, to hear news and talk politicks, whilst their wives and children wanted bread at home; and, their business being neglected, they were themselves at length thrust into gaols, or forced to take sanctuary in the army." The writer attributes the rise of newspapers to the public demand for news:

Hence sprung that inundation of *Postmen, Postboys, Evening Posts, Supplements, Daily Courants, Protestant Postboys,* amounting to 21 every week, besides many more which have not survived to this time. . . . Yet has not all this variety been sufficient to satiate the immoderate appetite of intelligence, without ransacking France, Holland, and Flanders, whence the foreign mails duly furnish us with the *Gazettes* or *Courants* of Paris, Brussels, Antwerp, Amsterdam, Hague, Rotterdam, Leyden, and some others not so common, besides the French and Holland *Gazettes-a-la-Main.*[9]

This "immoderate appetite of intelligence" not only shaped the production of newspapers and journals in eighteenth-century Britain, it also had a broad effect on the nature of reading. It made reading in general more often fast, more often piecemeal and fragmented, more often concerned with credibility, and more frequently associated with participation in public life.

I I

The development of the press in England greatly affected Samuel Johnson's career as a writer, as every student of Johnson knows, but its effect on his life as a reader has not been carefully chronicled. Johnson started his professional writing career with a Birmingham journal published by Thomas Warren, who soon commissioned him to write his first book, a translation of Jerónimo Lobo's *Voyage to Abyssinia*. In the mid-1730s Johnson began his crucial association with Edward Cave, founder and publisher of the *Gentleman's Magazine*. Johnson approached Cave as a student and a writer of scholarly poetry who could elevate the tone of Cave's journal, but he gradually accommodated his writing to the more general audience sought even by Cave's relatively erudite production. Johnson went on from book reviewing and translating, to writing parliamentary reports, to editing the journal and writing a large part of the copy himself in the late 1730s and early 1740s. Later, Johnson wrote or contributed to many other journals: the *Rambler*, the *Idler*, the *Adventurer*, and the *Literary Magazine*, to name only a few. Admittedly, the journals on which Johnson worked were entirely of the higher sort, the kind that tried to rise above mere news reporting by printing durable, moral essays, and news that aspired to history. However, in the middle of the eighteenth century there was a great deal of crossover among the various journals, as there still is today. Johnson's moral essays for the *Idler* and the *Rambler* showed up in lesser publications, and news reports from the *Gazette* or from cheaper, independent papers, such as the *London Evening-Post,* showed up in the *Gentleman's Magazine.* Publishers formed syndicates, as they do today, and the productions of a "columnist" like Johnson made their way throughout the system of journalistic production. In addition to writing journalism, Johnson himself was the subject of numerous reports, reviews, and advertisements in journals of all kinds, beginning in the 1730s and continuing throughout his life. All of this has been well documented and frequently discussed.[10] What is missing, and not easily recovered, is Johnson's experience as a reader of journals and newspapers.

For all his attention to hard reading and for all his engagement in self-help reading, Johnson was also a reader of a variety of journals. Even in his advice to students who needed encouragement to study, Johnson recommended some "lighter" journal reading. He wrote to young George Strahan at University College, Oxford:

> Do not tire yourself so much with Greek one day as to be afraid of looking on it the next; but give it a certain portion of time, suppose four hours, and pass the rest of the day in Latin or English. I would have you learn French, and take in a literary journal once a month, which will accustom you to various subjects, and inform you what learning is going forward in the world. Do not omit to mingle some lighter books with those of more importance; that which is read *remisso animo* is often of great use, and takes hold of the remembrance.[11]

Johnson himself read literary reviews; he designed one, and, although he never executed that production, his column on foreign books in the *Gentleman's Magazine,* as well as his book reviews in the *Literary Magazine,* do much the same work. Although such journals are a means of access to study and harder reading, they require a less concentrated, more piece-meal kind of attention. They can be read *remisso animo,* in a state of relaxation, like that assumed by the woman amidst the leaves in Kertész's photograph.

Johnson also recommended and read journals that were closer to the world of newspapers than to that of the learned reviews. He especially praised the *Tatler* and the *Spectator.* The closeness of these productions to the news is suggested in Johnson's recommendation of the *Tatler* to young Susanna Thrale, the younger sister of his goddaughter Queeney: "I cannot tell you much news because I see nobody that you know. Do you read the Tatlers? They are part of the books which every body should read, because they are the sources of conversation, therefore make them part of your library."[12] The connection here is not absolutely tight, but clearly Johnson associated newspapers with magazines like the *Tatler,* even though it was then more than seventy years since a fresh issue had been published. They were related vehicles, even though Addison's journal became more and more literary as its period of serial publication (1709–11) receded into the past and it was read in bound, reprinted volumes. It may be that Johnson was recommending the "higher," more durable news to Susanna, but that news was repeatable, contemporary, and suitable for conversation nevertheless.

In his life of Addison, Johnson locates the origin of the *Spectator* and the *Tatler* in the political pamphlets and newspapers of the Restoration. He argues that Addison and Richard Steele transformed the genre into a kind of fiction by their efforts at instruction and their nonpartisanship. Reading these transformed works of journalism is an experience that belongs in the lower reaches of newspaper reading, where fiction reading begins and credibility is a lesser issue. A series of excerpts from Johnson's life of Addison shows that his reading of Addison's journalism belongs in this region:

These *Mercuries* [early, partisan newspapers] were succeeded by L'Estrange's *Observator,* and that by Lesley's *Rehearsal,* and perhaps by others; but nothing had been conveyed to the people in this commodious manner but controversy relating to the Church or State: of which they taught many to talk, whom they could not teach to judge. . . . to minds heated with political contest [the *Tatler* and the *Spectator*] supplied cooler and more inoffensive reflection; and it is said by Addison . . . that they had a perceptible influence upon the conversation of that time . . . an effect which they can never wholly lose, while they continue to be among the first books by which both sexes are initiated in the elegances of knowledge. . . .

The Tatler and *Spectator* adjusted, like [Giovanni della] Casa, the unsettled practice of daily intercourse by propriety and politeness; and, like La Bruyère, exhibited the "Characters and Manners of the Age." The personages introduced in these papers were not merely ideal; they were then known, and conspicuous in various stations. . . .

It is recorded by [Eustace] Budgell that of the characters feigned or exhibited in *The Spectator* the favourite of Addison was Sir Roger de Coverley, of whom he had formed a very delicate and discriminated idea. . . . The reason which induced Cervantes to bring his hero to the grave, "para mi solo nacio Don Quixote, y yo para el," made Addison declare, with an undue vehemence of expression, that he would kill Sir Roger. . . .

It may be doubted whether Addison ever filled up his original delineation. He describes his Knight as having his imagination somewhat warped; but of this perversion he has made very little use. The irregularities in Sir Roger's conduct seem not so much the effects of a mind deviating from the beaten track of life by the perpetual pressure of some overwhelming idea, as of habitual rusticity, and that negligence which solitary grandeur naturally generates.[13]

There is some oscillation in this collection of observations. According to Johnson, Addison had a "discriminated idea" of Sir Roger, but Sir Roger is not merely ideal; he is like Don

Quixote, which makes Addison a kind of Cervantes, but Addison was also a La Bruyère depicting the characters of his day, and there were real people behind these literary artifacts. Moreover, the genre of the *Spectator* derives from the political broadsheet; it functions as its predecessors did, only more successfully and philosophically, but in doing so it tends to become fiction. Johnson's insecurity about where to place Addison's works arose from the variations in his own experience of reading them; he read them by turns as political journalism, self-help, and fictional narration. A descendant of this kind of journalism is the *New Yorker,* where the "friends" mentioned in "The Talk of the Town" or the "far-flung correspondents" come up with portraits of contemporary life that achieve some durability, some general and therefore moral character, while they also irradiate contemporary news.

The *Spectator* tested and stretched its audience's ability to decide how to read a given text. Johnson accordingly vacillated in his description of the experience, but one thing he was sure about was the *Spectator*'s effect on conversation. Other journals also contributed to conversation, in Johnson's view; one of the hallmarks of newspaper reading is its closeness to conversation, its nearness to actual participation in its implicit community of readers. This element of virtual conversation is again important in Johnson's most extended published account of reading a newspaper:

> One of the principal amusements of the Idler is to read the works of those minute historians the writers of news. . . . To us, who are regaled every morning and evening with intelligence [news], and are supplied from day to day with materials for conversation, it is difficult to conceive how man can subsist without a news-paper, or to what entertainment companies can assemble, in those wide regions of the earth that have neither *Chronicles* nor *Magazines,* neither *Gazettes* nor *Advertisers,* neither *Journals* nor *Evening-Posts.*"[14]

Johnson further discusses the way newspapers stimulate talk, and he finds some drawbacks in the way news "fills the nation with superficial disputants." But "filling," as ever in Johnson's rhetorical world, is an important sign of success, and the success of journalism in creating conversation is not trivial, even if the chatter it promotes is. Reading stimulates conversation, or provides a substitute for it; therefore, by capturing the forum of social conversation, the newspaper seizes power in the social construction of reading.

The reading of newspapers is especially closely related to the reading of other, competing contemporary productions. Its power is such, however, that the relation is more than one of resemblance: reading the newspaper influences the reading of contemporary writing to such an extent that it may be said to typify it. How Johnson felt about reading all kinds of contemporary works came out, appropriately enough, in his own conversation. For example, when Allan Ramsay (1713–84) remarked that Alexander Pope was more admired in his lifetime than after, Johnson replied, "Pope's poetry has been as much admired since his death as during his life; it has only not been as much talked of, but that is owing to its being now more distant, and people having other writings to talk of. Virgil is less talked of than Pope, and Homer is less talked of than Virgil; but they are not less admired. We must read what the world reads at the moment."[15] Johnson qualified the imputation that "this superfoetation, this teeming of the press in modern times, is prejudicial to good literature, because it obliges us to read so much of what is of inferiour value," but he saw the present as occupying us for mechanical, ultimately Lockean reasons. It occupies us and fills up our attention because it is present, not because its quality is high or low. It is not to Pope's enduring credit that he was so much talked of in his time, just as it does not demean him to have been less discussed after his death.

In a conversation earlier in 1778 Johnson roundly condemned a new poem by Richard Tickell which was read aloud to the company: "Sir, it has no power. Were it not for the well-known names with which it is filled, it would be nothing: the names carry the poet, not the poet the names." Dr. Samuel

Musgrave, a physician and classical scholar who was reading the new work to the company, interposed, "A temporary poem always entertains us," and Johnson replied, devastatingly, "So does an account of the criminals hanged yesterday entertain us."[16] The sensational presence of such accounts, their accessibility, and their way of nearly forcing attention are aspects of the experience that Johnson had in mind when he wrote that newspaper reading was "one of the principal amusements of the Idler." When he compares Tickell's poem to a sensational news story, Johnson suggests that contemporary writing, even poetry that aspires to greatness, enjoys some of the affective qualities of news. Contemporary writing is read as news is read, regardless of its pretensions to a different kind of reading and an eternal readership. This may always have been true, as, again, the word *gospel* may suggest, but the rise of newspapers in the seventeenth and eighteenth centuries made it clearer than ever.

As an aspect of its conversational and "amusement" value, the newspaper also supplies a kind of knowledge. Johnson emphasizes the solid value of reading the newspaper in *Idler* 7: "All foreigners remark," he writes, "that the knowledge of the common people of England is greater than that of any other vulgar. This superiority we undoubtedly owe to the rivulets of intelligence, which are continually trickling among us, which every one may catch, and of which every one partakes."[17] However, the quality of this knowledge is a matter of serious concern in *Idler* 30, which Johnson wrote a few weeks later. The newspaper offers a kind of reading in which both reader and writer are more irresponsible than they are in other networks of literary production and reception: "One of the amusements of idleness is reading without the fatigue of close attention, and the world therefore swarms with writers whose wish is not to be studied but to be read."[18] Clearly, Johnson distinguished journal reading from study, and he here assigned it a lower place in the world of reading, but it has a place nevertheless, and a power.

For the most part, when he is critical, Johnson prefers to

condemn those who pander to the interest in mere reading, rather than the lazy readers themselves. This is evident in his famous characterization of newswriters:

> In Sir Henry Wotton's jocular definition, "An ambassador" is said to be "a man of virtue sent abroad to tell lies for the advantage of his country"; a news-writer is "a man without virtue, who writes lies at home for his own profit." To these compositions is required neither genius nor knowledge, neither industry nor sprightliness, but contempt of shame, and indifference to truth are absolutely necessary. He who by long familiarity with infamy has obtained these qualities, may confidently tell to-day what he intends to contradict to-morrow; he may affirm fearlessly what he knows that he shall be obliged to recant, and may write letters from Amsterdam or Dresden to himself.[19]

Much of the foreign news in eighteenth-century papers, especially "features," appeared in the form of letters from correspondents or eyewitnesses. These "reporters" were often transparent inventions—literate (sometimes verbose) sailors, for example, who had been on burning ships or just happened to be in port during catastrophes such as the Lisbon earthquake.

When Johnson concludes his condemnation of news reporters, however, he does lay a little blame at the feet of their readers. Having discussed the great opportunities for journalism provided by war, Johnson says, "Among the calamities of war may be justly numbered the diminution of the love of truth, by the falsehoods which interest dictates and credulity encourages."[20] "Interest" on the part of the writers and publishers leads to the production of falsehoods, but "credulity" on the part of readers leads to their reception. The result of reading is a combination of the efforts of readers and writers. Popular "credulity" is partly the effect of the anxieties surrounding war, but it is supported by the growth of newspaper reading, with its kinship to looser forms of communication such as conversation and gossip.

Although he was a newspaper reader, Johnson was always

ready to apply the standards and principles of studious reading to journalistic productions. (Conversely, he could apply the speed of newspaper reading to books.) *Idler* 7 offers a better idea of how Johnson could use the papers for a variety of reading purposes. Johnson's essay for 27 May 1758 laments that

> journals are daily multiplied without increase of knowledge. The tale of the morning paper is told again in the evening, and the narratives of the evening are bought again in the morning. These repetitions, indeed, waste time, but they do not shorten it. The most eager peruser of news is tired before he has completed his labour, and many a man who enters the coffee-house in his night-gown and slippers, is called away to his shop, or his dinner, before he has well considered the state of Europe.

To remedy this situation, Johnson sarcastically proposes a collaboration among newswriters so that they can divide up their stories and tell them piecemeal over several issues of their various papers. This will not "intensify" the reading experience by packing more information into a smaller compass and getting the coffeehouse politician home well informed. It will, however, enhance the narrative and extensive qualities of the experience, "so as to vary a whole week with joy, anxiety, and conjecture."[21] In proposing this solution, Johnson reveals the real secret of compulsive news reading and successful news production.

In the Harleian Library catalogue Johnson lists collections of journals under the heading "Miscellaneous English History," and at the beginning of *Idler* 7 he calls news writers "minute historians," but in his solution to the problem of reading news he recognizes that news is a form of narrative and that it will be more effective and saleable (though not perhaps more laudable) if it is made engaging and absorbing, like a fictional narrative. It has to have a plot, and there must, therefore, be reversals of fortune as well as unity, a certain length of time, and other traditional features. The news story must have all this and yet retain credibility.

In the example that fills out the rest of *Idler* 7, Johnson divides a typical news story into twelve parts, one for each of the daily and evening numbers of journals for six consecutive days. On the evening of the last day, he provides the sort of account that was most common in the papers of the day. The whole thing is a parody; it does not correspond exactly to any particular news story, but it parallels some of them. Johnson's manner of telling faintly recalls the sad case of Admiral Byng, whom the ministry, to Johnson's horror and disgust, had scapegoated and executed two years before in an effort to mask its own failure of policy in the war with Spain.[22] But there is a stronger parallel between Johnson's made-up story and a real account that was in the papers at just about the same time. By comparing the two, it is possible to throw some light on Johnson's experience of reading the news.

Johnson sums up his story this way: "*Saturday Evening.* Capt. Grim arrived at the Admiralty, with an account that he engaged the Friseur, a ship of equal force with his own, off Cape Finisterre, and took her, after an obstinate resistance, having killed one hundred and fifty of the French, with the loss of ninety-five of his own men."[23] The corresponding news story was reported in the London papers, beginning on 12 May 1758 with this brief account in the *Public Advertiser:*

> Yesterday an Express arrived at the Admiralty office with Advice that the Dorsetshire Man of War, commanded by Capt. Dennis, had fallen in with a French Man of War of 64 Guns and 650 Men, 14 Leagues to the Westward of Scilly, and after a smart Engagement which lasted near two Hours, had taken her. The French lost 150 Men killed and wounded, and the Dorsetshire had 15 killed and 25 wounded.—She is called the Raisonable, and was commanded by the Chevalier de Rohan, Nephew to the Prince de Soubize.[24]

One important feature of Johnson's account is its relative freedom from jargon, but this stylistic feature and the likelihood that he was directing his satire partly at naval jargon is evident only when we read contemporary newspaper accounts of the incident, especially the full story of the Dorsetshire and the

Raisonable, as it was transmitted from the admiralty to the *London Gazette*, the official government organ of news reporting:

> On the 29th about Three o'Clock in the Afternoon, Capt. Pratten seeing a Sail to the S. W. made a Signal for the Dorsetshire, of 70 Guns, and 520 Men, commanded by Captain Denis, to give Chace; and soon after observing the Chace to be a large Ship, dispatched the Achilles, of 60 Guns, commanded by the Honourable Captain Barrington, also after her, and then followed them with the rest of the Squadron. About Seven o'Clock the Dorsetshire came up with the Chace, which proved to be the Raisonable, a French Ship of War of 64 Guns, and 630 Men, and Capt. Denis began to engage her very closely, and they continued warmly engaged til about Nine o'Clock, when the Enemy's Ship, commanded by the Prince de Mombazon, Chevalier de Rohan, struck, having suffered greatly in her Hull, and had 61 Men killed, and 100 wounded. She was going from l'Orient to Brest, a new Ship, not above four or five Months off the Stocks. The Dorsetshire's Masts, Yards, and Sails, were greatly shattered. She had 15 Men killed, and 21 Wounded.[25]

Johnson's version omits most of the statistics common in such stories, as well as jargon such as *chace, struck, stocks,* and *yards.* Only *strike* without the object *flag* would really be inadmissible, according to Johnson's *Dictionary,* but the difference in diction between Johnson's account and the admiralty's is clear. That Johnson intended to satirize the jargon is probable because of the frequency with which he used it in one of his twelve earlier "news releases": "Tuesday Morning. It was this morning reported, that the Bulldog engaged the Friseur, yard-arm and yard-arm three glasses and a half, but was obliged to sheer off for want of powder."[26]

Johnson's other releases suggest that there are other qualities of newspaper reports, besides their style, that he wishes to satirize: their uncertainty and vacillation, if not contradiction; their reliance on rumor; and their tendency to deviate into matters that we think of as belonging to the society pages.

However, not many of these ridiculous qualities show up in the real reports about the engagement between the Dorsetshire and the Raisonable. In fact, there is little in the papers except frequent redactions of the report of the admiralty office printed in the *Gazette*. The *Whitehall Evening-Post, or, London Intelligencer* for 13–16 May added the most when, in scattered parts of the paper, it reported the arrival of the Dorsetshire at Spithead and noted that "a few Hours after the Dorsetshire came in with her prize, Mr. Hook, Gunner, was brought on shore in a Cradle, being wounded in both Thighs."[27] The *Gentleman's Magazine,* which had the advantage of going to press much later, and only once a month, reprinted the story in its "Historical Chronicle," with only some slight additions from the French accounts of the episode: "By the French accounts, the Raisonable, with the Hero, Formidable, and Intrepide, and two frigates were designed for Canada; to which place and Louisbourgh [the Nova Scotia scene of important battles between the French and English] they have sent several little squadrons at different times; one under M. de Beaussier, sailed to the latter place on the 5th of April."[28]

What is most salient both in the real stories and in Johnson's mock twelve-part story is repetitiveness; this is the formal quality of the news that Johnson most severely satirizes. One reason for the repetition, however, is lack of information or knowledge, and Johnson may be pointing more angrily to the reliance of the newspapers on the official reports of the *Gazette,* an organ he despised, at least until receiving his pension in 1762. In his reviews for the *Literary Magazine* of some pamphlets concerning Admiral Byng, Johnson had recently alerted his readers to the unfair way in which the *Gazette* had abridged a letter from Byng to the admiralty and thereby curtailed the effectiveness of his defense of himself before the public.[29] One part of the lesson of *Idler* 7 is that newspapers do not tell us enough; the other part is that what they tell, they tell badly.

Are we then to conclude that Johnson's experience of reading the papers was often one of disappointment and disgust? Perhaps. He could certainly be critical, and he wanted more knowledge, more densely packed, than the papers offered, but he kept reading. His letters and essays show him to be continuously well informed, although direct references to the papers are few. John Woodruff has shown that even the Olympian essays of the *Rambler* were responsive in many cases to current events reported and advertised in the papers.[30] This is much more true of the *Idler,* and there are little suggestions throughout the body of Johnson's work that he read the papers faithfully, as he did, for example, when he warned Hill Boothby that the Johnson whose death the papers were reporting was not her loving friend.[31] The studious, critical reader that Johnson often was is evident in his written remarks on newspaper reading; the life he led as a consumer of the news has left fewer traces, but there is reason to believe that it existed and was, at least tacitly, more approving.

The conflict in Johnson's attitude towards journalism is apparent in his preface to the 1740 volume of the *Gentleman's Magazine.* He begins by praising the social role played by the papers:

> Every-body must allow that our News-Papers (and the other Collections of Intelligence periodically published) by the Materials they afford for Discourse and Speculation, contribute very much to the Emolument of Society; their Cheapness brings them into universal Use; their Variety adapts them to every one's Taste: The Scholar instructs himself with Advice from the literary World; the Soldier makes a Campaign in safety, and censures the Conduct of Generals without fear of being punished for Mutiny; the Politician, inspired by the Fumes of the Coffee-pot, unravels the knotty Intrigues of Ministers; the industrious Merchant observes the Course of Trade and Navigation; and the honest Shop-keeper nods over the Account of a Robbery and the Prices of Goods until his Pipe is out.[32]

Johnson approved of newspapers and read them because they filled time and conduced to social interaction. In the last part of his life, he put so much emphasis on the importance of such interaction that he even he wished he had learned to play cards to promote it. (Card playing, with its reliance on printed cards, might even be considered a form of community reading.)

However, when Johnson contemplated the writing in newspapers apart from their functional value, he had to be critical; characteristically, in his critical, studious mode, he thought of the classics. After subjoining examples of the Roman equivalents of the newspaper, the *Acta diurna,* Johnson remarks ironically:

> They want that sprightly Humour and diffuse Kind of Narration, which embellish the Compositions of our modern Diurnal Historians. The *Roman* Gazetteers are defective in several material Ornaments of Style. They never end an Article with the mystical Hint, *this occasions great Speculation.* They seem to have been ignorant of such engaging Introductions, as *we hear it is strongly reported;* and of that ingenious, but thread-bare, Excuse for a downright Lie, *it wants Confirmation.* It is also very observable, that the Prætor's Daughter is married without our being told, that *she was a Lady of Great Beauty, Merit, and Fortune.*[33]

In his studious mode Johnson felt much as the exiled Cicero did upon receiving a scrap of a Roman newspaper from his friend Caelius. As Johnson put it, Cicero declared himself an inveterate hard reader and replied, "Do you think . . . that I left it in Charge with you to send an Account of the Matches of Gladiators, the Adjournments of the Courts, and such like Articles, which even when I am at *Rome,* Nobody ventures to tell me? From you I expect a political Sketch of the Common-Wealth, and not *Chrestus's* News-paper."[34] Even if he felt as Cicero did, like Cicero, Johnson read on. By examining exactly what he found in some of the papers he read, it may be possible to learn more about his reading experience than he reveals in his critical statements.

III

In an article about changing methods of reporting State of the Union addresses, Michael Schudson discovers numerous ways in which "the news story today, as in the past, not only describes a world 'out there,' but translates a political culture into assumptions of representation built into the structure of the story itself."[35] By examining the conventions of news reporting in the late nineteenth and early twentieth centuries, Schudson shows how the news has not only reflected but actually participated in changes in American political life, fostering, in particular, a kind of professionalization of politics and the formation of a society of experts and expertise. The emerging elements of news stories involved in this change include the summary lead, the centrality of the president in the narrative, a focus on a single and, as far as possible, a singular event, the use of quotations, and the provision of enough interpretation to place the event in a larger historical time frame. Little of what Schudson finds in early-twentieth-century American news reporting was present in the British newspapers of 1758. However, inchoate forms of some of it are discernible, and the conventions of these earlier papers likewise bear "assumptions of representation" in their structure that "translate a political culture."

The *Gentleman's Magazine* and similar journals instituted the phrase "prime minister" by focusing attention on Walpole as the lead actor in accounts of political events; their practice may have anticipated twentieth-century journalism's focus on the president of the United States. To parallel another of Schudson's findings, interpretation and historical background were provided in some eighteenth-century British news stories, including many by Samuel Johnson, but the history and interpretation were usually separate from the news reporting itself and almost always lagged behind it. Johnson's reports of controversial parliamentary debates, for example, were published more than a year after the breaking stories. Again, eighteenth-century British newspapers differed from their late-nineteenth-century American counterparts because actual quotation was harder to come by, especially since no one was permitted to take notes on or to report sessions of Parliament. The papers, however, and probably their readers too, felt a need for eyewitness accounts. So, as ever, there were leaks, accidental and arranged; sometimes members of Parliament even arranged for the publication of pamphlets containing whole speeches that had been delivered on the floor. Finally, news stories in the eighteenth century, like those in the late nineteenth century, often focused on single and singular events, but the telling of them, as Johnson's parody suggests, often made them seem the same as yesterday's or last month's event.

Perhaps the single most glaring difference between eighteenth-century news reports and those of the late nineteenth century and later is the absence of the summary lead. In fact, there were no headlines in the papers that Johnson and his coevals read. Datelines and other indications of where the news originated provided the main sort of formal guidance in the reading experience. News stories gathered under a single dateline were not distinguished from each other by more than paragraphing. The stories generally were printed in a recognizable order from top left to bottom right, across three columns for the most frequently published sheets and two columns for some of the longer, less frequently published journals. The order of the stories varied a bit from journal to journal, but in most of them foreign news was followed by domestic news, which tended to descend from more-important happenings to announcements of deaths, social events, and crimes. London news was separate and most prominent among the domestic entries. The *Gazette* put "Present" news first, meaning news of the king or the court, and gave datelines of a kind to various branches of the government, including the Admiralty and the excise office. Clearly the *Gazette* implied a politics in its layout, but so did the other journals in theirs, and a politics in layout implies a way or ways of reading. As Michael Schudson has argued, the layout of the news is political in its implications, but this is only one aspect of its effect on readers. The politics of layout can reveal the ways in which the format and presentation of the news reflect and help shape broad intellectual changes going on in a culture at a given time. One family of these broad changes, all of which carry political implications, is the history of reading.

Perhaps the two most striking features of news reporting in mid-eighteenth-century newspapers are the complete separation between the editorial pieces and the news stories, and the relative absence of separation between stories. If he read the *London Evening-Post* for 13–16 May 1758, Johnson saw the account of the Dorsetshire and Raisonable in the third column of the front page amidst a group of other reports, all entitled "From the London Gazette" and subtitled with the dateline "Admiralty-Office, May 13." Two other stories also came under this subheading. The story ends with "and one of the wounded is since dead"; the next story begins after only a paragraph break:

> Advice is received from Rear-Admiral Broderick, who was on his Passage to the Mediterranean, that on the 13th of last Month, in the Latitude of 48: 00, his majesty's ship the Prince George, of 80 Guns, in which the Rear-Admiral hoisted his flag, took Fire at half an Hour after One in the Afternoon, and, after burning down to the Water's Edge, the Remnant of her sunk at a little before Six in the Evening.

To a modern reader of newspapers the shift is somewhat disconcerting because we have come to rely on slugs and headlines to guide us through the hodgepodge of news, just as we have come to depend on punctuation marks to clarify the sense for us in written prose. Punctuation was a relatively late development in the history of writing, and so was the appearance of headlines and summary leads in newspaper writing. Both are aids to reading that were only gradually added to the sparsely directed earlier forms of writing and publication.

The layout of eighteenth-century newspapers was a little like the *scripta continua* of the manuscripts produced in earlier times without word breaks or punctuation. In both cases the reader was expected to do more than twentieth-century readers of most books and journals in order to make even bare sense of the text. At a minimum, the reader of eighteenth-century newspapers was responsible for creating a pause and a sense of a fresh start. The need for this became even more emphatic as one descended further into the newspaper. Reading the *White-hall Evening-Post, or, London Intelligencer* on 13–16 May 1758, for example, required some interpretive efforts on the part of the reader, whose efforts are now more heavily supported by elements of format. The redactions from the *London Gazette*, including the Raisonable story, appeared in the upper left. Then came a group of foreign news items separated by date-lines, but not grouped by subject. The whole section was printed under the heading "*Yesterday arrived a* MAIL *from* Holland," and began as follows:

> Lisbon, April 5. Since the terrible Earthquake we some Time since felt, we have not been so sensibly affected as we were on the 19th of the last Month, when we had a most violent Storm of Wind, which did great Damage, and forced many Vessels out to Sea, which were upon the point of entering the Tagus.
>
> Stockholm, April 25. It is judged that our Army will soon be recruited, so as to exceed 30,000 men, and to be upon such a footing as it was in October last; besides which a Squadron of Russian Men of War will soon appear in the Baltick, and be joined by one of ours, not to prevent the English from passing the Sound, of which we are under no Apprehensions, but to undertake some other Enterprize.

Was the reader supposed to imagine a change in voice between these two reports? If one were reading the two reports, should one imitate a different foreign accent for each? That might be the World War II newsreel convention. What about the tone of "to undertake some other Enterprize"? Was this supposed to sound shifty and mysterious or nonchalant? Surely it was a cue to coffeehouse politicians, who might produce their military maps of Europe and start moving shot glasses around the Baltic to represent the movement of fleets. There seems to be a good deal of room for adaptation and interpretation in these stories.

Headlines, slugs, bylines, and recently instituted labels for "news analysis" may not thoroughly remove ambiguity from the papers, but they provide directions that were absent from eighteenth-century foreign news reporting. The problems continued for the eighteenth-century reader of national and local news.

In the *Whitehall Evening-Post,* after "Ship News," which was simply a list of arrivals and departures, came "London Intelligence." The variety of stories separated only by a new paragraph is bewildering. For example, in the second paragraph we read, "An embargo was laid on all shipping at Boston the 13th March last [two months before]." The next paragraph says, "Friday last the Lord Keeper set out from his House in Lincoln's Inn Fields, for his Lordship's Seat at Grange in Hants." Not all the transitions are this abrupt, but many of them are. Readers surely had to read this page in discrete pieces and do whatever assembling they wished outside the context of the paper—on a map, in a discussion, or in an essay.

The country news section made similar demands on the reader. Although, like foreign news, country (or county) news was broken up by datelines, the shifts required reading in discrete blocks. The section for this date began:

> Norwich, May 13. A few Days ago the Rev. Mr. Francis Jones was instituted to the Rectory of Huntingfield with Cookley in Suffolk, on the Presentation of Sir Joshua Van Neck, Bart.
> Bristol, May 13. Yesterday John Smith and Mary Holister (who lived together at Pensford, in the County of Somerset) having some Words whilst they were at Dinner, Smith ran a Knife into her Body, of which Wound she is since dead.

In section B of the *New York Times,* or on the local television news in most major American cities, there might be a similar juxtaposition of society stories and family murder, but headlines, pictures, or commentary would serve to separate such items more fully now. Such unframed and indistinct bits of news presumably put the reader on his or her mettle to make ethical and moral distinctions about what is grave and what is gay. This quality of the papers is analogous to the penchant for juxtaposing unlike elements, in eighteenth-century verse. When Alexander Pope wrote, "And Wretches hang that Jury-men may dine," he was asking his readers to make discriminations similar to those elided by the daily paper. He may even have been alluding to such elisions.

After some public service announcements and the inevitable advertisements in the *Whitehall Evening-Post,* there was a final column of news that included a guide to how it should be read. This column, called "Postscript," also represented an advance in clarity over what was offered in other newspapers of the day. Although the mixture of stories is still bewildering by modern standards, there are more traces of an organizing voice threading through the series. I think these rudimentary forms of organization are the formal ancestors of the relatively clear labels now used to signal a column of commentary or analysis. "Postscript" opens:

> By a private Letter from Dantzick, dated May 3, we are informed, that General Fermer is not thought more infalli-ble at the Court of Petersburg than his Predecessor; having received the Day before an Order from his Mistress to recall all Officers, of what Rank soever, to whom he had given Leave to be absent from their respective Corps but for a few Days, and to proceed vigorously in his Operations. The General, in Consequence of these Instructions, has trans-ferr'd his Head-Quarters to Brischau, which is within three Miles of Dantzick, has thrown a strong Bridge of Boats over the Wesel, and is preparing to pass that River with all his Army.

Again, we do not know how to interpret the meaning of the troop movements reported: a modern story would have inter-viewed generals, retired generals, or other experts in an effort to throw some light on the meaning of the reported facts. Here the journalistic silence is an embodiment of governmental secrecy, and of a relatively closed world of political insiders. We do have cues from the *Whitehall Evening-Post,* however, about how to hear the tone of the story. It is gossipy and tattletale rather than historical or "objective," as modern reports try to be. It is the latest intelligence from someone in the know, and a journalistic representation of some breach in the closed circle of power. The tone of the article is much closer to chat or coffee-house conversation than many of the other items in the paper, and it is closer to conversation than much modern newspaper reporting. It suggests a penetration of the inner circle by a friend of the reader rather than a modern, expert view of the facts.

"Postscript" news is chatty, but the syndicated editorials in the papers of the day used more-formal rhetorical techniques and distanced themselves from mere talk. Our contemporary situation is often the reverse: our news stories are usually more formal in structure than our editorials, in which wit and ambiguity are sometimes used to come obliquely to a point. Some of the most famous eighteenth-century essays (Defoe's *Shortest-Way* and Swift's *Modest Proposal,* for example) are ambiguous and ironic. Their success as irony may have arisen because, in general, eighteenth-century editorials are among the most legible, straightforward parts of the paper. They tend to be relatively carefully framed, both rhetorically and typographically. They stick out from the rest of the paper because of this. For example, on the day that it transmitted the Raisonable report, the *London Evening-Post* reprinted an essay from the *Monitor* in praise of William Pitt. There is a horizontal line separating it from the story above; the centered dateline "London"; and then the centered slug "From the MONITOR, No. 147." Even though the piece is wedged into the central ten inches of the left-hand column and there is no bottom dividing line, it has unusually definitive framing in comparison with the news stories in the paper.

The *Monitor* essay itself is full of propagandistic history about how Pitt was chosen by "the Voice of the People," and is entitled to "the Confidence of the People," because he is a defender of "the Rights of the People." "The people," who constitute the audience for this essay, could not have missed the rhetoric of the appeal. In other editorials the defense of the ministry took other forms that were just as obvious, if not so appropriate to the readership of a popular journal. On 25 December 1755, for example, about the time Johnson was writing to Hill Boothby about the mistaken newspaper reports of his death, the *London Evening-Post* ran its own editorial under a horizontal separator, with the heading "London." The piece begins with an attack on a particular rhetorical line:

> There is no Colour [excuse] for saying, if a War happens, that we have run into it rashly; there is much more Reason to ascribe it to Timidity. If we had resented the first Intrusion of the French in America, there it had stopp'd. They would not have quarrell'd with us about a Carrying-Place, or a Mud-wall Fort;[36] they were not indeed in a Condition to do it. Our tameness encouraged them to encroach gradually.

The way in which the editorial tries to encourage a particular manner of speaking about politics, while discouraging others, becomes clearer in the second paragraph when the writer attacks the "Doctrine . . . that we had too much Land in America; that we need not be solicitous about such trifling Encroachments. . . . Language absurd and ridiculous, even in the Mouths of those, who, for want of proper Lights, had really embraced such Sentiments."

The writer attacks one sort of rhetoric, implying that it is cant, like the obviously French, somewhat technical term "encroachment." He then proposes instead an equally rhetorical but presumably more profound language of stern morality:

> There would be no harm in laying before the *Multitude* a true *Representation* of their own thoughtless Conduct and *dissolute* Way of *Living*. There would be no harm if *Prelates* would set themselves to *preach* in this *Strain* in their respective *Dioceses*. There would be no harm if the numberless

Alehouses were *reduced;* if *Places of Diversion* were kept
within Bounds; if Men were put in mind of Sobriety, Diligence and Fair-dealing; if *Women* were exhorted to *revive*
the *good Customs* of their *Grandmothers,* mind their *Family*
Business more, and their *Amusements* less. Or if *young People*
were instructed as to the Advantages of *Study, Temperance,
Chastity, Modesty.*

The transition from politics to morality in this essay is not
easy, but its rhetoric, easily visible, is made to glow with the
electricity of italic type, which is much more sparingly and
more formulaically applied in the news stories. In its editorials,
the paper was trying to shape a way of speaking; the speakers
strain to be audible, whereas the news reports themselves are
barely legible. There are sharp contrasts in the way the page of
eighteenth-century newsprint is "voiced," but the contrasts are
crude rather than fine in some cases and nonexistent in others.
Similarly, shifts in voice tend to be either overemphasized or
inaudible. The layout of the page is generally obscure, but the
syndicated editorials stand out in sharp contrast to the rest.

There were other voices in the papers besides those behind
the dateline news and the editorials. There were letters from
supposed eyewitnesses, which were set off in inverted commas
(sometimes on every line in midcentury), and there were even
occasional letters to the editor. The authenticity of any of these
letters is hard to gauge, partly because the papers were using the
epistolary form so often as a backdrop for reporting. The letter,
a preexisting, better-known form of communication, was used
in these instances to lend credibility to a newer form; the relationship between the two forms in eighteenth-century newspapers is the reverse of their relationship today. The letter is
today much more closely linked to the editorial that expresses
an opinion than to the news story reporting the facts. The
eighteenth-century epistolary form of news was meant to suggest that the report emanated from the scene and was directed
privately to the paper; passing on the report was a fulfillment of
public trust for the paper, but it also smacked faintly of gossip

or unauthorized publication. The transgression was less serious than modern readers might think because the letter was then a more public form than it is now, although it was, for numerous reasons, becoming increasingly more private at that time. The letter was then also a broader form and included in its range the "newsy" kind of letter meant to be a source of public information.[37] Reading a letter and reading a newspaper were closer kinds of reading in the eighteenth century than they are now, although we recapture some of the flavor of earlier letter reading when we read a letter aloud to others or when we receive a letter that was sent to a host of correspondents. I find reading such letters difficult, however, because I expect a letter to be personal; this expectation was growing in the eighteenth century and may now be waning as more and more of what goes through the mail is mechanically produced.

Letters to the editor in the eighteenth-century papers were quite different from the news letters that appeared nearby: they served editorial or commercial purposes rather than the nobler purpose of providing the public with information, but they often tried to link themselves with the letters that served the papers' higher aims. In its issue of 29 April–2 May 1758, for example, the *London Evening-Post* printed a letter under the heading "London":

> To the Author, &c.
>   Sir, Your Paper frequently contains very useful Observations and Hints for the publick Good. As the following is entirely calculated for that laudable Purpose, I shall be glad to find it meets with Approbation, and be carried into Execution.

The proposal that follows would replace a flat tax of one shilling on houses worth more than ten pounds per year in rent and a somewhat progressive tax on windows (on houses with sixteen or more), with a truly progressive rate on the per annum value of houses up to a maximum of three pounds per year on a house worth three hundred pounds a year in rent. The writer concludes:

This Tax would be nothing to the Rich, who inhabit such noble Houses. And it is humbly requested our worthy Patriot Ministers will take this into their serious Consideration, and make an Alteration in the designed Tax agreeable to the Circumstances of the Persons who are to pay it.

I am; Sir, Your constant Reader,

J.W.

The tone of the phrases "worthy Patriot Ministers" and "those persons who are to pay it" is somewhat hostile. The word "Patriot" had been overused until it was beaten into a symbol of political cant by 1758. But perhaps the most striking thing about the letter from both a political and a critical standpoint is the writer's (or publisher's) identification of the newspaper and the proposal as instruments of the "publick Good." Moreover, as the "constant Reader" of the paper, one who read both frequently and faithfully, the writer was a user and, in effect, a coadjutant of the publisher in the use of this instrument of the public good.

Even if the politics of such a collaboration are not always so clear, newspapers usually reach out to the audience in a direct way: to talk about what is on the public's mind; to address its concerns; and to provide, or to seem to provide, a voice for its observations. In its way, the newspaper is an interactive medium, and the mere reading experience is more a matter of hearing oneself and reliving one's immediate perceptions than is study or perusal. (Self-help books are meant to be about oneself, but they are designed to transform rather than reflect the self; they are about ideal and demonic versions of oneself.) As Lennard Davis has shown, readers of eighteenth-century papers could sometimes find themselves in the text, and editors were eager to promulgate the sensation, even if it was fanciful.[38] It has since become part of the credo of the industry to provide news that is of special interest to its readership, even if that means demoting stories of greater global or historical significance.

Actual letters from real correspondents are so crucial to the makeup of eighteenth-century newspapers that their presence marks a periodical production as a genuine newspaper, rather than a magazine or literary journal. The true literary journals, such as the *Rambler,* the *Spectator,* the *Tatler,* or the *Female Tatler,* called for letters from readers, but the pieces they printed as correspondence were mostly written by the principal authors of the journals or carefully solicited, usually from their friends. The call for letters was merely a facade to lend the publication some of the comfortable feel of a newspaper for the public. The reading experience proffered in the literary journals was more fictional or sometimes more a matter of self-help than what was offered in the true newspapers. Real letters were rarer than contrived ones in any journal, however, and most of the real contributions by real correspondents appeared in the advertising sections of the newspapers.

I V

Advertisements are crucial to the reading experience fostered by newspapers, and we know that Johnson gave some time to this trivial, light kind of reading, despite the images of him as a studious and assiduous reader that are preferred by his biographers. Johnson dedicated *Idler* 40 to the subject of advertisements and issued some of the most durable statements ever made about the form. He begins characteristically with a note on the origins of the genre: "The practice of appending to the narratives of public transactions, more minute and domestic intelligence, and filling the news-papers with advertisements, has grown up by slow degrees to its present state."[39] The "minute and domestic intelligence" includes public service announcements concerning hospitals or turnpikes, notices to the creditors of deceased or bankrupt persons, descriptions of lost articles, and descriptions of thefts, thieves, and perpetrators of other crimes. How personal-sounding such notices could be is shown in a letter from one W. Webster printed in the *Public Advertiser* for 12 May 1758, the same issue in which the story of the Raisonable first appeared:

Sir, You may remember that some Time ago I acknowledged in your Paper the Receipt of some impudent Letters,
and desired the Authors to appear personally, and answer to
the Contents of them, which they never dared to do. I have
since made the Matter public, by shewing the Letters to
several People in my Parish, and defeated the most villain-
ous and cruel Scheme that ever was form'd against me and a
whole Family; which has so provoked the Villains, that I am
still pester'd with Letters, which I still as constantly return
to the Post-Office. Of this I thought fit to give Notice, that
my Friends, if they write to me, by a Hand that I do not
very well know, they will not be receiv'd by me.

Despite its apparent frankness, however, the notice turns out
also to be an advertisement for a book, the most common kind
of ad in all the newspapers of the day; in his postscript the
writer says, "If any one has the Curiosity to see the blackest
Iniquity and Impudence imaginable, I shall publish it at the
End of a Pamphlet . . . entitled A Plain Narrative of Fables &c.
sold by Mr. Noon at the White Hart in the poultry." The whole
letter might be a fabricated excuse for advertising a *roman à clef,*
a genre that took advantage of the dispersion of "domestic"
news. On the other hand, the letter could be serious about its
avowed intentions. It is hard to tell, and it is, in general, somewhat difficult to separate "personals" from "advertisements" in
the eighteenth-century press. This is sometimes still the case
today, of course, but in most newspapers an effort is made to
categorize ads so as to avoid such confusion.

Although they were sometimes delivered in epistolary form,
most bits of eighteenth-century "domestic news" were more
straightforward than W. Webster's ad: typically, they informed
the public of a theft and promised a reward. The aims of
informing and advertising may have been conflated, but they
were not often confused. On the other hand, the juxtaposition
of domestic news and separate ads in the same column of
newsprint can be disconcerting. A domestic news story in this

same number of the *Advertiser* was followed by an announcement. The two pieces together, separated only by paragraphing, could make for alarming reading:

> Wednesday last a little Boy was run over in Blackman-
> street, Southwark, by a Hackney Coach: The Child was
> carried to St. Thomas's Hospital, but died the next Day.
> Ranelagh House will be opened every Evening.

We live with such brutal miscellaneousness in newspapers
today, but the conventions, and our mastery of them, are such
that we are not usually so shocked as we must be by the colloca-
tion of the child's death and the socially exciting announcement about Ranelagh, where to "make one" (be present) in the
well-dressed crowd was the aspiration of London's smart set.
Making a similar observation about such confusion in the
newspapers, Terry Castle points out that

> in the second half of the century, the newspapers ran col-
> umns of "masquerade intelligence," lengthy descriptions
> of particularly elegant masquerades. The modern reader is
> jarred by the surrealistic prominence of these accounts,
> which are juxtaposed quite unself-consciously to reports of
> troop movements, Parliamentary sessions, and other more
> somber public doings. The hint is suggestive: on some level
> the masquerade was news as much as any other public occa-
> sion. Indeed an odd blurring sometimes takes place in the
> eighteenth century between the masquerade and politics:
> they absorb similar kinds of public attention.[40]

The miscellaneousness of the newspapers may, as Castle suggests, represent a correspondent miscellaneousness or mixture
of the serious and the comic in the minds of readers—that is, it
may embody cultural assumptions in a direct way. It is equally
likely, however, that the mixture required readers to make their
own distinctions and create their own pauses, just as they did
when they emended the punctuation in their more studious
reading, or just as earlier readers had had to find word breaks in
scripta continua before making sense of what was before their

eyes. Interpreting layout or any other nonverbal feature of a text as epistemology is problematic because it is never clear how much what is usually made explicit in modern typography was actually being supplied by earlier readers. However, it does seem clear that the readers either had to supply more distinctions than are now required, or that they lived with a lower degree of categorization in their understanding of newspaper content, or both.

Public service announcements in the eighteenth century were often introduced by datelines, making them look like news, but the true, longer-running, more expensive ads were separated from each other by horizontal lines running across the column. Additionally, the paid ads more than made up for their lack of datelines by containing much greater typographical variety than the news stories. This is so visibly the case that it is reasonable to conclude that the modern typography of news presentation derives from the conventions of advertising. But it must be remembered that in its early stages, advertising was itself imitating the narrative conventions of the news.

Most of the ads for books begin with the newsy declaration *"This Day is Published"* in italics, followed by the short title in large capital letters with the name of the author in small caps later in the ad. Other changes in font, type size, and the use of centering also vary the ads for books. The ads for patent medicines, the second most common kind of ad, also imitate news stories but use additional typographical variety. In the *Public Advertiser* for 12 May, we find the centered slug: "The great Discovery for the VENEREAL DISEASE, By his Majesty's most gracious Letters Patent, November 1757, called THE ROYAL MILITARY DROPS." Then follows the "story":

> A SURGEON retired from the ARMY, has discovered a most inestimable Remedy for the VENEREAL DISORDER, which he calls The ROYAL MILITARY DROPS. They are [*sic*] experienced a certain Cure from the slightest Case, to the most inveterate and malignant Degree of that baneful Distemper. . . .
> To show the great superiority of this Medicine over all oth-

ers, and to put the great Power of these Royal Military Drops beyond the Possibility of a doubt, he will undertake to cure with them, the Poor of every Parish in London (however deplorable) gratis: Hence it is plain that his Motives for publishing these drops are more from Principles of Humanity, than his own private Emolument.

Claims such as these are what led Johnson to declare in *Idler* 40 that "promise, large promise, is the soul of an advertisement."[41]

If promise gave advertisements a soul, certain journalistic forms provided the body. Eighteenth-century advertisements were so anxious to look like public service announcements that many of them carried banners reading "Address to the Public." Others begin, "To prevent any Impositions on the Public whatsoever. . . ." The public is always the paper's audience and its avowed raison d'être, so the ads are trying to blend in with their parent medium, but their typographical variety belies the attempt even as it draws desirable attention to them. Ross Perot gave the infomercial new prominence in the early stages of the 1992 United States presidential campaign, but the form was already highly developed in the eighteenth century.

The domestic news story is present in eighteenth-century medicine ads and also in that somewhat higher-class and older form, the book advertisement. One reason for this is that patent medicines and books were often produced and sold by the same people. Johnson's friend Robert James produced both the *Medicinal Dictionary* (to which Johnson contributed) and his famous fever powder. Both the medicines and the books were spoken of as "published," and a key feature in the advertisement of the medicines was the promise of a book of instructions. It is hard to say how much similarity between the two kinds of products was felt by eighteenth-century readers. As with the conflation of other forms now more clearly separated, it is unclear whether the similarities between book and medicine ads promoted confusion or required greater powers of discretion on the part of readers. However, consumers of medicine had to be readers, and reading was part of the consumption of both products. A better sense of how consumers viewed these products would no doubt make the equation more complex, but the conflation of the book ad and the medical ad in the medium of news suggests how reading resembled consumption in the middle of the eighteenth century. The resemblance was present in earlier times, and literature and medicine have been associated since antiquity, but advertising and the growth of a consumer culture, chronicled in the development of newspapers, tightened the connection between reading and ingestion. But the parallels between reading and pharmacology are also the product of an increasing sense that the members of the public could gain personal access to the secrets of education, which had earlier required the ministering help of doctors (of medicine or philosophy), if they could afford it.

Although it is difficult to know what the common reader thought, in *Idler* 40 Johnson is clear about how he read the ads: "Whatever is common is despised. Advertisements are now so numerous that they are very negligently perused, and it is therefore become necessary to gain attention by magnificence of promises, and by eloquence sometimes sublime and sometimes pathetic."[42] Johnson took his examples from the most respectable ads: soap, lottery tickets, a traveling zoo, cures for decent, common ills, such as Daffy's elixir and the "anodyne necklace" for teething children. Staying away from advertisements for studs and cures for venereal disease, Johnson correctly analyzes the psychological operations of the most common ads; he is especially sharp on the pathos in the ad for the "anodyne necklace," which says that "A MOTHER WOULD NEVER FORGIVE HERSELF" who could have kept her child from disaster with such a simple and inexpensive device.

Johnson could hone his reading to an analytical fineness and a professional sort of study when looking at ads, but the kind of reading they usually foster is a "negligent perusal." The other quality of reading ads that Johnson noticed is equally important:

It has been remarked by the severer judges, that the salutary sorrow of tragick scenes is too soon effaced by the merriment of the epilogue; the same inconvenience arises from the improper disposition of advertisements. The noblest objects may be so associated as to be made ridiculous. The camel and dromedary [in one raree show] themselves might have lost much of their dignity between "The True Flower of Mustard" and "The Original Daffy's Elixir"; and I could not but feel some indignation when I found this illustrious Indian warrior [in a different raree show] immediately succeeded by "A Fresh parcel of Dublin Butter."[43]

What Johnson says is true of the advertising section, but this miscellaneous quality was often more than matched by that of the news sections of the papers, and Johnson's complaint could be equally directed to any part of most of the dailies and twice- or thrice-weeklies. (The monthlies were better organized, although they simply reprinted some miscellaneous parts of the dailies.)

Despite Johnson's complaints, it is likely that the reading public was accommodating itself to a new kind of reading, or at least expanding its capacity to read in a way for which there had in the past been relatively little call. Advertising sections and newspapers in general called for a kind of browsing or negligent perusal that Johnson elsewhere called "mere" reading. This was a kind of reading at which he excelled, as he did at every kind of reading, and one that he could engage or disengage at will. He complained about it, but he did it, and it did not stop him from practicing all the other kinds of reading.

As usual, in *Idler* 40 Johnson is worried about the effect of publications on the general public rather than on himself. He could read Hobbes or Mandeville without danger, but he refused to put these writers in the hands of all readers when he excluded their works from the illustrative quotations in his *Dictionary*. Likewise, he was worried about the effect on the public of the reading of advertising, despite his own immunity. He ends *Idler* 40 with a plea for greater responsibility in adver-

tising, which quickly becomes an appeal to writers and publishers to keep newspapers on the high road of historical writing rather than descending further into their special realm in
which fact and fiction are confused and credence is constantly
at issue. Johnson made his appeal directly to individual advertisers, but he filled it with irony, and he was obviously speaking
to everyone involved in producing and purchasing the papers:
"Every man that advertises his own excellence, should write
with some consciousness of a character which dares to call the
attention of the publick. He should remember that his name is
to stand in the same paper with those of the King of Prussia,
and the Emperor of Germany, and endeavour to make himself
worthy of such association." This is ironic because Johnson did
not trust Frederick III, the king of Prussia, and he did not like
England's involvement in the diplomatic chess game he was
playing with Maria Theresa of Austria. Moreover, "Emperor of
Germany" had become only a nominal title by this time.[44]

Johnson's next remark in *Idler* 40 is even more broadly satirical: "Some regard is likewise to be paid to posterity. There are
men of diligence and curiosity who treasure up the papers of the
day merely because others neglect them, and in time they will
be scarce. When these collections shall be read in another century, how will numberless contradictions be reconciled, and
how shall fame be possibly distributed among the tailors and
boddice-makers of the present age."[45] What Johnson is really
laughing at here is the readers who might be stupid enough to
believe what they read in the papers or innocent enough to
think the papers a fit vehicle of the high seriousness of history. It
is a medium to be negligently perused, mistrusted, and trashed.
But it is nevertheless to be read. Johnson's own range of allusion
in the *Idler,* in the *Literary Magazine,* in the *Gentleman's Magazine,* in his letters, and even in the *Rambler* proves that.

The newspapers not only fostered a new kind of reading
habit; they also had an effect on other kinds of reading. We are
all newspaper readers now, whatever other kinds of readers we
are. The habit of negligent perusal is available for us to apply to
any kind of book, although we are more likely to apply it to the

unavoidable displays of print that assail us in contemporary society, on the roadways, on our packages of provisions, and on our clothes. Indeed, without the habit of negligent perusal, or mere reading, it would be difficult to get from one end of a city street to the next. If we tried to read the print around us as hard readers or self-help readers, we would surely be at a standstill, overwhelmed with interpretive suggestions or confused by conflicting advice. We have to read it all negligently and with measured or minimal credence. To a degree, we have all become masters of this, and this mastery must come into play in at least some other parts of our lives of reading. The obvious example for the present is reading on the World Wide Web, or browsing, as it is aptly called.

The kind of reading on which ads and newspapers probably have had the greatest effect, however, is narrative fiction. Newspaper reading prepared the public for new kinds of narrative fiction and a new appreciation of fiction. In general, advertising enabled readers better to read fiction as fiction, to read happily and swiftly without extending credence. But for all its untrustworthiness, the news could also be true, and it was concerned with being credible. Hence, by becoming acquainted with newspapers, readers of fiction gained a new way of believing what they read as well as a new way of distrusting it.

CURIOUS READING

The typical material of curious, inquisitive, and addictive reading is romance and other kinds of fiction. When a reader is "lost in a book," the book is most often a novel or a romance; this had been true for at least a couple of generations by the third quarter of the eighteenth century. John Adams, America's second president and a great reader in later life, described reading romances as an "incredible delight." Not content with that justification of this much-maligned form of reading, however, he self-consciously defended his expenditure of valuable time: "These Scottish and German romances," he told Dr. Rush, "show in a clear light the horrors of the feudal aristocracy as the histories of Genghis Khan and Tamerlane shew the same anarchy in the Asiatic aristocracy."[1] In effect, Adams argued, his "incredibly" pleasurable reading was also a form of study. Adams did not explore the psychology of pleasure that he derived from his reading of romances, but his phrase "incredible delight" suggests that, for him as for others addicted to the genre, there was something fantastic in the experience.

Adams's successor as president of the United States examined the question a bit more closely. Like many readers, Thomas Jefferson grew away from reading romances and gradually rejected fiction reading altogether. In 1771, at the age of twenty-eight, Jefferson was still recommending some fiction in his "model library": Henry Fielding, Tobias Smollett, Laurence Sterne, Oliver Goldsmith, Jean-Jacques Rousseau's *Eloise,* and others. By 1818, however, he had changed his mind: "A great obstacle to good education is the inordinate passion prevalent for novels, and the time lost in that reading which should be instructively employed. When this passion infects the mind, it destroys its tone, and revolts it against wholesome reading. . . . The result is a bloated imagination, sickly judgment, and disgust towards the real business of life."[2] Like Jefferson, Samuel Johnson grew increasingly contemptuous of the improbable and unprovable as he grew older. He also felt there were dangers in what I call "curious reading," but he never entirely rid himself of the "incredible delight" or "inordinate passion." He tried to shift the focus of his reading passion to works that were more profitable or studious, but never did he entirely give up reading in the genre that most encourages such wildness in reading.

Although there are a few books on the subject, such as Janice Radway's *Reading the Romance* and Victor Nell's *Lost in a Book,* the psychology of curious reading has not been thoroughly explored. It is safe to say that this psychology is complex: the common analogy to dreaming has its limits, and readers "lost in a book" are probably not always lost. Common sense tells us that readers seldom give over completely to belief in the world of their texts. Nevertheless, there is some "willing suspension of disbelief," in Coleridge's famous phrase, or, as I suggest in my scheme of the types of reading, credence is allowed to become irrelevant in this kind of reading. The situation is oddly similar to that in study or hard reading, where credence is also irrelevant. An important difference between the two kinds of reading, however, is the speeds at which they are usually done. The slow speed of study, the concentration on text as text, the isolation of portions of the text for reflection and recollection, all remind the reader of the intangibility of the world of words under consideration. In the rapidity of curious reading and its ability to transport the reader into the worlds of fiction or romance, aesthetic and intellectual considerations tend to be lost as the reader follows the unfolding events of the story. If one paused to reflect on it, one might reject the credibility of the tale and execrate the fiction; one does pause from time to time, but the experience is best without such reflection.

I think most readers have had the experience of reading in this uncritical way, at least at times, through parts of certain books. In fact, there is reason to believe it is the most popular kind of reading. It is certainly a kind of reading that Johnson did. To adapt the famous claim of the Roman dramatist Terence, no human reading experience was alien to him. But Johnson's experience as a curious reader was not like that of a modern reader. This is in part because of the different collection of books that Johnson read with curiosity; in part because of changes in social circumstances and the social construction of reading; and in part because of Johnson's own special qualities as a reader.

Johnson confessed to reading romances throughout his life, and there is also evidence of compulsive, impassioned reading of the sort that romances foster. Both forms of this experience—reading *Hamlet* until he was frightened, and hearing romances on his mother's lap—are more common in childhood, but even in later life Johnson had reading experiences that engaged him so completely that he forgot himself. Hester Thrale, who only knew Johnson in his last twenty years of life, reported: "He had sometimes fits of reading very violent; and when he was in earnest about getting through some particular pages . . . he would be quite lost to company, and withdraw all his attention to what he was reading, without the smallest knowledge or care about the noise made round him." Thrale added, with real disgust, "He advised the same conduct to others."[3] There is no indication that these "fits" of reading focused on one kind of book rather than another, and it is certainly possible that Johnson, like some other readers, applied habits of curious reading to texts other than novels.

Most, but not all, of the reading matter that Johnson described as captivating was fictional. Nevertheless, the works that provided him with material for a similar style of reading should have similarities, and those similarities might offer clues to the nature of Johnson's experience as a reader. Johnson said he read Henry Fielding's *Amelia* straight through without stopping, and on another occasion Hester Thrale "heard him say he

Joseph Baretti, c. 1780, mezzotint by John Watts after Sir Joshua Reynolds (courtesy of the Yale Center for British Art, Paul Mellon Collection).

never read but one book, which he did not consider as obligatory, through in his whole life (and Lady Mary Wortley's Letters was the book)."[4] His report to another friend that Robert Burton's *Anatomy of Melancholy* was the only book that ever got him out of bed early suggests that the list may have been a little longer than any one deposition indicates.[5] But, even adding up all the favorites, the list is not long. Johnson did an immense amount of his reading in books that he wanted to study for humanistic reasons and in books that he perused for the purpose of making other books. To invoke a broad distinction

Portrait of Dr. Samuel Johnson, c. 1783, attributed to Frances Reynolds (courtesy of the Albright-Knox Art Gallery, Buffalo, New York—a gift of Mrs. R. B. Adam in memory of Mr. R. B. Adam).

ventured by Northrop Frye, Johnson was more an Iliad than an Odyssey reader.[6] But he was also a great Odyssey reader, as his friends were continually discovering to their surprise. For all his seriousness as a student and writer, Johnson was also an idle reader who could be found sitting alone reading the admittedly tedious *History of Birmingham* and roasting apples to pass the time, or indulging in an inspection of *The Charmer: A Choice Collection of Songs* (1749) in the home of a Hebridean host.[7]

Despite his critical seriousness and his professional practicality, Johnson often wished for both pleasure and transport

Dr. Johnson Perusing the Manuscript of The Vicar of Wakefield, 1843, by E. M. Ward (courtesy of the Board of Trustees of the National Museums and Galleries on Merseyside, Walker Art Gallery, Liverpool).

in his reading. His penchant for absorption is registered in Sir Joshua Reynolds's famous picture of him reading in 1775 (see frontispiece). Although the picture does not show it, Johnson's worst deficiency of sight was in his left eye, and some of the concentration is evidently meant to convey this deficiency (though Reynolds may have the picture turned about). But an absorption that goes beyond the physical is also conveyed, especially in comparison, for example, to Reynolds's portrait of Giuseppi Baretti, who obviously suffered from some sort of nearsightedness. There are two other paintings of Johnson reading. They are not so startling as Sir Joshua Reynolds's, but they also suggest a strong degree of concentration. Neither of them shows the pages of Johnson's book so bent and mangled, as though he were actually consuming the book, as though he were exhibiting the power attributed to him by Mary Knowles to "tear out the heart of a book."[8]

The attitude of the 1775 Reynolds portrait was taken later by an imaginative painter who recreated the scene of Johnson reading the manuscript of Goldsmith's *Vicar of Wakefield* in a tavern, looking as if it would be a close contest between the food and the book. Balancing these stories of consumption are tales of disgust. Johnson's eagerness to be pleased could turn to contempt if he were disappointed: there is evidence of this reaction in Boswell's account of Johnson throwing a book down in disgust on the journey to the Hebrides, his frequent announcement that he seldom read books through, and the copious evidence of Johnson not reading books, including many for which he wrote dedications and of some of which he wrote short reviews.[9]

Even without a violent reaction, Johnson could easily turn aside from a book. There is a nice image of how thoroughly Johnson could neglect a book in a pair of letters he wrote to Joseph Craddock in 1783. Craddock evidently lent Johnson a folio manuscript that contained poems by James I and others. When Craddock solicited its return, Johnson wrote, "Mr. Johnson has no remembrance, and can hardly think he ever received it." Anxious to get the volume, which he himself had on loan, Craddock sought the help of George Steevens, Johnson's coeditor on the revised edition of Shakespeare and a serious book collector. Steevens replied, "That then . . . is the book, which now lies under his inkstand; it is neatly packed up and sealed." That is how it arrived and that is how it was returned.[10]

It is worth noting, however, that Johnson was more likely to leave manuscripts unread than printed books, and he did not like receiving manuscripts from aspiring writers or even from friends.[11] Johnson also did not collect manuscripts, although at various times in his life he displayed a considerable antiquarian interest and sometimes requested copies of manuscripts from the Bodleian Library; he even owned a copy of *Bernard's Catalogue* (1697), so that he could get the pressmarks right in his requests.[12] But Johnson had a decided preference for printed works, and this conveniently registers his place in the history of the technology of writing and reading. He preferred the look of print, and its regularity suited his reading habits. Although he was capable of studious behavior as a reader, he was also infected with a wish to read quickly. He absorbed print more quickly than handwriting, and thus was more absorbed in it. Johnson's predilection for print may have arisen in part because of his nervous and ocular disabilities, but it was not wholly dictated by those disabilities. He adapted his life of reading to his infirmities in a special way that was suited to his place in the history of reading and his particular mentality. Because he was a great reader, Johnson's special accommodation defines a moment in the history of reading, just as his overall literary sensibility defines an age in literary history.

I I

There are several classes of books among those that Johnson read with great absorption. The most important group is composed of romances. Like John Adams, Johnson said he liked those that could be read allegorically, but he preferred moral to political allegory, and named as his favorites *Robinson Crusoe, Don Quixote, Pilgrim's Progress,* and the *Iliad.*[13] These books provided Johnson with some of the pleasure of more trivial romances such as *Don Bellianis of Greece* or Richard Johnson's *Famous History of the Seven Champions of Christendom,* the book with which he probably learned to read.[14] Johnson's own "incredible delight" certainly included a "lower" interest in the fantasies of sexual as well as military conquest that dominated the romances he began reading as a child, perhaps in the simple chapbook versions in which the popular and children's literature of the time was printed.[15] Bishop Percy heard Johnson "attribute to these extravagant fictions that unsettled turn of mind which prevented his ever fixing in any profession."[16] This "unsettled turn of mind" is associated throughout Johnson's diaries with his "melancholy" and with the "tyranny of vain imaginations" that he struggled to control.[17] Like Jefferson, Johnson worried about the psychological effects of curious reading, and he condemned it, but such reading, like some of his other habits, was too deeply ingrained in his inner life to be extirpated.

Johnson both evinced his knowledge of romances and analyzed their dangerous consequences for readers in a chapter that he either wrote himself or substantially revised as a conclusion for his friend Charlotte Lennox's comical *Female Quixote*. The protagonist of Lennox's book is Arabella, the only child of a widowed marquis, who goes to school on romantic fare and imagines that it describes the real world. Her misconceptions lead to many funny adventures; in the end, she has to be kept from drowning herself to prevent an innocent approach that she fears will end, as such approaches threaten to do in romances, in rape. In Johnson's chapter, Arabella's cousin, a minister, convinces her that her beloved novels are "Senseless Fictions . . . which at once vitiate the Mind, and pervert the Understanding."[18] Such a lesson is to be expected from the great moralist. However, on his way to proving his point about the dangers of romance reading, Johnson ironically displays a broad familiarity with the genre. For instance, he has Arabella say

> Why . . . should I not dread the Misfortunes which happen'd to the divine Clelia, who was carry'd to one of the Isles of the Thrasymenian Lake? Or those which befell the beautiful Candace, Queen of Ethiopia, whom the Pyrate Zenodorus wander'd with on the Seas? Or the accidents which imbitter'd the Life of the incomparable Cleopatra? Or the Persecutions which made that of the fair Elisa miserable? Or in fine, the various Distresses of many other fair and virtuous Princesses: such as those which happen'd to Olympia, Bellamira, Parisatis, Berenice, Amalgantha, Agione, Albysinda, Placidia, Arsinoe, Deidamia, and a thousand others I could mention.[19]

Johnson himself may not have known "a thousand others." He may not even have known all these; some were well known in chapbooks and other forms, and some may have been invented. But there is evidence here and elsewhere that Johnson knew the genre of the romance well and had read many examples of it.

Johnson's ironic indictment of the reading of romances in his chapter of Lennox's book is various, but he comes closest to expressing his fears about the genre's dangers for himself when he has the minister say, "It is the fault of the best fictions, that they teach young Minds to expect strange Adventures and sudden Vicissitudes, and therefore encourage them often to trust to chance."[20] This may be part of what he meant when he ascribed his own "unsettled turn of mind" to reading romances. It represents an indictment of fiction in general, and perhaps of writing in general, of which Johnson grew more and more aware through the 1750s and which he expressed strongly in his thirty-nine book reviews for the *Literary Magazine* from 1756 to 1757. In this record of his reading it is clear that he was increasingly likely to approve of literature that served practical purposes, such as teaching a method of bleaching or desalination, and to reject mere fiction as, at best, a waste of time.[21]

Johnson sometimes acknowledged that fiction could be safely read, but only if it were recognized as fiction. In *Rambler* 4, for example, he describes the "heroic romances" of an earlier age as safer than his day's more realistic fiction because "the reader was in very little danger of making any applications to himself; the virtues and crimes were equally beyond his sphere of activity; and he amused himself with heroes and with traitors, deliverers and persecutors, as with beings of another species, whose actions were regulated upon motives of their own, and who had neither faults nor excellencies in common with himself."[22] Johnson may say this in his role as the stoical and professional Mr. Rambler, but his more casual remarks, as well as his practice in the *Literary Magazine,* suggest that his fears about the influence of fiction were not just part of the monitory persona he adopted in his most famous essays.

However, in the *Rambler,* as in his chapter of *The Female Quixote,* Johnson was careful to exempt Samuel Richardson from the caveat against reading fiction. Introducing Richardson, the anonymous but well-known guest author of *Rambler* 97, the anonymous but well-known regular author of the *Rambler* describes him as "an authour . . . who has enlarged the knowledge of human nature, and taught the passions to move at the command of virtue."[23] But even in this accolade one sees the danger that Johnson felt fiction posed: it moves the passions, and to be safe, it had better move them in accordance with virtue, but only the best writers can achieve that, and only the best human beings wish to achieve it.

In reading as well as in other solitary activities (or in inactivity), Johnson worried about his passions or his imagination running away with him. Some of the fantasies in which he engaged, whether reading or not, were obviously of a sexual nature. Romances, from *Daphnis and Chloe* to *Don Bellianis of Greece* to Spenser's *Faerie Queene,* and even *Pilgrim's Progress,* take advantage of the seductive nature of sexual fantasies, even if their object is to help us control them. Johnson could announce books like Bunyan's and Richardson's as his favorites because they justify and redeem their pleasures with moral teaching, but the pleasures may have been what kept him reading. It was not for the story alone, nor only for the morality, that he read *Clarissa, Amelia,* and *The Vicar of Wakefield.* He said directly about *Clarissa* that one who read it for the story would be so fretted that he would hang himself, and he must have encountered a similar problem in *Amelia.*[24] The most sentimental performance of Fielding's pleased him much more than *Tom Jones,* which he disparaged, saying "there was more knowledge of the heart in one letter of Richardson's."[25] He even preferred the didactic fictions of Fielding's sister Sarah (*The Governess,* for example) to Henry's picaresque tales.[26] But if Johnson liked pure morality in fiction, he might have said something kinder about William Congreve's *Incognita,* the object of his deathless pronouncement "I would rather praise it than read it."[27]

After *Rambler* 4 (1750), Johnson made several famous critical statements on the dangers of writing that presents life as it is, without the mediating influence of a strong, moralizing authorial voice. For his admiring but sober editor, it was Shakespeare's as well as Fielding's greatest fault that he failed to draw the moral of his tales with sufficient clarity. As usual, however,

Johnson's critical statements did not necessarily coincide with his practice in his life of reading. What really attracted Johnson to Shakespeare, as well as to *Clarissa, Amelia,* and *The Vicar of Wakefield,* was partly the feelings that the works evoked in him. For the same reason that he liked Nahum Tate's happy ending to *King Lear* (Cordelia lives and marries Kent) and found Shakespeare's ending unendurable, Johnson found a certain satisfaction in *Amelia* and *The Vicar of Wakefield.* But it is worth looking more closely at *Amelia* for a moment to see if the nature of Johnson's attraction can be deduced from specific features of this novel, which he wishfully believed to be immensely popular and which he personally liked better even than *Clarissa,* despite his admiration and affection for Richardson and his contempt for Fielding. Is it only the sentiment in *Amelia* that Johnson liked so much? How could he have found it so compelling that he read, as he says, the two long volumes through without stopping?

Fielding obviously hoped to induce "curiosity" in his readers, and one sign of his intention is that he or his publishers started a rumor, only lately discredited, that the book went into a second printing within twenty-four hours. Johnson believed the rumor, and was a curious reader of the novel himself. Overall, the greatest inducements in *Amelia* to such curious reading are the numerous descriptions of violated chastity and the perpetual although always ineffectual threats to Amelia's chastity. The worst debaucheries are told by tellers within the tale, and it is intriguing that Fielding uses the word "curiosity" when describing the audience for these tales within the tale.

The novel opens inside a debtors' prison, where the hero, Booth, is eventually found in conversation with one Miss Matthews. They tell their life stories to each other with much animation. To Booth's great shock, Matthews triumphantly declares that she has murdered a man. Reacting to Booth's horror, she says, "Whatever you may have heard, you cannot be acquainted with all the strange Accidents which have occasioned your seeing me in a Place [prison], which, at our last

Parting, was so unlikely that I should ever have been found in; nor can you know the Cause of all that I have uttered, and which, I am convinced, you never expected to have heard from my Mouth. If these Circumstances raise your Curiosity, I will satisfy it."[28] The response Fielding wants from his audience is given by Booth: "He answered, that Curiosity was too mean a Word to express his ardent Desire of knowing her Story."

Matthews's story concerns her affair with a young officer, the loss of her chastity, his rejection of her and marriage to another, her torment and rage, and the grief of her father. As Fielding's description of her in terms of a catalogue of wicked women suggests, Matthews is an excessively passionate woman, and she makes plenty of trouble for Booth, beginning with her seduction of the otherwise faithful husband that first night in prison. Another passionate woman, Mrs. Bennet, later Mrs. Atkinson, also tells a story of murder and adultery. Her auditor is Amelia, who, despite her horror at the utterance of such words, must admit, "Indeed, Madam, you have raised my Curiosity to the highest Pitch, and I beg you will proceed with your Story."[29] Mrs. Bennet then goes on for some chapters to tell how, under duress of poverty, she submitted to the entreaties of a certain peer, who has been courting Amelia. Her indigent husband discovers her infidelity because he contracts venereal disease from her. In his madness he injures himself and dies later of causes that Mrs. Bennet cannot be fully convinced are medically unrelated either to gonorrhea or to his self-injury.

Although he consciously tries to arouse it in his readers, Fielding declares that "Curiosity . . . when thoroughly roused is a very troublesome Passion."[30] Particular stories of debauchery are said to arouse this emotion in the auditor, but much of the novel is about curiosity in a slightly broader sense: it is perpetually concerned with the varieties of uneasiness and the feelings incident to our failure to know what is in the minds of others. Appropriately, the central social event in the book is a masquerade at Ranelagh, the deceptions at which are not all sorted out until the end of the novel.[31] Curiosity is often the emotion raised by untold tales, incomprehensible notes, and other formal sources of information, but suspicion is the more common response to the unknown in *Amelia*.

Suspicion is the darker side of curiosity, as Fielding suggests in one of the many reflections on human nature he inserts in his novel: "So great a Torment is Anxiety to the human Mind, that we always endeavour to relieve ourselves from it, by Guesses however doubtful or uncertain; on all which occasions Dislike and Hatred are the surest Guides to lead our Suspicion to its Object."[32] Despite its affinity with ugly passions, suspicion plays an important role in Fielding's conception of communication. In one instance, Booth fails to "read" Amelia's response to his news; she is above suspicion, and Fielding remarks that "Suspicion . . . indeed, is the great Optic Glass helping us to discern plainly almost all that passes in the Minds of others, without some Use of which nothing is more purblind than human Nature."[33] Fielding's dark view of human nature, modeled on writers such as Mandeville, made it hard for Johnson publicly to admit Fielding's attractions. In his role as public monitor and moralist, Johnson was much more often and more solidly on the side of Mandeville's antagonist, William Law, who took a bright view of individual human potential. However, as an individual, Johnson was a reader of Mandeville; he both understood and entertained such dark views of the human animal. Fielding's description of curiosity and suspicion interested Johnson, and, like other eager readers of *Amelia,* he enacted and endorsed Fielding's views in greedily consuming the novel.

It is an overstatement to say that *Amelia* is a tale about curious reading and the difficulties in "reading" others, but the novel embodies these themes. Amelia herself is "unreadable" because she is so nearly perfect. Because of an accident in which her nose was crushed, the Amelia of Booth's earliest account is masked, undergoing a lengthy surgical reconstruction. Booth fell in love with her one day at tea when he "begged her to indulge my Curiosity by shewing me her Face. She answered in the most obliging Manner, 'Perhaps, Mr. Booth, you will as little know me when my mask is off as when it is on.'" Booth does not know how truly she has spoken, and he is virtually blinded with passion when she takes off the mask: "The Surgeon's Skill was the least I considered. A thousand tender Ideas rushed all at once on my Mind. I was unable to contain myself, and eagerly kissing her Hand, I cried—'Upon my Soul, Madam, you never appeared to me so lovely as at this Instant.'"[34] Because she has plastic surgery but also because she is above suspicion, Amelia is always virtuously masked, always unreadable, always an object of pure curiosity. For some readers, including Samuel Johnson, Fielding succeeded in giving his book the same virtue.

Even if Johnson did not see *Amelia* as an allegory of reading, there is much in it that he must have admired as well as much that aroused his curiosity. Booth's tenderness for women and all the sentiment poured forth in the novel had their attractions for Johnson, whose wife declared him the most "sensible," meaning sensitive, man she had ever met. Booth describes Amelia likewise as "the most sensible Woman in the World."[35] But the word he uses most to describe Amelia is "angel." He calls her "my dear Angel" and says she has the "Sweetness of an Angel."[36] The four volumes of *Amelia* were published not long before the death of Johnson's wife Elizabeth, and they may have been on Johnson's mind three years later when he courted Hill Boothby and addressed her in letters as "My Sweet Angel."[37] Whether or not Johnson was alluding to *Amelia* in his love letters, I think *Amelia* was a book about romance as he understood it, and that was part of its attraction for him. As there is, at times, for modern readers of romance, there was an element of identification for Johnson in his reading of *Amelia,* and this is one of the distinctive features of curious reading in any age.

Of course, we do not have to imagine Johnson swooning over *Amelia* like a teenager reading a romance novel. The novel also contains a good deal of "manly" moral generalization, and a good deal of literary allusiveness that appealed to the student in him. But identification of some kind was at work in his reading. This feeling may have been furthered by the figure in the book who bears a resemblance to Johnson himself. There is a hack writer in the prison frequented by Booth whose occupation is described by the bailiff Bondum in satirical terms: "He writes your History Books for your Numbers, and sometimes your Verses, your Poems, what do you call them? And then again he writes News for your News Papers." Booth replies, "Ay indeed! he is a most extraordinary Man truly—How doth he get his News here?" "Why," replies Bondum, "he makes it, as he doth your Parliament Speeches for your Magazines. He reads them to me sometimes over a Bowl of Punch.—To be sure it is all one as if one was in the Parliament House—It is about Liberty and Freedom, and about the Constitution of England."[38] Such Tory concerns fill the parliamentary debates that Johnson wrote for the *Gentleman's Magazine* in the early 1740s. The imprisoned hack does not exactly resemble Johnson, but on this point he certainly does, and the book contains enough real people, real events, and real addresses to fill a contemporary reader with curiosity or suspicion about whom a given character might represent. This mixture of reality and fiction is one of the qualities that made novels compelling for Johnson and for other curious readers in the eighteenth century.[39]

Johnson's attraction to *Clarissa* can be explained in similar terms, although Richardson's novel is more complex and a greater work of art than Fielding's *Amelia*. Like *Amelia*, *Clarissa* combines some of the pleasures of sentimental fiction with some of the pleasures of romance. Both works also justify themselves by their moral teachings, although Richardson, according to Johnson, achieves the higher goal of teaching "the passions to move at the command of virtue." But making them move in the first place is an important part of pleasing Johnson that is not necessarily coherent with the moral design. In fact, the passions are moved against the commands of virtue in much of *Amelia* and even in parts of *Clarissa*. As contemporary and modern commentators have easily seen, *Clarissa* indulges prurience in the way it reveals the private life of an attractive young woman, and there is plenty of sexual titillation. Like more-conventional romances, *Clarissa* exposes a beautiful young woman to the danger of rape. The coffin, the tomb of the apartments in which she is kept, the illusions, and the masks all belong to the world of romance in which Richardson himself was probably schooled. Johnson's public critical remarks about *Clarissa* and his letters to Richardson all stress the important moral and ethical lessons of the book, but if he took pleasure in the book (and he probably did, judging by his repeated readings), it seems likely that he found in it an appeal to some of his underlying susceptibilities as a reader, the same susceptibilities that gave romance their appeal for him, including what Fielding describes as the "serio-comic romance" of *Amelia*.

The French writer Denis Diderot gave perhaps the nicest account of the sort of pleasures available in *Clarissa* for Johnson and other contemporary readers. Tom Keymer adduces this passage among many others in his book on *Clarissa*'s eighteenth-century readers: "Une idée qui m'est venue quelquefois en rêvant aux ouvrages de Richardson, c'est que j'avais acheté un vieux château; qu'en visitant un jour ses appartements, j'avais aperçu dans un angle une armoire qu'on n'avait pas ouverte depuis longtemps, et que, l'ayant enfoncée, j'y avais trouvé pêle-mêle les lettres de Clarisse et de Paméla."[40] Diderot described his reading experience as one that demanded a good deal of activity on his part. He had to sort out the letters in his dream of *Clarissa* and in his real reading of the book. Richardson did not do everything for him. Johnson undoubtedly also felt that much was left to the reader, and the contemporary comparisons between *Paradise Lost* and *Clarissa* were founded to some extent on the ways in which both books presented readers with ethical questions in the form of problems of comprehension. But Diderot's description also displays Richardson's reader as a kind of prurient dreamer investigating someone else's house and getting into his or her private things. Johnson probably felt some of this unspeakable pleasure.

Diderot also remarked that part of the experience of Richardson was a renewed awareness of his solitude as a reader: "A la fin, il me sembla tout à coup que j'étais resté seul."[41] As Keymer shows, this separation from society is a prelude to deeper involvement in the text. The more illicit pleasures of reading *Clarissa* required this solitude and the dreaming that it permits. Read in company, especially mixed company, as it was read by Richardson and other paternal figures, *Clarissa* could become a moral manual, but read in solitude it could yield the pleasures of romance. Johnson undoubtedly read it both ways, as did many of his contemporaries, including Lady Mary Wortley Montagu, who abused the work in her letters and wept over it in private.[42] It would come as no surprise to sociologists or philosophers that perception is altered by group dynamics. As a kind of perception, reading too is subject to change, even if its object remains the same, when the circumstances surrounding the reading change.

I I I

In some ways the *Letters* of Lady Mary Wortley Montagu is the most interesting of the entries on the short list of books that Johnson described as most compelling. The other works are all clearly fictional except Burton's *Anatomy of Melancholy*, which is hard to classify. With its dense texture of classical quotation and its farrago of wisdom and pseudodoxia about melancholy, it undoubtedly struck responsive chords in Johnson, who was constantly bringing classical wisdom to bear on an examination of his own melancholic temperament. Because Johnson says he got out of bed to read Burton's *Anatomy of Melancholy*, it may have been a book for study, whereas he may have stayed in bed and "read like a Turk" when his fare was *Amelia* or Montagu's Turkish letters. But why Montagu's letters?

The letters published in Johnson's lifetime provide a record of the journey the author took from 1716 to 1718 as the young wife of George I's ambassador to Turkey. The letters were prepared for publication by 1724, when they were outfitted with a preface by Mary Astell, but they were not published until 1763. This is close to the date at which Johnson told Hester Thrale how much he enjoyed them, and it was a year after Johnson received his pension and with it his freedom from reading and writing for a living. There may have been an element of celebration in Johnson's thorough reading of Montagu's letters that had to do with his changed position in life, and he may have been naming a book that his new friend, Mrs. Thrale, might easily enjoy herself, but there was undoubtedly more to his stated preference than this. The reason Johnson found the *Letters* so compelling is that it contains several of the elements of all the books that engaged him. It combines the appeal of letters, a documentary part of biography, the genre Johnson once said he liked best, with elements of romance: descriptions of distant, exotic, usually "Oriental" places, sensuous descriptions of women, and suggestions of sexual encounters or possibilities for such encounters. Moreover, unlike romances but like some other travel literature, these letters could be believed—an added incentive to approbation, as well as a greater inducement to fantasy. It is easier to entertain fantasies about a situation that may be real, although fantastic in itself, than about one that is patently unreal, because incredulity does not interfere so readily, even when the fantasy involves the falsehood of one's own presence and power in faraway places and unlikely positions. Johnson's internal censors guarded against the admission of the incredible as sternly as they watched for the immoral, but then his powerful curiosity and his great imaginative range (his expansive sense of self) put these guards frequently to the test.

Travel literature is likely to engender a sort of reading halfway between the mere reading associated with newspapers and magazines and the absorbed reading most closely associated with fiction. In reading the accounts of travelers, Johnson, like his coevals, extended and withheld credence in a volatile combination. For Johnson, writing that was both exotic and credible was the most desirable. The qualities of credibility and exoticism work against each other, however, and I think that where they were both strong Johnson found greatest pleasure. In addition, it is likely that Montagu's attention to descriptions of beautiful women, their bathing habits, and in some cases their sexual lives gave rein to Johnson's imagination. The description of the baths at Adrianople provides a good example of

Montagu's mixture of the credible and the sensually exotic. It begins with the ride to the baths in a remarkable coach, "cover'd all over with scarlet cloth, lin'd with silk, and . . . richly embrodier'd and fring'd." Inside, she continues,

> I was in my travelling Habit, which is a riding dress, and certainly appear'd very extraordinary to them, yet there was not one of 'em that shew'd the least surprize or impertinent Curiosity, but receiv'd me with all the obliging civillity possible. I know no European Court, where the Ladys would have behav'd them selves in so polite a manner to a stranger.
>
> I believe in the whole, there were 200 Women and yet none of those disdainful smiles or satyric whispers that never fail in our assemblys, when any body appears that is not dress'd exactly in fashion. They repeated over and over to me, Uzelle, pek uzelle, which is nothing but, charming, very charming. The first sofas were cover'd with Cushions and rich Carpets, on which sat the Ladys, on the 2nd, their slaves behind 'em, but without any distinction of rank by their dress, all being in the state of nature, that is, in plain English, stark naked, without any Beauty or defect conceal'd, yet there was not the least wanton smile or immodest Gesture amongst 'em. They Walk'd and mov'd with the same majestic Grace, which Milton describes our General Mother. There were many amongst them as exactly proportion'd as ever any Goddess was drawn by the pencil of a Guido or Titian, and most of their skins shineingly white, only adorn'd by their Beautiful Hair divided into many tresses, hanging on their shoulders, braided either with pearl or riband, perfectly representing the figures of the Graces.[43]

This is certainly not pornographic, but it contains sensuous "incredible delight." Moreover, the high tone of the comparisons to Milton and Titian gives way in the next paragraph when Montagu reflects on her sensations. This turn inward leads to a kind of writing that resembles the somewhat pornographic response of a reader wishing to indulge his or her own fantasies:

I was here convinc'd of the Truth of a Reflexion that I had often made, that if 'twas the fashion to go naked, the face would be hardly observ'd. I perceiv'd, that the Ladys with the finest skins and most delicate shapes had the greatest share of my admiration, tho' their faces were sometimes less beautifull than those of their companions. To tell you the truth, I had wickedness enough to wish secretly, that Mr. Jervas [a painter famous for his pictures of beauties] could have been there invisible. I fancy it would have very much improv'd his art to see so many fine Women naked in different postures, some in conversation, some working, others drinking Coffee or sherbet, and many negligently lying on their Cushions, while their slaves (generally pretty Girls of 17 or 18) were employ'd in braiding their hair in several pretty manners.[44]

The scene has descended from Titian to Jervas and settles down close to the boudoir fantasies of François Boucher. Montagu herself does not remove all her clothes, but she takes off enough for her hosts to examine her stays, which they interpret as some kind of chastity belt. The direction of the gaze is momentarily reversed and the Westerner becomes the exotic object, but the looseness of the Eastern life is also suggested by this scene. For a man reading this, for Johnson, there is a double kind of exoticism in that both the world of "the Orient" and the world of women are exposed to his forbidden view.

Montagu devotes a great portion of her correspondence to descriptions of women. As one of the only women in the eighteenth century to visit Turkey and many of the places through which she passed to get there, she provided an unusual view of certain sights she had seen, and most unusual of all, perhaps unique, was her glimpse behind the chadors and caftans that hid Islamic women from the view of men. The dress, figures, and faces of Islamic women are frequently described, and one climax of the book occurs when Montagu is introduced to the "fair Fatima," lady of the Kahya, the powerful deputy of the grand vizier:

I was met at the door by 2 black Eunuchs who led me through a long Gallery between two ranks of beautifull young Girls, with their Hair finely plaited almost hanging to their Feet, all dress'd in fine light damasks brocaded with silver. I was sorry that Decency did not permit me to stop to consider them nearer, but that Thought was lost upon my Entrance into a Large room, or rather Pavillion, built round with gilded sashes, which were most of 'em thrown up; and the Trees planted near them gave an agreeable Shade, which hinder'd the Sun from being troublesome, the Jess'mins and Honey suckles that twisted round their Trunks, sheding a soft perfume, encreas'd by a white Marble fountain playing sweet Water in the Lower part of the room, which fell into 3 or 4 basins with a pleasing sound. The Roof was painted with all sorts of Flowers falling out of gilded baskets, that seem'd tumbling down.

On a sofa, rais'd 3 steps, and cover'd with fine Persian carpets, sat the Kahya's lady, leaning on cushions of white Satin, embrodier'd, and at her feet sat 2 young Girls, the eldest about 12 year old, lovely as Angels, dress'd perfectly rich and almost cover'd with Jewels. But they were hardly seen near the fair Fatima . . . so much her beauty effac'd every thing. . . . I was so struck with Admiration that I could not for some time speak to her, being wholly taken up in gazing. That surprizing Harmony of features! that charming result of the whole! that exact proportion of Body! that lovely bloom of Complexion unsully'd by art! the unutterable Enchantment of her Smile!—But her Eyes! large and black, with all the soft languishment of the bleu! every turn of her face discovering some new charm.[45]

Montagu then endeavors, "by nicely examining her face, to find out some imperfection," and becomes convinced of the "Error of that vulgar notion, that a face perfectly regular would not be agreeable."

Like a Renaissance sonneteer, Montagu finds that Fatima achieves the beauty of Apelles' famous painting of a woman composed of the best features of several women. But the presence of such conventions makes it difficult to say precisely what is going on in Montagu's description. There is passion in the description, but it is consistently displaced in terms of art. Montagu's Fatima is not a flesh-and-blood person but a work of art, as she concludes after carefully surveying her body: "I took more pleasure in looking on the beauteous Fatima than the finest piece of Sculpture could have given me."[46] But she frankly says this is a rationale for her rapture, and her description is sensual: "She was dress'd in a Caftan of Gold brocade, flowered with Silver, very well fitted to her Shape and shewing to advantage the beauty of her Bosom, only shaded by the Thin Gauze of her shift."[47] Is this what one would notice in a work of art, or is the attention there diverted to the skill of the artistic performance? It depends on the kind of "reading" being done. In curious reading or viewing, the artfulness of the object is less important than it is in studious reading or viewing. Curiosity focuses the attention and the fantasy on the object described or delineated, and for all her aesthetic training, Montagu was curious about Fatima.

Sensuousness and curiosity are even more evident as Montagu describes the dance of Fatima's twenty maids:

> This Dance was very different from what I had seen before. Nothing could be more artfull, or more proper to raise certain Ideas, the Tunes so soft, the motions so Languishing, accompany'd with pauses and dying Eyes, halfe falling back, and then recovering themselves in so artfull a Manner that I am very positive the coldest and most rigid Prude upon Earth could not have look'd upon them without thinking of something not to be spoke of.[48]

"Artful" in the language of curious viewing becomes a synonym for "realistic." The women look as if they truly are in the throes of erotic ecstasy, so their gestures are, ironically, artful for Montagu. Not many of the novels popular in Johnson's time reveal much more than this, even if they are about loose women, rape, or incest. Moreover, there is no evidence that Johnson read libertine literature; he may have felt inhibited from doing so, as he evidently felt inhibited in his sex life. But Montagu's letters undoubtedly passed the test of censorship; they are full of redeeming value, especially because they communicate new knowledge, and the character of the writer is in many respects both literarily and socially admirable. At the same time, the letters satisfy an appetite for the exotic, the sensual, the feminine, and the wonderful that was part of Johnson's nature as a reader.

With one or two important additions, the appetite satisfied by Montagu's letters is much the same appetite that was satisfied predominantly by the novel in the latter part of Johnson's lifetime. In *Before Novels,* J. Paul Hunter has thoroughly discussed the importance of readers' desires in forming eighteenth-century British fiction. Johnson's desire to read Montagu's letters may be seen as part of a constellation of wishes that Hunter finds common among readers at this time:

> The taste for surprise in a world seen scientifically—the desire to wonder in a world increasingly explored, understood, and (it seemed) conquered—led to many cultural and literary phenomena in the late seventeenth and early eighteenth centuries, from voyages to exotic or unknown places to imaginary voyages in the mind, from Grand Tours to minute analyses of the antiquities of England, from Royal Society experiments to freak shows at fairs and festivals, from the founding of museums for curiosities and rarities to a domestic taste for orientalism and gothicism in gardens, houses, and storytelling, from the reading of wild but "true" collections of wonders and curiosities and miraculous events to fictions that probed the unusual and bizarre in the world of everyday. Novelists both before and after Fielding turn aside the wilder wish to make readers gape at any cost, channeling reader desires into a wonder about human events that—if not really marvelous, miraculous, or magic—still provides a sophisticated outlet for that human curiosity.... The novel is only the most successful of a series

of attempts to satisfy, in a context of scientific order, the itch for news and new things that are strange and surprising.[49]

The "new things" that the novel could provide, as Hunter perceives, came not only from external wonder but, preeminently in the end, from "forbidden, repressed, or secret arenas of human activity, as well as those private recesses of the human mind, will, and appetite that produce them."[50] Montagu's *Letters* provides both the external, male world of the exotic and a more domestic but equally exotic world of women's shapes and female desires. Inextricable from this world are the "private recesses" of Johnson's own highly active imagination. Johnson's own "recesses," however, although "private," were far from unique. On the contrary, they may have been what united him most with other readers of the time.

Johnson once confessed to vain fantasies of life as a sultan in a seraglio.[51] Surely these fantasies were fueled, although probably not created, by Montagu, who describes the sultan's choice of a woman for a given day in some detail:

> The story of the Sultan's throwing a Handkercheif is altogether fabulous, and the manner upon that occasion no other but that he sends the Kuslir Aga, to signify to the Lady the honour he intends her. She is immediately complemented upon it by the others, and led to the bath where she is perfum'd and dress'd in the most magnificent and becoming Manner. The Emperor precedes his visit by a Royal present and then comes into her apartment.[52]

The fantasy of the power of sexual choice is amplified beyond the sort of temporary monogamy implied in the formal selection of a partner when Montagu adds, "Sometimes the Sultan diverts him selfe in the Company of all his Ladies, who stand in a circle round him, and . . . they were ready to die with Jealousie and envy of the happy She that he distinguish'd by any appearance of preference." It is impossible to tell if Montagu intended this passage specifically to raise curious interest, but she could hardly have succeeded better if she had.

Montagu's *Letters* probes or stimulates exploration of at least three exotic regions: one public, one private but external (the hidden lives of others) and a third internal (the reader's own world of fantasy and imagination). Johnson was deeply suspicious of this internal, imaginative world; he had trouble controlling his mind and thought it needed control, but he was also drawn to explore its "private recesses" and "secret arenas." This is part of the scholar's melancholy life, as scholars such as Robert Burton and Christopher Marlowe suggest in their works. For the most part, Johnson rejected the whispers of fancy in his public writings and his public doings, but he listened nevertheless. As Montagu at least intuitively perceived, catching the reader's ear for such whispers is the secret to stimulating curious reading.

I V

From a reader's point of view, Montagu's *Letters* is closely related to the novels on the short list of books that Johnson read with the greatest curiosity because they satisfied the same "itch" for the "strange and surprising." The letters have the additional virtue of being believable, although, as Johnson might have guessed, they are not exactly what they appear: for one thing, they were never sent as letters but only written in that form. *Robinson Crusoe, Don Quixote,* and even *Pilgrim's Progress* all resemble the *Letters* in their concern with exotic places, especially "hidden recesses" of the soul, and all these, plus *Amelia,* are alike in their fascination with masking and unmasking, an important element of the exotic. They also all justify their explorations of strangeness by offering the material for ethical lessons, which are easily drawn by a sober, conscientious reader. The truth of Montagu's letters, although it is not impeccably above the truth of the "true stories" sometimes at the center of popular fiction, makes them a better key than the novels to much of the other reading that Johnson performed in an absorbed and concentrated manner.

In addition to Montagu's *Letters,* Johnson did a great deal of other reading in books about the Near East and India—"the Orient," as it was then called. He once said that if he had gotten his pension early in life he would have gone to the Near East, like the great scholar Edward Pococke, and learned Arabic. Later in life he contemplated a trip to India to join his great friend Robert Chambers and to visit the most accomplished Sanskritist of his day and also a member of Johnson's Club, William Jones. He owned an Arabic dictionary and consulted it while writing his *Dictionary of the English Language.* He had a copy of the Qur'an and some other Islamic works. He also had a copy of Nathaniel Halhed's *Code of Gentoo* [Hindu] *Laws,* which provides an introduction to Sanskrit with plates of the letters and the first Sanskrit texts reproduced in an English book. Richard Knolles's *Historie of the Turks* was a favorite book of Johnson's and one of many on the Islamic Near East that he read in preparation for writing *Irene.* Both *Rasselas* and his early translation of *A Voyage to Abyssinia* carried him close to "the Orient."

Johnson read about the East in order to acquire knowledge, and he considered the region particularly important because it was the cradle of Christianity. Johnson was also interested in the East because it was a scene of the fabulous, a literary scene, even a set, but he understood that it was usually fictionalized in order to serve in that capacity. Montagu was also aware of how much the East had been fictionalized, and she paused in many letters to ridicule the falsehood of the accounts of Turkey given by men pretending to have seen what was certainly forbidden to their eyes. Johnson undoubtedly shared Montagu's skepticism about many of the earlier reports and valued Montagu for her direct access to privileged information. He found a similarly skeptical approach in Richard Chandler's *Travels in Asia Minor* (1775). Johnson owned this book in an impressively produced edition, and he undoubtedly appreciated Chandler's resistance to wonders. In Miletus, for instance, Chandler found a storied but ruined theater too choked with bats and "dry filth" to permit further exploration. He provides a description of what he really saw and juxtaposes it to stories about the place in question; in this respect Chandler's method resembles Johnson's in his *Journey to the Western Islands of Scotland* (1775).

Chandler was dry, however, and Johnson must have read his book with more approbation than curiosity. At the other end of the spectrum of Johnson's "Oriental" reading is a work he must have consumed with curiosity, but not much approval, *The History of Thamas Kouli Kan*, translated from the French in 1740 and abridged by Johnson himself in the same year.[53] The French bookseller's preface to *Thamas Kouli Kan* cannily declares the qualities of the book likely to make the reader curious or "addicted to enquiry": "The author of this history . . . captivates the Reader by his Stile, and by the lively, sensible, and now and then malicious Reflections, with which he adorns his Stories. Moreover, the subject of this present History of Thamas Kouli Kan, is the most likely to raise Curiosity: A Man, who from a mean Birth, raised himself, in our own Days, to the throne of Persia."[54] The author is an engaging interlocutor; he has gossip to retail, but only rarely does he become malicious. That a rarely manifested aspect of the narrative is prominently advertised suggests how important that element was in satisfying the eighteenth-century reader's appetite. Montagu certainly did not neglect such "malicious Reflections," and her epistolary method is designed to make the reader feel included in a kind of private discussion. Her remarks about Islamic women and Eastern European social customs often include unflattering comparisons to English women and English customs. She rises at times to grand reflections that must have pleased Johnson on the vanity of English or European wishes. A view of the battlefield at Carlowitz is a "proof of the irrationality of mankind," for Johnson as well as Montagu, and he certainly saw the wisdom in her query, "Considering what short-liv'd weak animals men are, is there any study so beneficial as the study of present pleasure?"[55] As evidenced in their taste for *The Turkish Spy*,[56] the fictional reflections of an "Oriental" on Europe, Montagu's readers certainly had a desire for this kind of instruction, but the story of *Thamas Kouli Kan* appealed to another, perhaps even deeper, kind of curiosity.

Thamas is portrayed as a modern-day Tamerlane who rises from obscurity to ride in triumph through the streets of Persepolis as king of Persia. As Christopher Marlowe realized, the story of Tamerlane is about triumphant self-creation, and *Thamas Kouli Kan* is a Bildungsroman that celebrates an apotheosis of everyman. The story maximizes the potential for reader identification, an important feature of curious reading, by making much of the mysterious origins of Thamas: "Many nations having adopted this extraordinary Man, it would be difficult to decide what was his native country."[57] The author considers the various possibilities and entertains at some length the claim of the Germans in a letter from the marquis de Villeneuve dated 8 September 1736. But the hero could be from any nation; in fact, he could be anyone. His resolution and success are unbelievably great, and despite his brutality, he has a kind of ethical superiority. When he is proclaimed king of Persia it seems as though he has been duly elected or at least authorized by the people. The effect of this confirmation is partly to sanitize and authorize the fantasy of power for Western readers. Thamas is like the king in the English constitutional monarchy, so the story is adapted to the sort of fantastic longing for self-realization that an English reader might entertain without engaging internal moral censors.

The final description of the hero, the "faithful character," is a piece done in imitation of a standard element of biography in the eighteenth century, observed by both Johnson and Boswell, although stemming from the earlier genre of the "character." In this recognizable set piece, the adaptation of the hero to Western readers is tacitly completed. However, the curious history of the hero has taken less than half the book, although it is advertised as its central story. The foil for the Bildungsroman, the exotic setting of the East, takes up the other half of the book, and it is just as important as the "triumph of the will" in the story proper. The author spends most of his pages on a trav-

eler's account of the locale in which the story occurs, complete
with digressions designed to heighten curiosity and desire. Of
the town of Thamas's origins, for example, the author says:

> It is reported that Mahomet did not love to visit this town,
> because he found there a Satisfaction of all his senses too
> alluring. And in reality, nothing can be more agreeable to
> the sight, than the various objects which this country pre-
> sents to the view of travellers. The smell is delighted by the
> alleys of orange-trees with which their gardens abound. The
> taste is feasted by the juicy flavour of the Meat, their wild
> and tame Fowl. Their Wives are excellent and much es-
> teemed. As to the rest, which this pretended Lawgiver val-
> ued most, the Women of Schiras were very likely to give
> him all the satisfaction he could desire.[58]

Other conventional wonders and exotic bits of information
come in throughout. Wood heavier than water and stone
lighter than water are spotted, as are "Brachmans" and "gaurs,"
Brahmins and gurus, although this mixes up the cultural tra-
ditions of the region as badly as Disney's *Aladdin*. Then there
is a history of the Persian empire, which only gradually leads
up to the central story of the meteoric personal rise of Thamas.
The combination of the exotic background and the curiously
Westernized or "naturalized" central story makes *The History
of Thamas Kouli Kan* a prototype of the novel, displaying the
ancestry of the appetites it satisfied, as well as aspects of the
genres that it displaced and mimicked in its competition for
those appetites—travel, news, and romance.

V

Another aspect of *Thamas Kouli Kan* that makes it fit for
curious reading is the way it straddles the boundary between
fact and fiction and sets up in readers a tension about credulity
that produces curiosity. This is a quality that the novel has in
common with Montagu's *Letters* and with much travel literature of the time. In the eighteenth century the East was the
setting for so much fiction masquerading as fact that when

William Jones published his landmark *Poems consisting Chiefly of Translations from the Asiatick Languages,* he felt ill at ease in making his claims of fidelity to the original texts, which he was the first to translate into English:

> The reader will probably expect, that, before I present him with the following miscellany, I should give some account of the pieces contained in it; and should prove the authenticity of those *Eastern* originals, from which I profess to have translated them: indeed, so many productions, invented in *France,* have been offered to the publick as genuine translations from the languages of *Asia,* that I should have wished, for my own sake, to clear my publication from the slightest suspicion of imposture: but there is a circumstance peculiarly hard in the present case; namely, that, were I to produce the *originals* themselves, it would be impossible to persuade some men, that even *they* were not forged for the purpose, like the pretended language of *Formosa.*[59]

Jones refers to a hoax perpetrated by George Psalmanazar, who pretended to be a native of Formosa and whose fictional description of that largely unknown place was so respectfully received that he lectured at Oxford on the subject and was regarded as a great authority for decades before the hoax was revealed. The members of the English reading public, or at least its increasingly professional monitors, improved their ability to detect fraud during the course of the century, but they were sorely tried: Thomas Chatterton's Rowley poems, James Macpherson's *Ossian,* and William Henry Ireland's Shakespeare are only the most famous attempts to fool the public with the literary equivalent of Piltdown man.

Along with the hoaxes that depended on ignorance of Eastern or Celtic or medieval English culture, there were many books that mingled fact and fiction concerning contemporary events. The private lives of others constituted another kind of mysterious "Orient," ignorance of which writers could exploit to stimulate curious reading. In writing novels about scandals real and imagined, eighteenth-century writers appealed to an appetite for gossip that was fostered in the newspapers but was closely related to the appetite for all sorts of wonders, which had been the target of travel books and broadsheets for a long time. The interesting and somewhat new aspect of the situation in the eighteenth century was an increased anxiety about the confusion between the areas of fact and fiction. At least from the time of Bacon and the New Science, literate British culture began placing stronger emphasis on the need to separate the factual and the hypothetical. At the same time there was more exploration into the unknown and a wider, somewhat less discriminating audience for accounts of such exploration. As ever, books mixed the false with the true, but the new, wider audience, with a redefined interest in knowledge, made for a new polity between fact and fiction.

Although he could be as satirical and as ironic as Swift when he wished, generally Johnson was quite clear about whether his literary representations were fact or fiction. He was usually openly and broadly fictional about his presentation of Eastern culture. He made it clear in most of his works that he did not want to contribute to confusion: in *Rasselas,* for example, the pretense of truth about the cultures represented is conscientiously thin, if not transparent. In this, Johnson followed such writers as Robert Dodsley, whose transparently fictional *Oeconomy of Human Life* (1750) displays a sense of humor about itself by pretending to be a Hindu treatise, transmitted to a Chinese scholar, who passed it on to the author's source. Earlier in his career, Johnson danced a bit more on the edges of believability in a couple of "Oriental" tales that he probably wrote (or excerpted from other works): a life of Confucius and a history of the Amazons. Johnson was not immune to the temptation to mix fact and fiction in the representation of "the Orient," but he resisted it later.

However, the East was not the only scene of the unknown concerning which Johnson had to decide about the politics of fact and fiction. For all his interest in the East, Johnson was more fully engaged in presenting the mysterious world of what he called "domestick privacies," and his biographies are accordingly his most compelling, most "curious" works. The best of all is his *Account of the Life of Mr. Richard Savage.* Joshua Reynolds read this work with such curiosity that he remained in a single position throughout the several hundred pages of the book and found his arm dead asleep against the mantel in the end. The truth of some of the *Life of Savage* is hard to judge, especially when Johnson describes the walks about Grosvenor Square, which begin with reforming governments and founding nations and end with sleeping outside the glassworks. Johnson was an eyewitness to these events and ought to be believed, but there is rhetoric and, in particular, a kind of defense of Savage running subtly through the whole piece that competes with its fidelity to truth. In his reading, however, Johnson encountered more-volatile and more-mendacious accounts of real events than those he wrote. These wilder mixtures of fact and fiction seem calculated mainly to stir the mind with curiosity rather than to let it "repose on the stability of truth,"[60] as the mature Johnson said the mind could do in reading the works of Shakespeare. It is important to look at some of these "unstable" works in order to understand Johnson's life of reading.

One of the problems in trying to discuss Johnson's reading of popular fiction, however, is that he said so little about it. There is plenty of evidence that he read such books, but it is not completely clear which ones. The few I have chosen for brief analysis here recommend themselves for two reasons: it is extremely likely that Johnson read them because the authors and the subjects were of interest to him, and they exemplify features of the sort of books that made the best material for curious reading in the middle of the eighteenth century.

Herbert Croft, who contributed the biography of Edward Young to Johnson's *Lives of the Poets,* wrote at about the same time a kind of fiction interlaced with fact entitled *Love and Madness: A Story Too True In a Series of Letters between Parties, whose Names would perhaps be mentioned, were they less known, or less lamented.* The identities of the principals may or may not have been generally known, but in any case the book was designed to stimulate speculation. Things heat up right away as the letters show that the correspondents are in love and that the woman is married to an older, unsatisfying man. By letter 7 the male correspondent is addressing her as "My Life and Soul!" and Croft is implicitly acknowledging his torrid pace in what the correspondent says about his own form of address: "But I will never more use any preface of this sort—and I beg you will not. A correspondence begins with 'Dear,' then 'My dear,' 'Dearest,' 'My dearest,' and so on, till, at last, panting language toils after us in vain."[61] Complications arise, and in the end the man is preparing for suicide, but he changes his mind and kills his mistress instead. He is rapidly hanged by the law, to the relief of author and readers alike.

What most fills Croft's book, however, is not the matter of love and the feelings that lead to the disastrous outcome; the bulk of it is composed of reports of real news and true literary anecdotes. For example, the male lover, sojourning in London, reports the death of the Reverend William Dodd, the dashing minister who was hanged for embezzling funds from his former employer, the fifth Lord Chesterfield, although Johnson assisted him in his attempts to obtain clemency by petition. Other genuine news items included are the speech of Logan, a Shawnee Indian chief, to Lord Dunmore, and Mrs. Dixon's letter on her suicide at age nineteen. The bulk of the material concerns literary history, however, and the largest inclusion is a life of Chatterton based on documentary sources, especially letters that Croft somehow extracted from relatives of the poet who were later infuriated by their publication in *Love and Madness*. The male lover also makes literary observations on his reading, although most are mere declarations, such as "Robinson Crusoe. Now—what Nature! It affects us throughout." This is evidently meant to show that he is a man of passion and sensibility. To prove it further, he is displayed reading Johnson's *Dictionary* with equal heat: "What must have been Johnson's feelings, when in his wonderful work, the English Dictionary, he cited the following passage from Ascham, as an instance of the use of the word Men? 'Wits live obscurely, men care not how; or die obscurely, men mark not when.' "[62] Croft had once planned to do a revised edition of Johnson's *Dictionary,* and throughout *Love and Madness* he draws on his own literary interests in creating the sensibility of his principal character. It may be that the book is, like Charlotte Lennox's *Female Quixote,* a monitory work on the dangers of reading, but part of the point of Croft's extensive references to real people, real events, and real reading experiences (shared in many cases by his audience) was to mix an element of truth into the otherwise thin and rapid romantic tale. In doing so, he was, I think, taking advantage of the appetite for curious reading that existed in his time.

Love and Madness is designed both to encourage curious reading and to give an example of it; it does the former by means of the latter. The principal character is a reader with whom Croft's readers were meant to sympathize; he reads much of what they read, and he alludes consistently to events in the real world, events with which real readers were presumably familiar. The character sometimes knows more than the readers (about Chatterton in particular), but he is more believable as a reader than as an actor in the romance. It may be that Croft invented his fiction primarily to produce Chatterton's letters and life in a context that shielded him from prosecution by the family. No matter what his priorities, however, Croft's blend of fact and fiction, his presentation of a curious reader and his attempt to stimulate curious reading, make a combination that reflects the situation of curious reading towards the end of the century. Indeed, Fielding seems to note the prevalence of this kind of writing in his caricature of the Grub Street hack in *Amelia* who resembles Johnson in his production of fictional parliamentary debates. Fielding offers a satire on novelists of the day when he declares that he has given up other kinds of writing because,

> in Truth, the Romance Writing is the only Branch of our Business now, that is worth Following. Goods of that Sort have had so much success lately in the Market, that a Bookseller scarce cares what he bids for them. And it is certainly

the easiest Work in the World; you may write it almost as fast as you can set Pen to Paper; and if you interlard it with a little Scandal, a little Abuse on some living Characters of Note, you cannot fail of Success."[63]

In 1755, twenty-five years before Croft's *Love and Madness,* and three years after Fielding's *Amelia,* Benjamin Victor published a work called *The Widow of the Wood* that displays another mixture of fact and fiction that fed the appetites of curious readers in Johnson's day, one with more than a minor interlarding of scandal. As the treasurer of the Drury Lane Theatre, Victor knew everyone in Grub Street, and Johnson sought him out for information when he was writing his *Lives of the Poets.* Since it was written by a person he knew and was based on a scandal involving a prominent Staffordshire family, Johnson was almost sure to have read *The Widow of the Wood,* although, like most novels and other "lower" kinds of literature, it is not listed in the catalogue of his library or recorded in his journals. Victor uses dashes to conceal the names of his principals in the thinnest possible way. He even conceals his own name in this transparent fashion. Such pro forma concealment is an important feature of eighteenth-century writing that takes advantage of readers' anxieties about the boundary between fact and fiction. As in Johnson's own *Debates in the Senate of Magna Lilliput,* the disguise in *The Widow of the Wood* lends a literary character and a literary license to the proceedings of the author, but it does not hide the identity of his target. It confronts the readers with just enough of a barrier to make them feel they have been admitted to a jolly coterie, but it does not exclude anyone. Even the common reader can have the satisfaction of distinguishing fact from fiction, or at least of feeling that he or she is so distinguishing. And the reader reads on partly to complete the process of making the vital distinction.

Transparent *romans à clef* such as *The Widow of the Wood* belong to a form of public literature masquerading as coterie performance. The earliest examples of the genre in England, such as Delarivière Manley's *New Atalantis* (1709), were closer to coterie performances because they required more inside information, and keys had to be produced to afford access to the gossip. Once the expectation of a "real story" beneath the fiction is aroused, there is little satisfaction in the fictional story itself. Victor realistically discusses his readers' expectations in his preface:

> If the following narrative had been sent forth into the World without those Advantages to prove the Veracity of the Facts, I am certain it would not only be received as a Romance, but by the judicious Part of its Readers, despis'd for its Absurdities: for even the many fictitious Stories that have lately been published (from the very fertile Brains of our present Set of Novel Writers) have all, at least, this Merit, that their Incidents are within the Pale of Probability.[64]

Learned readers perhaps appreciated Victor's allusion to Aristotle's distinction in the *Poetics* between the probable fiction and the improbable reality. Although Victor's improbable reality may have been the wrong choice artistically, from the point of view of the news-hungry, curious reader it was right. Victor therefore attached to his account all kinds of affidavits and finally the judgment of the court that tried the case of the widow who was, spectacularly, married four times.

Victor knew the intimate details of his story because he was a confidant and almost a participant; he was therefore able to place the readers in close proximity to the unfolding events, and even to bring them right into the rooms when important decisions were made. The sexually adventurous and wily widow ensnares the men around her and fools the minister so badly that he dies of consternation. This is a plot that appealed to readers for a variety of reasons, including prurience and astonishment that such wiles were performed by a woman of quality. There is also misogyny in the tale, as in many successful tales of the time, including Johnson's *Life of Savage,* where the sexually active and perfidious mother of the poet is Johnson's villain. Sexuality in the plot and misogyny were often part of the formula for success in creating curious reading, but it also depended on the combination of the authorized and proven with the catty and gossipy, the publicly demonstrated and the privately whispered, the legal and the libelous. Like *Amelia* and *Love and Madness, The Widow of the Wood* can be read as an allegory of curious reading. Unlike the former it has little artistic merit, and unlike the latter it does not concern figures who are of much interest to modern readers. But Victor's book has the volatile combination of fact and fiction that won readers, and it has the splendid fact/artifice of a narrator who performs both in the fact and in the fiction. This is a device Johnson used in his most curious work, *An Account of the Life of Mr. Richard Savage,* and it deserves a place in the paradigm of curious reading in the eighteenth century.

Like the other kinds of reading I have identified, curious reading can attach itself to all kinds of books. It certainly can occur with newspapers and magazines, and many of the fiction-reading experiences that I call curious are closely related to newspaper reading. This is partly because the situation of reading fiction in the middle of the eighteenth century was conditioned by the problems of credibility encountered in the reading of newspapers more than it was by either studious reading or practical perusal. As the etymological similarities suggest, news *(nouvelles)* and novels were emergent forms at about the same time in history. Both forms, however, especially in their beginnings, were compounded of recognizable literary forms, including the romance, the travel narrative, and the letter. I think Johnson was inclined to read novels that demonstrably retained their ties to some of the older forms of which they were composed. The novel as self-help manual, as in the case of *Clarissa;* the novel as news, as in Ben Victor's work; the novel as travel narrative, as in Defoe—these were all more attractive to Johnson than the more-recent novels, such as Fielding's *Tom Jones* or, in a different way, Sterne's *Tristram Shandy*, that sought rules of their own and were on the way to becoming a new genre.

There is a parallel to the emergent forms of eighteenth-century fiction in Hogarth's drawings. As Richard Dorment points out, "To his contemporaries . . . Hogarth's stories were as fresh as the morning newspaper." However, some readers wished to elevate or justify the "stories" by allegorizing them. Dorment considers it "ironic, then, that only a few years after the artist's death in 1764, the Rev. John Trusler published a moralizing exegesis on the prints which emphasized the ways in which the Harlot's or the Rake's progresses were like that of Bunyan's Pilgrim."[65] The cleft stick in which Hogarth's work is either news or allegory, but not what it really is, corresponds to the situation of fiction for readers in the eighteenth century. But writers were able to profit from their readers' uncertainty in this regard, as the need, the compulsion, or the satisfaction of distinguishing kept them turning the pages.

Romance continued to appeal to Johnson, despite its arrant fictionality, because it could be a form of self-help, as in the case of *Pilgrim's Progress* or (in contemporary interpretations) the *Odyssey* or *Don Quixote*. Moreover, the genre was old enough to have an antiquarian interest (it was useful in editing Shakespeare, for example), and it could provide opportunities for study when it was written in a foreign language. Although Johnson enjoyed *Il Palmerino d'Ingleterre,* he probably also read it for the language, as Boswell eagerly reported. Romance as mere fiction, however, was unappealing to Johnson, at least as he got older. Most pastoral seemed ridiculous to him; novels he described likewise as reading matter for the young, the ignorant, and the idle.

Although Johnson sought and had experiences of curious reading, he was also wary of them. There is some evidence of this in the books he took with him when traveling and those he resorted to when forced into idleness on journeys. For the most part these were all works for study. Unlike most modern travelers, Johnson read classical works and classical commentaries in coaches. For example, he read Erasmus's *Ciceronianus* on a coach ride to Lichfield in 1784.[66] Journeying in Wales, he noted a typographical error in the edition of Martial that he had taken with him; on the same trip he also read Phocylides and St. John Chrysostom.[67] John Wesley had a bookshelf in his traveling coach so he could make the best use of his time.

Johnson was not so organized as the minister, but he used his pockets with equal seriousness. Unfortunately, he was not always thoroughly prepared. Caught unprovisioned in a storm on Col, he was delighted to find a copy of *Gataker on Lots,* a humanistic commentary that allowed him to get through a tedious day.[68] In the Harwich stagecoach in 1763 he "had in his pocket '*Pomponius Mela de situ Orbis,*' in which he read occasionally and seemed very intent upon ancient geography."[69] Several of these works slide over from studious hard reading to perusal for the purposes of self-improvement, but even studious travelers in modern times have been more likely than Johnson to take fiction on the train or plane with them. E. R. Dodds, for example, a Hellenist out of Johnson's league, was not unusual in reading mysteries on the train. The practice is so common among academic readers today that it has spawned its own genre—the academic murder mystery, with titles like *Murder in a Tenured Position* and *The Vassar College Murders.* Among general readers too, the books that while away traveling time are mainly fiction, and fiction generally of a sort that does not display firm connections to genres of self-help or news. The change was occurring in Johnson's time; fiction valued on its own terms was emerging from fiction valued as moral allegory or consumed as news, but an appreciation for it was largely outside Johnson's life of reading.

In *Australian Readers Remember,* Martyn Lyons provides an oral history of reading in Australia in this century.[70] Lyons discovered that Charles Dickens was the author whom the greatest number of older readers freely remembered from their youths. Looking at the later history of reading from Johnson's point of view, it is remarkable that a writer of novels is the best-remembered author among a generation of readers. More remarkable still, many older readers remember that Dickens's novels were considered important books in the library and appropriate for collection and display in uniform editions. These works had by the late nineteenth century assumed something like the prestige reserved for classical study in the eighteenth.

Although this is not the place for it, there is a complex story to be told of how novels achieved the status of serious literature and came to replace not only Shakespeare but also Euripides and Homer on the shelves of many readers. The departure of these new "greats" from the world of compelling or curious reading is an important moment in their elevation. As reading experiences, novels began to leave the realm of curious reading towards the end of the eighteenth century; they then moved into the area of hard reading. It is a peculiarity of novels in the history of reading that they have made this particular transition. What they left behind them in the world of curious reading has continued to evolve, however, and we now have many popular forms that mix fiction with some of the other kinds of literature of which novels are made. The mixture of fiction and news is especially popular today and has certainly been fostered by television and other media of mass communication. The docudrama about Amy Fisher or Princess Di makes for highly curious consumption in our day, much as *The Widow of the Wood* did in Johnson's time. The romance in its modern form, as love story, gothic mystery, or medieval adventure story, has also inherited a field of reading once partly occupied by "serious fiction," a phrase Johnson would have considered largely self-contradictory.

Curious reading requires material that has either the capacity to make the reader dream (to live in a world that is obviously fictional but appeals to a seductive inner voice of fantasy) or the capacity to make the reader believe in the fiction because it is draped over a skeleton of known and reported truth. Another direction taken by fiction more than any other form, however, is into the new screen-oriented media—movies and television, of course, but also computer programs in the form of games and hypertexts. Whether or not these forms suggest new directions for the history of reading is the question I ask in the next and final chapter. Even to this question about reading, which has only arisen in the past ten years or so, I think an understanding of Johnson's life of reading and the changes in the history of reading that occurred in the eighteenth century can help provide answers.

SAMUEL JOHNSON AND THE
FUTURE OF READING

*A*ny contemporary study of an important cultural practice would seem woefully out of step these days were it not based on the postmodern belief that such practices are socially constructed. At the risk of dutifully following the crowd, I have assumed throughout this book that reading, like literature itself, is socially constructed. On the other hand, I believe there may be some "natural" aspects of reading, facets of the practice that do not change with changes in culture and language, and I hope my view of reading encompasses some of them, even though it was not designed with that purpose in mind. Such remarks as I have offered on the psychology of reading (mostly drawn from others) hint at natural aspects of reading. But more importantly, Johnson was a reader of such profound range and talent that his life of reading touched on virtually every possible aspect of the practice. This hypothesis is unprovable without a full psychology of reading, however, and I can comfortably claim to have described reading only as it is shaped by certain social circumstances, beliefs, and assumptions. Even though such circumstances are not determinative, and not everyone operating in roughly the same cultural circumstances has the same life of reading, the circumstances are crucial.

The welter of cultural and social circumstances in which reading occurs is not easy to analyze or disentangle, but, to the extent that it can be isolated, the technological context of any life of reading is one essential part of its construction. The idea of reading that I have developed here on the basis of Johnson's life of reading is highly dependent on the existence and the spread of printing. Study, perusal, mere reading, and curious reading either do not exist or do not exist in the same relation to each other in a culture that depends mainly on oral reports or manuscripts for the production and transmission of its verbal artifacts. We may be able to imagine an auditor, a rich one, engaged in study with a group of tutors who comment on each other's statements, and an auditor might, in some respects, be a curious reader, but the middle categories of perusal and mere reading would be largely impossible. Because of this, the relation between study and curiosity would be different, and my description of reading would be distorted, if I tried to apply it to a culture that was still mainly oral.

A manuscript culture presents similar problems. As in a predominantly oral culture, in a manuscript world the implicit community of readers and the social circumstances of reading are dramatically different from those in a world dominated by print. Curious reading was certainly possible in the age of manuscript production, for example, but it was less common. Under those technological conditions, reading in general was less likely to be solitary, partly because of the scarcity and cost of manuscripts; but whether or not it was solitary, the virtual community of other readers that one joined in reading most manuscript books was relatively small and select. That means that some of the features that define modern curious reading were missing in earlier versions of such reading. Because of changes in the communities of readers, for example, the curious reading of manuscript romances in the fourteenth century may have been more like eighteenth-century coterie reading than eighteenth-century curious reading.

It is impossible to be categorical about such distinctions. One can always think of counterexamples to defeat the neat application of historical categories of reading. In the seventeenth century, for example, William Temple and Dorothy Osborne read romances as a form of coterie reading that harkened back to earlier practices. Temple sent manuscript copies of books from the Continent to his beloved, and the romances shared by the two of them became part of their epistolary lovers' discourse. Their reading existed in as small and closed a coterie as the one in which Paolo and Francesca misread themselves to destruction, in Dante's retelling of the famous tale.

More could be (and has been) said about reading in the days before print. There are a thousand qualifications to add, but it is still true that the development and spread of print culture in the sixteenth and seventeenth centuries helped produce the conditions that defined Johnson's life of reading, just as they shaped his life as an author. Even the "new" kinds of reading Johnson did, such as "eye-reading," were possible in antiquity, but the social construction of reading at that time, with its expectation (though not requirement) of vocalization, was different. Then, as in Johnson's time and in our own, social and technological conditions constructed reading experiences but did not determine them.

Although my scheme for describing reading is flexible and will be of some use in describing lives of reading at other times in history, it works best for Johnson and the eighteenth century. Moreover, it is possible to think of cultural situations, such as those that existed before the spread of print and the widespread existence of literacy, that render the scheme inappropriate. I will not try to put my finger on the moment when my notion of reading becomes appropriate, or "shimmers into life," as Michel Foucault says of certain neoclassical conceptions. Instead, in this final chapter, I wish to examine the possibility that we are approaching a period in which reading, as I have described it and as Johnson practiced it, is about to disappear. There have been a number of jeremiads on this subject in recent years.[1] I do not intend to add another. In fact, on balance, I find a great deal of continuity between Johnson's life of reading and our own, even though there are important changes now underway.

Screen-oriented technologies tend to make reading significantly different than it was for Johnson in terms of the categories I use to describe reading. The "characteristic texts" of electronic reading, for example, need not be texts at all in the conventional, "printed" sense of the term. Whereas printed texts are fixed and unchanging compared to manuscript texts or oral performances, electronic texts are susceptible to alterations imposed by the reader's method of access or by his or her intervention. On the other hand, the "fixity" of the printed text has been exaggerated; it is merely a superficial quality, if one thinks of reading as the experience of an individual free to interpret and even to turn pages as he or she wishes. It is also true that consumers of books have often had the ability to change the nonverbal formats of the works they read: by buying large-paper editions, by having them interleaved, by hiring professional readers to annotate them, and in countless other ways. Even though it has been exaggerated, however, there remains a contrast between the fixity of print and the fluidity of electronic transmission.

One family of electronic works that relies heavily on this fluidity is called hypertext. *StorySpace* is one of the most popular programs for creating works of this kind. Readers are explicitly invited to "navigate" these texts in individual ways and even to assume a measure of responsibility for their creation. Hypertext readers are confronted by a "web" on their screens composed of boxes within boxes of texts. (The World Wide Web is in many ways just a large hypertext, collaboratively produced by thousands of contributors.) In a hypertext web there are rubrics over the various boxes, and the links between the boxes sometimes have titles also. One can read the texts in almost any order, and at any given moment there is a choice available between following the default path (one selected by the author or perhaps by a reader intermediate between the author and the present reader) and a path that one selects. Instead of the fixity of print we have the fluidity of an electronic text, the writers of hypertexts argue, and instead of an authoritative text written by an author who directs our responses we have a changeable text, subject to the whims of the reader. The hypertextual critic and novelist Michael Joyce offers the following account of reading in the hypertext mode:

In the course of what is seen the writer is replaced by the reader (the writer who will be). This is the claim of constructive hypertext, and by extension any system of electronic text, from hypertext to virtual reality to ubicomp. The fossil word, which on the computer screen is always tilted to the light and constantly replaced, again takes its place within the universe of the visible and the sensual. Print stays itself, electronic text replaces itself. With electronic text we are always painting, each screen washing away what was and replacing it with itself. The shadow of each dead letter provides the living form of what replaces it.[2]

Joyce describes the experience of a hypertext reader who is extraordinarily active. The trick of turning writing into a form of painting is not so easy as he makes it sound. Moreover, if such transformations are possible in the actual physical medium of hypertext, they have first to be conceived in the more fluid medium of the mind, where readers have always had the prerogative of misreading or rewriting their texts. The possibility of creative reading is part of the story of Carlo Ginzburg's famous study of the life of reading of a sixteenth-century miller named Menocchio.[3] However, both within hypertext novels and in works about hypertext, great claims have been made for the importance of the new medium to reading. Even if these claims are exaggerated, they deserve a hearing because it stands to reason that reading will change as the medium through which it is practiced changes.

The hypertext *Izme Pass* contains several blocks of theory along with the 231 blocks relevant to the tale of a murder, around which the dreams and doings of several young men and women circulate. One of these blocks of theory is called "The Dryden Statement: Principles Regarding Interactive Multiple Fictions":

I) No interruptions
   Reading should be a seamless and uninterrupted experience. Its choices proceed from the expression of possibilities as a narrative medium and depend upon the complicity of

the reader in the creation of a narrative. Reading is design enacted.

II) Any person

Interaction manifests itself through recognition, sympathy, and witness as much as through impersonation, perception, and exploration. Apprehension of character is participatory design.

III) Every ending

Closure has been described as the completion of self by the reader. It is, in this sense, design determined.

IV) A read-write revolution

Interactive narratives are "evolving narratives," written, whether by reader or writer. Authorship is an invitation to active design.

The piece is identified by a citation that reads "TINAC / Dryden, New York and elsewhere / 1988." It is unclear what this means, but it looks like a bit of information on the publication of this statement. It is tempting to read "and elsewhere" as indicating that in this electronic world there really is no fixed place of publication, just as there is no fixed text. The place of publication is in electronic space, and every reading, in effect, produces a new place of publication because every reader alters the text. In fact, like many other aspects of electronic production, this is only an extension of a trend that has been visible in conventional books for years. Because of changes in technology and in the corporate life of the publishing industry, publication data has changed its meaning over the years; place of publication in printed books is not nearly so determinative a piece of information as it was when it pinpointed a place of origination and, with the help of press figures, even the particular printing presses and compositors in the place where the impression of type on paper was made. Publishers now are not so easy to locate, and places of manufacture are even harder to pin down. Electronic publication aggravates the problem of locality. Likewise, the principles of the "Dryden Statement" should be taken seriously even if they apply mainly to reading and writing in the print world. It seems safe to reject the claim that we are undergoing a "revolution," but there may nevertheless be a process of change under way.

J. David Bolter, classicist, coauthor with Michael Joyce of the hypertext program *StorySpace,* and an eloquent spokesperson for its cultural significance, is more measured in his assessment than is the "Dryden Statement." Bolter says that "the reader of an electronic text functions like the writer of a genre text, or like a poet in the Greek oral tradition."[4] The readers' creative power is not limitless; they work within certain constraints with given material; but each of them composes a narrative differently than the others do, given the same materials and the same constraints. In this description, the reading of hypertext does not sound much different than the imaginative reading of a printed text. Indeed, Bolter might agree that electronic reading need not be fundamentally different, but I think he would argue that hypertext encourages and facilitates an active sort of reading that print often discourages. This may be true, at least in principle, but it is important to remember that reading in the medium of print is not one uniform activity. Samuel Johnson's highly varied life of reading was conducted largely in the medium of print, and it should stand forever as a warning against looking at reading print as a monolithic activity. It is more useful to compare electronic reading to some of the specific kinds of reading I have described as parts of Johnson's life of reading than to contrast it with print-world reading in general.

My sense is that the kinds of reading encouraged by hypertext fiction correspond fairly closely to the fourth category in my outline of Johnson's reading. Reading a hypertext fiction, or reading/writing it, seems to me to be a form of curious reading, although it may be that the electronic environment incites and extends curiosity in ways that are more difficult or less obvious in the older medium of print. The boxes-within-boxes format of hypertext fiction is itself an incitement to exploration and curiosity; one is looking through veils and into previously unopened chambers.

Izme Pass and other hypertext novels address subjects answerable to this formal incitement by concentrating often on the inner lives of women, including that of the author; the story itself is feminine, we are often told, emanating from a female web and an expression of a female consciousness. For example, in a box called "stories" we read, "When a woman tells a story she is remembering what will be. What symmetry or asymmetry the story passes through the orifice beneath the widespread antlers, curved horns of ritual at her head, just as it passes through the orifice between her legs. Labrys. How could she not know?" This is not crystal clear, but the author is suggesting a female version of the mythological gate of horn that gives entrance to the dream world, and other passages similarly suggest a connection between the female and the webs of this mythic hypertext world. Hence, exploring this hypertext is a little like exploring the female world of Lady Mary Wortley Montagu's *Letters.* There is even a box of narrative in *Izme Pass* called "harems": "Their bodies glowed with cooling sweat, the moist fever of arms and legs undulating in movement. One of them would be taken." (One could draw similar connections to other works in Johnson's curious reading: the boxes within boxes of the prison cells in *Amelia,* for example; the rifled drawers in Amelia's bedroom; the violated escritoire in *Clarissa.*)

However, for hypertext to fulfill its greatest promise of reader participation, it would have to be possible for one to spend time in the harem—to go into the next room in a way Montagu does not allow. This is not possible, however, and although one has the sense of opening the harem door by choosing the box of narrative with that name, one can only find what the author has written there. Even if one extends the technology to virtual reality—the system by which the action of the book could be simulated, like the flight of an astronaut—the same thing holds true. A computer program only displays what has been input. The author makes the menu, even if he or she no longer prescribes the order in which the dishes will be served. It remains to be seen if a vast increase in the options available to a reader can eventually create a sense of independent, free exploration or navigation. My sense is that this will never happen, but the reasons are as much social and intellectual as they are technological. Bolter's description of the hypertext reader as a kind of oral poet composing a performance out of existent materials may be valid, but it ought to be remembered that oral poets in different cultures at different times perform with different degrees of freedom. The situation of the *imbongi* in South Africa in 1994 was different from the situation of the scop in tenth-century England. The freedom of the oral poet is sometimes not so great as the freedom that readers of printed texts have to misremember and recreate their reading in privacy. The social circumstances of reading and writing always have their effect; technology never exists in a vacuum. It still probably means more to the freedom of the reader to live in a free society, to have a liberal education, and to be intelligently imaginative than it does to read in the medium of hypertext or virtual reality.

What applies to fiction can be transferred, by and large, to other genres written in the hypertext format. In the new medium, classical texts are given new fluidity because a reader can examine many versions almost simultaneously, as well as a vast amount of commentary and literary context. The fixity of the text is reduced by the efflorescence of alternative readings that surrounds it, or by the wealth of information that can be drawn from the World Wide Web. But do these vastly expanded resources encourage a kind of reading that is fundamentally different from conventional study?

The answer is a firm yes and no. Expanded electronic resources extend study by putting the reader in command, potentially, of a huge "page." This electronic page resembles the format tried in the sixteenth century, in which a text was placed in the center and surrounded by commentary that still left room for margins (and marginalia) all around. With the right kind of equipment, the screen (full of commentary and other sorts of information) is a more flexible format for study than the page. One can put just the assortment of documents one wants in view at a time, and one composes one's own "page."

The screen is also a less clumsy work space than the conventional desktop because the "books" stay open and can be moved into view or to the periphery more easily.

And yet the space of even a large screen is limited, and the documents waiting in the wings (or on the Web browser's "hotlist") are not much more present than the documents in a library waiting to be fetched, although one can fetch them faster by computer than by recruiting a book pager in a major research library. A library also is less flexible about permitting one to open a number of pages at a time than a CD-ROM library or World Wide Web browser is about allowing one to open a variety of screens. In any medium, however, one only finds what has been put there by someone else or by oneself; it is going to take a long time before electronic resources have accumulated the kinds of reserves that exist in real libraries. And then it is still going to take intelligence, imagination, and education for readers to assemble them and read them profitably.

Theoretically, electronic space can more easily hold the kinds of reserves now enclosed by brick-and-mortar libraries. Whether or not they will depends on the decisions of librarians and funding agencies. The electronic space for exploration then created will be different from the spaces of a library, and it makes sense to believe that readers will move differently in it. Contrary to the fears of some old-fashioned scholars, browsing will still be possible. We may still encounter other researchers, although in disembodied forms. There will be no dust on the books, and they may not bear any evidence of having been touched before. The words of our books will outlive their margins, spines, and endpapers. On the other hand, it may be easier than ever to trace the movements of earlier readers across the library because traces can be left without damaging the material of the books, and because a single "copy" might be "handled" by a vastly greater number of readers. In either case, the new medium is going to make a difference, both to readers and to research on reading. This difference does not in my opinion add up to a revolution, but it is a difference.

It is already significant that a beginning scholar using electronic information can now perform some acts of study with greater proficiency than Joseph Scaliger or Johnson did after a lifetime of brilliant study. Anyone who owns the *Thesaurus Linguae Graecae* on CD-ROM can, in a matter of minutes, bring into view all the uses in Greek literature of a particular word or phrase, hence perfecting the hard-won humanistic practice of using parallel places to illuminate a text. Still, the kind of reading that the new format for classical texts encourages is a form of study because the focus is still on a central text and resources are brought to bear for the illumination and possible revision of that text. Could this method of reading eventually undermine the centrality of the text or the notion of a central text by providing too much readily available ancillary material, as some hypertext theorists have claimed?[5] Possibly, and that would mean important changes in reading, but it has not happened yet.

George Landow's hypertext course on Victorian literature and nineteenth-century British culture is a system of more than a thousand links to a central text, Tennyson's *In Memoriam*. Students following the links are repeating, in their own order, the connections perceived by Landow and some associates between a key text and its cultural context. The centrality of the text is certainly not compromised in this kind of study. Indeed, the models of text and commentary, or text and context, seem natural in the electronic medium. Navigating *Context 32* is easier than pulling books down from the shelf and finding materials in their indexes (for example, the indexes to *Notes and Queries*), but it is similar. It affords more opportunity for independence on the part of the reader, compared with the use of a single book, even a variorum commentary, but it does not give one freedom to do something substantially different from what a good library allows, if one is willing to navigate its less fluid spaces.

But even if study and curious reading remain fundamentally unchanged for the time being, electronic media are having a greater impact on my two middle categories of reading, perusal and mere reading. These two categories were thinly represented in preprint culture; they rose along with the spread of print, and they are being substantially expanded in the electronic world. This expansion promises to continue, and it seems likely to me that the two extremes of reading in my scheme—study and curious reading—will be pinched inward towards the means—perusal and mere reading—by electronic media. Such a distortion in the scheme may be a sign that electronic media will eventually change reading in a fundamental way. In electronic media, because of the ready availability of vast amounts of information, study has a tendency to become the sort of perusal that occurs in reference reading: reading a text can become a matter of scanning lexicons, commentaries, and "parallel places," although that has not happened yet. Likewise, with so much material available in any order, curious reading can tend towards mere reading. The recent proliferation of World Wide Web sites has accelerated the process.

Study can tend to become perusal in hypertext (or on the World Wide Web) because it is so easy to move on to the next bit of commentary or context and because the bits tend to be small and relatively less related than the bits in a conventional commentary. Moreover, the commentary and the links themselves have the status of a self-help work rather than the status of a primary text. So to the extent that one is following the links rather than learning about the text, one is perusing. Applied to education, hypertext is a kind of exalted self-help scheme (the characteristic reading experience of perusal) in which, as in conventional self-help reading, one must give oneself over to the system. One may argue with any patch of text within the system or add one's own patches, but the whole activity of linking and the given material of study are unimpeachable, unless one decides to shut down the computer.

In this respect, reading hypertext offers no increase of freedom over reading a printed text. In fact, hypertext encyclopedias (such as the electronic *Britannica* or even the *Oxford English Dictionary*), with their prominent outlines of each article, resemble the expanded charts and tables of neoclassical books of knowledge. They can be "rolled out" to display their structures and "accessed" at any point, but they always have such "layouts." The tyranny of this kind of layout inspired Swift and led to a whole age of satire directed at scholarly apparatus. Happily, satire is being stimulated again by the presence of a new medium for communicating knowledge. There are parodic Web sites out there already; among the first to arrive were those imitating and parodying the sites set up by presidential candidates. But it is reasonable to assume there will be others, and these will increase the skill of electronic readers, just as Defoe's and Swift's parodic pamphlets forced print-world readers to make new and more subtle distinctions in their time. Readers will have to retain some of the qualities of study because the relatively less intense practice of perusal will lead them into laughable errors.

If, overall, nonparodic electronic texts cause study to descend to perusal, at the other end of my scheme of reading they may cause curious reading to press up towards mere reading. Partly because it can make so much material available, electronic transmission encourages swift, inattentive, and cursory reading. Curious reading in the electronic mode is like reading a newspaper or journal full of fictional stories. In both cases, bits and pieces of stories are spread out for selection in an order determined by the reader. The headlines and slugs in newspaper stories are like the titles or rubrics on the boxes of text in hypertext. In each medium one can either select a thread and follow it or turn pages, following the given construction of the "text," and see what catches one's eye. There are important differences, of course. The "links" in a newspaper are much simpler than those in a hypertext; they generally only go on to the continuation of the same story, rather than, as in hypertext, to the beginning of new, though related, stories. I find in myself a tendency when reading in either medium to skip over a great deal of text. I get the gist of the box or the story and go on to something else until I hit on something that I want to read more closely. I pay no price for this in reading the newspaper or a hypertext because the stories are somewhat independent.

Moreover, in hypertext there is almost a surety that I will cover the same ground again and again.

Frequent repetition, both planned and accidental, is an important feature of hypertext, and it too encourages skipping and other features of mere reading. There is less sense of a beginning in hypertext fiction than in a book with numbered pages, and much less sense of an ending than in a book, the conclusion of which one can see approaching as the thickness of the pages on the right-hand side of the spine decreases. For me, this formlessness encourages extensive wandering in reading; it leads me to mere reading. In addition, the screen still seems to me a more public medium than the pages of a book: it is lit up; someone might look at it from a distance, as people often try to read newspapers from a distance. It is also, so far, difficult to bring a hypertext to bed or to some other personal retreats, and that too makes the reading of hypertext more like the mere reading of newspapers and journals.

Another sign that electronic reading tends to be mere reading is that the traditional sources of mere reading have been among those most readily converted to electronic production and reception. Newspapers are becoming electronic faster than other kinds of printed material. They are rapidly produced, and they are modified to suit the region in which they are distributed. California's weather is printed above the banner on editions of the *New York Times* distributed in that state, for example, and stories of limited local interest, such as sports stories about local teams, are eliminated in out-of-town editions. The ultimate end of such customizing could be electronic papers in which everyone draws out of electronic space a bucket full of stories on subjects of particular interest to themselves. The press would go on producing stories, but "publication" could become a matter of availability rather than printing, a little like home shopping on interactive TV. This is already happening on the many sites devoted to news on the World Wide Web. The searching system called WAIS, which is employed by the electronic *Britannica,* uses the convention of newspaper headlines to present the results of searches. In effect, WAIS creates custom newspapers for its users after searching through whatever banks of information it attacks, whether or not they are newspaperlike. Hence it presents all reading in the format customary for mere reading.

Although curious reading may be pinched up towards mere reading by electronic devices, mere reading seems likely only to expand. In a highly fluid buyer's market for information, it is also likely that an awful lot of what we read will take the form of advertisements, invitations to read further or to navigate in one direction rather than another through the maze of information. We do not read many advertisements with intensity because we know what they want, and this carelessness about reading such things is likely to grow. Here again the World Wide Web is showing the way. It is filling up rapidly with advertisements, which are the material par excellence of mere reading. Other kinds of reading are going to survive, clearly, but the emphasis on mere reading, even if it derives from the new medium, is going to have its effect on all reading. One sign that electronic production has encroached on the printed and manuscript worlds is that mail now goes unopened as well as unread, something that was unthinkable for most private citizens as recently as a generation ago.

I I

Having tried to apply my scheme to the present and future state of reading as it may be altered by hypertext and other electronic media, let me return to Johnson and his age, and let me try to relate Johnson's life of reading to the present and future. One important aspect of hypertext fiction, or any other kind of electronic book or web, is random access. This is the key to the decentering, the nonlinearity, the fluidity, and most of the other qualities that theorists say separate the new reading from the old. In some respects, however, random access does not represent a radical departure from earlier forms of reading. The history of literary formats is a story of increasingly random access. Writing increased the accessibility of "texts" (and created them in the modern sense) because one could draw on them without a rhapsode being present. The codex, especially after it was paginated and indexed, represented a vast increase in accessibility over the scroll. Indexing and cross-referencing improved during the eighteenth century; this both fostered and was nourished by an attitude towards reading that favored the use of such shortcuts. Traditionalists such as Jonathan Swift resisted such shortcuts to knowledge; Swift deplored "mere index learning," but it took hold nevertheless.

Unlike the kind of modern writer Swift satirized, Johnson's mind was more full than his commonplace book, but this was because of his laziness about writing and the vastness of his mind rather than because of any doctrine about reading. Despite his largely empty commonplace books, Johnson is an important figure in the growth of random-access reading, and for that reason he may be seen as having prepared the way for much of what appears new in the electronic reception of texts. This is one of the particular ways in which the example of Samuel Johnson is helpful for understanding recent as well as earlier developments in the history of reading.

A great deal of what Johnson wrote is itself suitable for reading in the bits and pieces needed for random access. *Rasselas,* with its discrete chapters, susceptible, to a degree, of being read in any order, makes a suitable hypertext fiction. Thanks to an enterprising research assistant, Simon Rakov, I have read it in this form and have had my students so read it. So far, the results are not surprising, but the "text" did seem to engage curiosity, and the inclusion of illustrations and other ancillary material had the effect of encouraging further reading or navigation. Some students also enjoyed being able to "mark up" the text for succeeding readers, and some enjoyed seeing the trails and marks left by their predecessors. Because the unviolated text is always available, one can accept the "reading copy" as a sort of wall for graffiti much more happily than one can see a library book ruined with scribbling. Because they are not sacred themselves, electronic texts are immune to desecration. This may be frightening in some respects, but there are advantages in it for the teacher hoping to stimulate active and creative reading.

Johnson's *Dictionary* is an even better text for random access than *Rasselas,* and it will certainly enjoy renewed life as a machine-readable text now that it has appeared on CD-ROM. The independence of Johnson's paragraphs and their brevity in many numbers of the *Rambler* make them also suitable for the closed but linked boxes of hypertext and for random access. Throughout his career, the genres in which Johnson worked were often ones that tend to encourage random-access reading, and this is important to me because Johnson's writing reflects his reading style. Johnson often spoke of reading as essential to writing, and we should expect to find connections between the two in any literary person.

The most famous aspect of Johnson's reading by random access is implicit in his frequent claim not to have read books all the way through. Boswell reported many instances in which Johnson made the claim, partly because they helped him build up a picture of his hero's superhuman intellectual strength. Boswell says that Johnson "had a peculiar facility in seizing at once what was valuable in any book, without submitting to the labour of perusing it from beginning to end."[6] As G. B. Hill suggests in his note, Boswell may have been adapting Johnson's own description of the child prodigy Philip Barretier: "He had a quickness of apprehension, and firmness of memory, which enabled him to read with incredible rapidity, and, at the same time, to retain what he read, so as to be able to recollect and apply it. He turned over volumes in an instant, and selected what was useful for his purpose." Johnson's mind is described in these cases as having the power of a computer to search through large bodies of text; he was a kind of human WAIS. In other cases, Johnson's failure to read books through seems a reflection more of impatience than of intensity:

> In the morning of Tuesday, June 15, [1784] while we sat at Dr. Adams's, we talked of a printed letter from the Reverend Herbert Croft [author of *Love and Madness*], to a young

gentleman who had been his pupil, in which he advised him to read to the end of whatever books he should begin to read. Johnson. "This is surely a strange advice; you may as well resolve that whatever men you happen to get acquainted with, you are to keep to them for life. A book may be good for nothing; or there may be only one thing in it worth knowing; are we to read it all through? These Voyages, (pointing to the three large volumes of "Voyages to the South Sea" [*Cook's Voyages*] which were just come out) who will read them through? A man had better work his way before the mast, than read them through; they will be eaten by rats and mice, before they are read through.[7]

Johnson reacted this way to many books, but he was especially hard on travel books. The way he treated Richard Twiss's *Travels in Spain* was particularly disrespectful of the sanctity of the text. After passing a fairly favorable judgment on the work, he announced, "I have not, indeed, cut the leaves yet; but I have read in them where the pages are open, and I do not suppose that what is in the pages which are closed is worse than what is in the open pages."[8] This episode is reminiscent of the occasion on which he read to his amanuensis Robert Shiels from James Thomson's *Seasons,* skipping every other line and exclaiming ironically, "Is not this fine?"[9] Then there is Johnson's famous angry retort to those who doggedly read books through and try to impose such a rule on others: "Mr. Elphinston talked of a new book that was much admired, and asked Dr. Johnson if he had read it. Johnson. 'I have looked into it.' ' "What (said Elphinston,) have you not read it through?' Johnson, offended at being thus pressed, and so obliged to own his cursory mode of reading, answered tartly, 'No, Sir; do *you* read books *through?*' "[10]

So much for the absolute authority of the printed text, and so much for the linearity and other restrictions it is said to impose on the reader in contrast to the freedoms permitted by the electronic text. Johnson felt at liberty to read the pages of a book in piecemeal fashion, either flipping through them or using an index. He "navigated" in texts, as in the whole "web" of books available in his time, in a manner that he once described as "fortuitous and unguided." In comparison to Johnson's methods, hypertext reading may seem more guided and restrictive than its counterpart in print. In fact, by the use of "guard" files, a hypertext writer can exert controls over access that are unavailable to print-world writers. The hypertext writer can prevent readers from looking at one box before they have opened a certain other box; it is easy to imagine how Johnson would have reacted to such a restriction, when he could not be bothered even to cut the pages of some books.

Johnson followed his desultory methods of reading partly because of his natural tendencies, but he also exalted them into a kind of theory of education and recommended them to others:

> Snatches of reading (said he) will not make a Bentley or a Clarke. They are, however, in a certain degree advantageous. I would put a child into a library (where no unfit books are) and let him read at his choice. A child should not be discouraged from reading any thing that he takes a liking to, from a notion that it is above his reach. If that be the case, the child will soon find it out and desist; if not, he of course gains the instruction; which is so much more likely to come, from the inclination with which he takes up the study.[11]

With some exceptions, Johnson extended this advice to adults as well:

> He said, that for general improvement, a man should read whatever his immediate inclination prompts him to; though, to be sure, if a man has a science to learn, he must regularly and resolutely advance. He added, "what we read with inclination makes a much stronger impression. If we read without inclination, half the mind is employed in fixing the attention; so there is but one half to be employed on what we read." He told us, he read Fielding's "Amelia" through without stopping. He said, if a man begins to read

in the middle of a book, and feels an inclination to go on,
let him not quit it, to go to the beginning. He may, perhaps,
not feel again the inclination.[12]

Johnson's notebooks show that he did a great deal of resolute
and regular reading, or study, as I call it. He listed page numbers and line numbers and schemes of progress on important
texts, such as the Bible, that he wanted to get through.[13] However, the great variety of books that often appears in a single
notebook entry also shows that he was reading by inclination at
any particular time, and with some impatience. The practice
was certainly not new with Johnson. In earlier times study
tended to confine readers to a single book; in some cases, the
confinement was literal because the book was chained to a
shelf. But even such confined readers found ways to practice
cursory and curious kinds of reading. In earlier times it was
common to have a variety of books bound between one set of
covers. Commonplace books of the seventeenth and eighteenth
centuries also show that readers dipped in here and there as
often as they read straight through.

The simple truth is that print-world readers have read in
a variety of ways, although there exists an ideal of "reading
through" that corresponds to the vaunted linearity of the
printed text and that was highly significant in the eighteenth-
century construction of reading. John Locke took the importance of straight, complete, linear reading to an extreme in his
paraphrase of St. Paul's epistles, and he wrote a manifesto for
this kind of thorough reading in his preface to that work (post-
humously published in 1704). Exalting the place of the author,
in contradistinction to essays on hypertext such as Michael
Joyce's "(Re)placing the Author," Locke says, for example:

> When the eye is constantly disturb'd with loose Sentences,
> that by their standing and separation appear as so many
> distinct Fragments; the Mind will have much ado to take
> in, and carry on in its Memory an uniform Discourse of
> dependent Reasonings. . . .
> The way to understand the Mind of him that writ it,

every one would agree, was to read the whole Letter through from one end to the other, all at once, to see what was the main Subject and Tendency of it. . . .

He that would understand St. Paul right, must understand his Terms in the Sense he uses them, and not as they are appropriated by each Man's particular Philosophy. . . . That is what we should aim at in reading him, or any other Author.[14]

Other readers extended Locke's assumption of unity and completeness even further. One thinks of Coleridge's notion that it would be easier to move a stone in the base of the great pyramid at Gaza than it would be to change one word in Shakespeare without making him say something different or say the same thing worse than he did. It is possible that print implies an ethos of linear procedure, of authorial control, and of a correspondent reading procedure of submission, that Locke epitomized in his treatise and Coleridge took to new heights in *Biographia Literaria*. However, this ethos has never been applied to all kinds of reading by all readers, and the theory or ethos itself has never gone unchallenged, not even in the periods when print was made the standard for all language. The world of print was never coherently or unanimously dedicated to a single doctrine of literary production or reception, nor is such unanimity likely to arise in a world dominated by electronic media.

As great a hero of the print world as he was, Johnson (like Swift and Sterne) had a stubborn, healthily subversive streak. Much as he admired Locke, he did not apply his method to all his own reading. He regarded print as the form par excellence of language and considered the print revolution the most important event in intellectual history, but in some ways he resisted the authority of print, just as he resisted many other kinds of authority; he did so, in part, by reading in a desultory fashion. It looks as if he anticipated some of the qualities of reading that electronic formats have made more prominent, but he was simply exercising a power of resistance that readers of texts have always had available to them. It is a source of some concern that hypertext tends to incorporate this resistance into its aesthetic, for, in so doing, it must seek to structure the reader's resistance and subordinate it to the artistic vision of the writer. But I am optimistic: I think the spirit of resistance will survive all changes in the media of communication, even though I am not sure what forms it will take should its older forms—"random access" or "fortuitous and unguided excursions" into books—become parts of package tours on the World Wide Web, arranged by hypertextual authors.

III

Samuel Johnson was not the first to practice and encourage random access to literature, but he asserted the reader's right to it in a post-Lockean age when greater strictness was settling in on the print world. Now typographic variety has given way, for the most part, to regularity in the production of books, and anomalies in spelling and grammar have gradually been reduced to largely homogeneous house standards. For all the talk about the death of the author among the elite practitioners of literary criticism, the cult of the author and his or her authority are stronger than ever. And authority and cult status are not reserved for the likes of St. Paul alone. We live in an age of biography, and most best-sellers reach that status on the strength of the author's name. Moreover, sales are especially brisk in highly formulaic genres, such as romance and self-help; for most readers these books depend on submission to the control of the author.

Although studies such as Janice Radway's *Reading the Romance* show that readers are not entirely passive in their reception of romances and other popular literary forms, they certainly are not the reader/writers envisioned by hypertext theorists. But at any given time in the history of reading many movements are taking place at the same time, and many kinds of reading are being practiced. This does not mean that we are helpless to describe the current situation or that it is ever shapeless or anarchic. I believe that my scheme of the four types of reading can be applied to the present situation. The proliferation of printed things and the greater accessibility fostered by electronic transmission has pinched the four kinds of reading towards the middle categories of perusal and mere reading, but there is still plenty of life at the extremes of study and curious reading. That situation is subject to change, but for the time being the four kinds of reading that I propose are all standing. At certain hours in nearby classrooms in my English department building some professors are wheeling in television sets and VCRs; others are booting up computers containing hypertexts; some are discussing the plots or meanings of novels; others are looking closely at a poem; others carry dictionaries and grammars as they prepare to go over the text of *Beowulf* word by word, four students and a teacher all with their heads bent solemnly over the text. The scene vividly displays the variety of kinds of reading supported by the literate environment in which we now live. It is true that the proportions may be changing; it is possible that such variety may not flourish forever; but it also seems unlikely that reading will ever become one homogeneous activity.

Despite the variety and vitality that exists in some quarters of the literate world, there is still plenty of alarm and plenty of cause for alarm about the future of reading. We need to ask if there is any possibility that reading will disappear altogether. The villain in today's jeremiads about reading is usually television or some other medium of communication that relies on images rather than words. Even the hypertextualist Michael Joyce worries about the future because he loves language, and, as he says, "hypertext is, before anything else, a visual form."[15] The fear is that screen-oriented "literature" will, like television, become less and less verbal, or at least less and less literate. Johnson was a supremely literate man in a literate age. His insensitivity to visual media has been exaggerated,[16] but he certainly felt that words were the best medium of communication, and, for all his skill in talking, it was printed language that he favored. It was said by his hearers that his conversation could have been printed without any correction.[17]

Speech was in retreat as a dominant medium in Johnson's day; he described preliterate or nonwritten language as "merely oral" in his *Dictionary*. Written and (especially) printed words were also displacing visual forms of communication. It was not until 1762 that the pictorial signs that were used as addresses in London were replaced, by governmental directive, with numbering systems for the use of the postal service. Before that time the streets, especially along the Strand where Johnson lived, were hung with innumerable pictures—remnants and reminders of a less literate age. Neither from this quarter nor from live speech is it likely that Johnson saw a threat to reading. Literacy seemed to be propelling society away from pictures and speech in his day. He was convinced, for example, that the lecture was doomed as a form of instruction because anyone would prefer to have books, which were increasingly available, in hand.[18]

Despite the growing prevalence of print, Johnson too worried about a decrease in reading in his own day. Paradoxically, he saw the vast increase in writing as the great danger to reading. In this he seems to have anticipated Italo Calvino's *If on a Winter's Night a Traveler,* but in one form or another the worry is ancient. Johnson is recorded as saying in 1783, "It is strange that there should be so little reading in the world, and so much writing. People in general do not willingly read, if they have any thing else to amuse them."[19] He was more insistent about the relationship and less puzzled by it in some of his literary essays. In *Adventurer* 115, for example, he lamented recent increases in publication and foretold how it would all end:

General irregularities are known in time to remedy themselves. By the constitution of Aegypt, the priesthood was continually increasing, till at length there was no people beside themselves; the establishment was then dissolved, and the number of priests was reduced and limited. Thus among us, writers will, perhaps, be multiplied, till no readers will be found, and then the ambition of writing must necessarily cease.[20]

In another place, Johnson satirically imagined that all English-men would be authors and "every man must be content to read his book to himself."[21] This complaint, however, is as old as Ecclesiastes. Moreover, Johnson was simply wrong about there being less reading in the world, at least from a statistical point of view.

The situation has not changed today. There is (statistically) more reading; there is certainly more reading matter; but there are plenty of worries about the survival of reading. It has been true for centuries that an individual reader can peruse only a small percentage of what is produced, much less study it, but the trend has dramatically increased in recent years and is likely to increase exponentially as electronic systems become more widely available. In the sense that he or she is likely to read a smaller and smaller part of what the culture produces, the participation of each individual reader in culture is diminishing. We may read little in common, and there may be no common readers.

The common reader that Johnson imagined was already an abstraction spanning ages and cultures to reside in an aesthetic space. It is possible that Johnson constructed such a reader to compensate for the lost possibility of anyone keeping up with everything that was published even in his day. Earlier, a great scholar—a Scaliger or an Erasmus—could personally read almost all that was worth reading from earlier times and from the scholar's own day. By late in Johnson's life, only a timeless, placeless abstraction such as the common reader could do that. Today the notion of a common reader is impracticable in theory as well as in reality. The canon is a discredited idea, and there is so much to read that we all read our own tiny fractions of what is out there. This reflects not only a change in what is read, but a change in reading itself, because reading itself is changed when the community of fellow readers changes. More reading now, whether in specialized English courses or in specialized journals, is coterie reading. (Even the book catalogue *The Common Reader* represents a kind of coterie reading, excluding everything technical or religious, for example.) I think

Johnson resisted this change, and his construction of the common reader is evidence of this resistance, although he distinguished himself from the common reader and would defend another's right so to distinguish himself or herself.[22]

The prospect of further fragmentation in the community of readers is the feature of the current scene of reading that I find frightening. Just what will it mean for the existence of a public sphere in America if everyone can have his or her own customized newspaper with his or her own news? Or if everyone reads a different or even a differently organized hypertextual novel, as theorists are predicting? We might then reach the point that Johnson foresaw, in which every writer must be content to read his or her own book. Even to approach this condition of isolation is to change the nature both of reading and of society, because reading is not separable from society. Despite the isolation in which it is often practiced, reading will always be a social activity, unless we literally read only our own books. At that point, reading would truly cease to exist, and it would become something it is now impossible to describe. The real threat to reading is the breakdown of the community of readers implicit in each of the various acts of reading. Loneliness was Johnson's greatest fear, and isolation, paradoxically, presents the greatest threat to the often solitary practice of reading.

NOTES

ABBREVIATIONS

Gleanings Reade, Aleyn Lyell. *Johnsonian Gleanings.* 11 vols. London: Francis, 1909–52.

Handlist Fleeman, J. D. *A Preliminary Handlist of Copies of Books Associated with Dr. Samuel Johnson.* Oxford Bibliographical Society Occasional Publication no. 17. Oxford: Oxford Bibliographical Society, 1984.

Letters *The Letters of Samuel Johnson.* Ed. Bruce Redford. 5 vols. Princeton: Princeton Univ. Press, 1992–94.

Life Boswell's Life of Johnson. Ed. G. B. Hill; rev. L. F. Powell. 2d ed. 6 vols. Oxford: Clarendon Press, 1934–64.

Lives *Lives of the English Poets by Samuel Johnson, LL.D.* Ed. G. B. Hill. 3 vols. Oxford: Clarendon Press, 1905.

Miscellanies *Johnsonian Miscellanies.* Ed. G. B. Hill. 2 vols. New York: Harper and Brothers, 1897.

Yale *The Yale Edition of the Works of Samuel Johnson.* Vol. 1, *Diaries, Prayers, and Annals,* ed. E. L. McAdam Jr., with Donald Hyde and Mary Hyde. Vol. 2, *The Idler and The Adventurer,* ed. Walter J. Bate, John M. Bullitt, and L. F. Powell. Vols. 3–5, *The Rambler,* ed. Walter J. Bate and Albrecht B. Strauss. Vol. 6, *Poems,* ed. E. L. McAdam Jr., with George Milne. Vols. 7–8, *Johnson on Shakespeare,* ed. Arthur Sherbo, with an introduction by Bertrand Bronson. Vol. 9, *A Journey to the Western Islands of Scotland,* ed. Mary Lascelles. Vol. 10, *Political Writings,* ed. Donald J. Greene. Vol. 14, *Sermons,* ed. Jean H. Hagstrum and James Gray. Vol. 15, *A Voyage to Abyssinia,* ed. Joel J. Gold. Vol. 16, *Rasselas and Other Tales,* ed. Gwin J. Kolb. New Haven: Yale Univ. Press, 1958–.

PREFACE

1. Italo Calvino, *If on a Winter's Night a Traveler,* trans. William Weaver (New York: Harcourt Brace Jovanovich, 1981), 97.

2. *Yale* 2:459.

3. Samuel Johnson, *The Universal Visiter and Memorialist*, ed. Donald Eddy (1756; reprint, New York: Garland, 1979), 162.

4. Calvino, *If on a Winter's Night*, 145–46.

5. See *Handlist*; G. W. Nicholls, curator of the Lichfield Birthplace Museum, was kind enough to pass on to me J. D. Fleeman's manuscript list of additions and corrections to his *Handlist*, through 1990. The many other sources of my information on Johnson's books will be noted in due course.

6. Samuel Johnson, *A Dictionary of the English Language*, 2 vols. (London: Strahan et al., 1755), preface, par. 28.

7. William Field, *Memoirs of the Life, Writings, and Opinions of the Rev. Samuel Parr, LL.D.*, 2 vols. (London: H. Colburn, 1828), 1:164; this passage has been cited by other students of Johnson's reading, including Lawrence Lipking and Paul Korshin, to both of whom I am indebted.

CHAPTER 1. THE LIFE OF READING

1. *Letters* 4:428.

2. Robert DeMaria Jr., *The Life of Samuel Johnson: A Critical Biography* (Oxford: Blackwell, 1993).

3. Janusz Slawinski, "Reading and Reader in the Literary Historical Process," *New Literary History* 19 (1988): 527.

4. Ibid., 535.

5. See Alvin Kernan, *The Imaginary Library: An Essay on Literature and Society* (Princeton: Princeton Univ. Press, 1982). I am also indebted to the other two books in Kernan's trilogy: *Samuel Johnson and the Impact of Print* (Princeton: Princeton Univ. Press, 1989) and *The Death of Literature* (New Haven: Yale Univ. Press, 1990).

6. *Miscellanies* 1:156.

7. Ibid., 158.

8. Victor Nell, *Lost in a Book: The Psychology of Reading for Pleasure* (New Haven: Yale Univ. Press, 1988).

9. See Janice Radway, *Reading the Romance* (Chapel Hill: Univ. of North Carolina Press, 1986), and Jean Wyatt, *Reconstructing Desire* (Chapel Hill: Univ. of North Carolina Press, 1990). But the association of women with romance reading in England is at least as old as Chaucer: see Derek Pearsall, *The Life of Geoffrey Chaucer* (Oxford: Blackwell, 1992), 58, who refers to Elizabeth Salter, "England and the Continent during the Thirteenth Century: Royal and Aristocratic Patronage," in *English and International Studies in the Literature, Art, and Patronage of Medieval England*, ed. Derek Pearsall and Nicolette Zeeman (Cambridge: Cambridge Univ. Press, 1988), 75–100. An association between women and light reading can be traced back at least to Juvenal (*Satires* 6.453).

10. *Miscellanies* 1:332.

11. *Letters* 4:130.

12. Cited in Marshall Waingrow, ed., *The Correspondence and Other Pa-*

pers of James Boswell Relating to the Making of the Life of Johnson (New York: McGraw-Hill, n.d.), 88.

13. *Life* 4:13.

14. *Letters* 1:350 and 3:288.

15. *Yale* 1:233.

16. *Life* 4:409.

17. Ibid., 2:121.

18. Ibid., 4:218.

19. *Lives* 3:309.

20. On the possibility that Johnson suffered from Tourette's syndrome, see John Wiltshire, *Samuel Johnson in the Medical World* (Cambridge: Cambridge Univ. Press, 1991), 29–32.

21. James Clifford, *Young Sam Johnson* (New York: McGraw-Hill, 1955; reprint, New York: Oxford Univ. Press, 1961), 65 (page citations are to the reprint edition).

22. *Miscellanies* 2:297.

23. *Life* 3:285.

24. John Hawkins, *The Life of Samuel Johnson, LL.D.* (Dublin: Chamberlain et al., 1787), 14–15.

25. *Miscellanies* 2:254.

26. Richard Brown, *Knowledge Is Power* (New York: Oxford Univ. Press, 1989), 201.

27. *Life* 4:31.

28. Ibid., 2:156.

29. See M. B. Parkes, *Pause and Effect: An Introduction to the History of Punctuation in the West* (Aldershot, Hants.: Scolar Press, 1992), 21, and, for the best discussion of the issue, Paul Saenger, "Silent Reading: Its Impact on Late Medieval Script and Society," *Viator* 13 (1982): 367–414. For an excellent analysis of the meaning of the new activity, see Saenger, "Books of Hours and the Reading Habits of the Later Middle Ages," in *The Culture of Print,* ed. Roger Chartier (Princeton: Princeton Univ. Press, 1989), 141–73; Saenger suggests that the shift took place in the fifteenth century and, in the reading of books of hours, coincided with a relocation of the essence of prayer from the lips to the heart.

30. For these and other descriptions of Johnson reading aloud, see *Life* 2:84, 212, and 5:115.

31. *Yale* 2:94.

32. Calvino, *If on a Winter's Night,* 176.

33. Preface, *Yale* 7–8:62; Johnson's reliance on Locke is registered in the *Dictionary* (s.v. "to rest," sense 8): "The philosophical use of words conveys the precise notions of things, which the mind may *rest* upon, and be satisfied with in its search after knowledge."

34. Preface, *Yale* 7–8:67.

35. Rolf Engelsing, "Die Perioden der Lesergeschicte in der Neuzeit,"

Archiv für Geschichte des Buchwesens 10 (1969): 946–1002; also see his *Der Bürger als Leser* (Stuttgart: J. B. Metzlersche and Carl Ernst Poeschel, 1974). Those who have made good use of Engelsing include David Hall, "The Uses of Literacy in New England, 1600–1850," in *Printing and Society in Early America* (Worcester, Mass.: American Antiquarian Society, 1983), 1–47, and Kernan, *Samuel Johnson and the Impact of Print.* However, for my introduction to Engelsing I am particularly indebted to Robert Darnton, "First Steps towards a History of Reading," *Australian Journal of French Studies* 23 (1986): 5–30. Lawrence Lipking applies Engelsing to Johnson in "Inventing the Common Reader: Samuel Johnson and the Canon," in *Interpretation and Cultural History,* ed. Joan H. Pittock and Andrew Wear (London: Macmillan, 1991), 153–75.

CHAPTER 2. NOTES AND MARGINALIA

1. D. F. MacKenzie, *Bibliography and the Sociology of Texts* (London: British Library, 1986).

2. Thomas Tanselle, "Libraries, Museums, and Reading," *Raritan* 12, no. 1 (1992): 66.

3. Seneca, *De tranquillitate animi* 9.6–7, in *Moral Essays,* trans. John W. Basore, Loeb Classical Library, 3 vols. (London: Heinemann, 1932), 2:249.

4. Lucian, *Works of Lucian,* trans. A. M. Harmon, Loeb Classical Library, 5 vols. (London: Heinemann, 1921), 2:179, 181.

5. The most famous expression of the tradition in Johnson's day was Alexander Pope's portrait of Timon in his study in his "Epistle to Burlington"; see Pope, *Epistles to Several Persons,* ed. F. W. Bateson (London: Methuen, 1951), 145–46:

His Study! with what Authors is it stor'd?
In Books not Authors, curious is my Lord;
To all their dated Backs he turns you round,
These Aldus printed, those Du Suëil has bound.
Lo some are Vellom, and the rest as good
For all his Lordship knows, but they are Wood.
(ll. 133–38)

6. *Life* 3:7.

7. Ibid., 2:192–93.

8. Ibid., 193 n. 2.

9. *Handlist* no. 245.

10. *Letters* 3:127.

11. *Life* 2:120.

12. Ibid., 5:206.

13. Ibid., 296.

14. Plutarch, *Lives* 5.846.24–25; Demosthenes 2.3.

15. Isaac Watts, *On the Improvement of the Human Mind* (London, 1741), 77.

16. *Life* 2:364–65.

17. Ibid., 364 n. 3.

18. Johnson took Charles Sheridan's *Account of the Late Revolution in Sweden* to the dining table and kept it on his lap wrapped in the tablecloth (*Life* 2:285); both this history and the volume of the *Encyclopédie* are books for perusal, and this is characteristically the kind of reading Johnson did in public.

19. *Letters* 3:159.

20. See O M Brack, *Bred a Bookseller: Samuel Johnson on Vellum Books, a New Essay* (Los Angeles: Privately printed for the Samuel Johnson Society of Southern California, 1990).

21. The extant binding is on a work of British antiquity, *Florus Anglicus* by Lambert van den Bos, a duodecimo volume published in Amsterdam in 1652, and the provenance suggests that Johnson did the work while still in Lichfield, before 1737; see *Handlist* no. 29.

22. *Life* 4:84.

23. *Letters* 4:395–96.

24. Ibid., 1:310.

25. *Life* 4:279.

26. *Letters* 1:313–14.

27. See G. J. Clingham and N. Hopkinson, "Johnson's Copy of the Iliad at Felbrigg Hall, Norfolk," *Book Collector* 37 (1988): 503–21. Some of the books bought by Windham at the sale of Johnson's library are in very poor condition, yet some are quite sound, and all are impressive volumes. See R. W. Ketton-Cremer, "Johnson's Last Gifts to Windham," *Book Collector* 5 (1956): 354–56.

28. See *Life* 2:57–58.

29. Martial, *Epigrams*, trans. Walter C. A. Kerr, Loeb Classical Library, 2 vols. (London: Heinemann, 1968), 1:165.

30. Ibid., 2:505.

31. Ibid.

32. Ibid.

33. Richard de Bury, *Philobiblion*, ed. and trans. Ernest C. Thomas (New York: Lockwood and Coombes, 1896), 178.

34. John Dryden, *MacFlecknoe*, l. 101.

35. *Life* 2:274 and *Letters* 2:129; the book has been identified as *Opus aureum* (1577) by Michael Neander (1525–95).

36. Darnton, "First Steps," 16.

37. Hawkins, *Life of Samuel Johnson, LL.D.*, 157.

38. *Yale* 1:233.

39. Richard Johnson, *The Famous History of the Seven Champions of Christendom* (n.p.: R. Scot et al., 1687), is in the possession of Peter Stockham of Lichfield. It contains a note saying that it was bought at the sale of

Johnson's books in 1785; if this is true, it shows that some books not listed in the catalogue were sold at that time. Alain-René LeSage, *The Adventures of Gil Blas,* 3d ed. (London: J. Osborne, 1751), and John Newbery, *The World Displayed* (London: J. Newbery, 1760), are in the British Art Center.

40. The relevant passages in a codicil to Johnson's will are reprinted in *Life* 4:402 n. 2.

41. Published as *A Course of Lectures on the English Law,* ed. Thomas M. Curley, 2 vols. (Madison: Univ. of Wisconsin Press, 1986).

42. Cited in *The Library of John Locke,* ed. John Harrison and Peter Laslett (Oxford: Oxford Univ. Press, for the Bibliographical Society, 1965), 1.

43. Ibid.

44. De Bury, *Philobiblion,* 239.

45. *Life* 3:43.

46. Pliny, *C. Plinii Cæcilii Secundi Epistolae et Panegyricus* (Oxford, 1703), Beinecke Rare Book and Manuscript Library.

47. John Milton, *Paradise Regain'd: A Poem* (London: J. Tonson, 1725), Hyde Collection.

48. Philip Melanchthon, *Epistolarum D. Philippi Melanchthonis Farrago in Partes tres distributa* (Basel, 1545), Hyde Collection.

49. Robert DeMaria Jr., *Johnson's Dictionary and the Language of Learning* (Chapel Hill: Univ. of North Carolina Press, 1986).

50. Bryan Duppa, *Holy Rules and Helps to Devotion Both in Prayer and Practice* (London: W. Hensman, 1675), Beinecke Rare Book and Manuscript Library, 185.

51. Samuel Johnson, "Considerations [by the late Dr. Samuel Johnson] on the Case of Dr. T[rapp]'s Sermons, abridged by Mr. Cave, 1739," *Gentleman's Magazine* 57 (1787): 555–57.

52. John Norris, *A Collection of Miscellanies,* 3d ed. (London: S. Manship, 1699), Beinecke Rare Book and Manuscript Library, 9. There is a similar expression of feeling in Johnson's copy of Joseph Butler's *Fifteen Sermons* (London: Robert Horsfield, 1765), now in the Trinity College Library. Johnson found a note saying "Memor Heighij" and he matched it with the note "Memor Elizabethæ," feeling as he read the sermons grief for his wife, who had died at least thirteen years before.

53. *Yale* 1:67.

54. The book is on deposit in the Bodleian Library (Dep. C. 25), 22. I owe the correct decipherment of Johnson's handwriting to Bruce Redford.

55. *Life* 3:358 n. 3; *Miscellanies* 1:284.

56. *Chancellor's Court of the University of Oxford,* Beinecke Rare Book and Manuscript Library MS. book (z117 115v), 4.

57. William Camden, *Remains concerning Britaine* (London: Thomas Harper for John Waterson, 1636), Folger Library, 386.

58. Inocui Sales, *A Collection of New Epigrams* (London: T. Hodgkin for Matth. Gillyflower, 1694), Hyde Collection, 15 and 26.

59. Sir Thomas Browne, *Pseudodoxia Epidemica: or, Enquiries into very many received tenents, and commonly presumed truths* (London: T. Hodgkin for Edward Dod, 1646), New York Public Library, 82.

60. Camden, *Remains concerning Britaine*, 202, 326, and 400.

61. *Life* 4:402 n. 2.

62. *Yale* 6:43.

63. British Library MS. 54225, fol. 59.

64. I am indebted to Bruce Redford for deciphering Johnson's handwriting in this note.

65. Jonathan Swift, *The Prose Works of Jonathan Swift*, ed. Herbert Davis, vol. 5, *Miscellaneous and Autobiographical Pieces, Fragments, and Marginalia* (Oxford: Basil Blackwell, 1962), 266−94.

66. See Elizabeth Eisenstein, *The Printing Press as an Agent of Change*, 2 vols. (Cambridge: Cambridge Univ. Press, 1979).

67. Indeed, Michael Warner believes print was socially constructed in such a way that it both received and gave strength to republicanism. The situation is more complicated than either Habermas or Warner acknowledges. The politics of print is beyond the scope of my study, but Swift, Johnson, and other readers having assumed a variety of stances in relation to the public carries implications for our understanding of the transformation of the public sphere. My sense of Johnson's life of reading generally fits Habermas's model, and is clarified by it, but the variety of Johnson's relations and nonrelations to the public world of other readers makes me hesitate to accept the sweeping generalizations found in the works of both Habermas and his followers. The example of Johnson and many others shows, for example, that Warner is wrong (or merely conceptual) when he says that "the mutual recognition promised in print discourse was not an interaction between particularized persons, but among persons constituted by the negating abstraction of themselves" (*The Letters of the Republic* [Cambridge: Harvard Univ. Press, 1990], 62).

68. British Library Add. MS. 5159.

69. *Letters* 1:119−20.

70. Cited by Stephen Parks, ed., *Sale Catalogues of Libraries of Eminent Persons*, vol. 5, *Poets and Men of Letters* (London: Mansell with Sotheby Parke-Bernet Publications, 1972), 389.

71. Lisa Jardine and Anthony Grafton, "Studied for Action: How Gabriel Harvey Read His Livy," *Past and Present* 129 (1991): 77.

72. *Idler* 74, *Yale* 2:231.

73. See Jesper Svenbro, *Phrasikleia: An Anthropology of Reading in Ancient Greece,* trans. Janet Lloyd (Ithaca, N.Y.: Cornell Univ. Press, 1993).

74. J. D. Fleeman, *A Preliminary Handlist of Documents and Manuscripts*

of Samuel Johnson, Oxford Bibliographical Society Occasional Publication no. 2 (Oxford: Oxford Bibliographical Society, 1967), no. 59.

75. The manuscript of this notebook is in the Royal Library, Windsor Castle; see *Life* 4:381–82.

76. Jonathan Swift, *A Tale of a Tub,* ed. A. C. Guthkelch and D. Nichol Smith, 2d ed. (Oxford: Clarendon Press, 1958), 148.

77. *Life* 5:272.

78. See the fine article by Thomas Mallon, "Memories Held in Check: Perusing a Lifetime of My Father's Expenditures," *Harper's,* October 1993, 75–82. Mallon chooses the word "perusing" with preternatural insight.

79. *Yale* 1:27.

80. Ibid., 159.

81. *Life* 5:294–95.

82. Ibid., 295.

83. Ibid., 302.

CHAPTER 3. STUDY

1. *Yale* 1:293–94.

2. For a description of this kind of reading, see James N. Baker, "The Presence of the Name: Reading Scripture in an Indonesian Village," in *The Ethnography of Reading,* ed. Jonathan Boyarin (Berkeley and Los Angeles: Univ. of California Press, 1993), 98–138. Also see Sylvia Scribner and Michael Cole, *The Psychology of Literacy* (Cambridge: Harvard Univ. Press, 1981).

3. *Life* 2:189.

4. *Yale* 1:147.

5. *Gleanings* 5:216; *Life* 4:403 n. 1.

6. See *Handlist* nos. 14, 15, and 258, for example.

7. This book is now in the Hyde Collection, which also includes a 1768 octavo, two volumes in seven.

8. *Gleanings* 2:78; *Handlist* no. 16.

9. *Handlist* no. 19; cf. the similar gift to "Suzy" Thrale, no. 25.

10. *Life* 1:445.

11. Ibid., 446 n. 3.

12. Ibid., 1:57.

13. Ibid.

14. Ibid., 70.

15. Ibid., 71.

16. *Lives* 3:348.

17. James Henry Monk, *The Life of Richard Bentley,* 2 vols. (London: J. G. and F. Rivington, 1833), 1:3.

18. *Life* 1:57.

19. *Lives* 1:2.

20. Michael Wilding, "Michael Johnson: An Auction Sale," *Notes and Queries* (May 1969): 181–82.

21. See British Library Add. MS. 71692; also see Clifford, *Young Sam Johnson,* 66 and 332 n. 15.

22. *Yale* 7–8:6, 755.

23. Lynne Sharon Schwartz, "True Confessions of a Reader," *Salmagundi* 88–89 (fall 1990–winter 1991): 203–4.

24. Joseph Spence, *A Parallel in the Manner of Plutarch: Between a most celebrated Man of Florence; and one, scarce ever heard of, in England* (Twickenham, England: Strawberry Hill Press, 1758), 85, 76–77, 43–44.

25. Ibid., 9, 21, 26.

26. *Yale* 6, 4.2.106–11.

27. Samuel Johnson, *The Poems of Samuel Johnson,* ed. D. N. Smith and E. L. McAdam Jr., 2d ed. (Oxford: Oxford Univ. Press, 1974), 353.

28. Spence, *Parallel,* 15.

29. Claudian Claudianus, *Cl. Claudiani quae exstant,* ed. Nicolaas Heinsius, 2 vols. (Amsterdam: Elsevir Press, 1665), 2:865.

30. For this remark in particular and throughout this section on Eliot I am indebted to conversations with Joanne DeMaria.

31. *Yale* 3:353, which follows Johnson's surprising accentuation of the Greek.

32. George Eliot, *A Writer's Notebook, 1854–1879,* ed. Joseph Wiesenfarth (Charlottesville: Univ. Press of Virginia, 1981), 96.

33. Ibid., 141; George Eliot, *Daniel Deronda* (1876; reprint, Harmondsworth: Penguin Books, 1967), 420.

34. *Yale* 3:358.

35. *Lives* 1:416 n. 4.

36. Ibid., 417.

37. Macrobius, *Opera* (Venice, 1521), fol. Cvii^r, and *Yale* 15:3, where the connection is noted by Johnson's editor, Joel Gold.

38. Macrobius, *Opera,* fol. Biiii^v.

39. Ibid., fol. Dviii^v; Macrobius, *Saturnalia,* trans. Percival Vaughn Davies (New York: Columbia Univ. Press, 1969), 27.

40. Macrobius, *Opera,* fol. xxxx; Macrobius, *Saturnalia,* 75–76.

41. Hawkins, *Life of Samuel Johnson, LL.D.,* 16.

42. Rulon-Miller Books, St. Paul, Minnesota; I have lost the catalogue number.

43. I discuss the "future of reading" in chapter 7 below.

44. For an extended discussion of the antagonism to scholars such as Bentley, see Simon Jarvis, *Scholars and Gentlemen* (Oxford: Clarendon Press, 1995).

45. Samuel Taylor Coleridge, *Marginalia,* ed. George Whalley, 3 vols. (Princeton: Princeton Univ. Press, 1980–), 1:221.

46. The poem was by Edmund Smith, a friend and favorite of Johnson's beloved Gilbert Walmesley; perhaps these volumes were gifts from the avuncular Lichfield gentleman.

47. *Life* 3:251, 4:182, and 3:346, respectively.

48. *Lives* 3:182–83.

49. For Woolf's debt to Johnson, see Beth Carole Rosenberg, *Virginia Woolf and Samuel Johnson, Common Readers* (New York: St. Martin's Press, 1995).

50. *Letters* 3:299; *Yale* 4:144.

51. The very book is now in the Pembroke College Library; Johnson left a few bits of marginalia in it, just enough to show that his reading was a little more active, critical, and participatory than his reading of undisputed champions such as Euripides.

CHAPTER 4. PERUSAL

1. William Powell Jones, *Thomas Gray, Scholar: The True Tragedy of an Eighteenth-Century Gentleman* (Cambridge: Harvard Univ. Press, 1937), 36; letter of December 1738.

2. *Lives* 3:429–30.

3. Ibid. 429 n. 5.

4. Ibid., 2:26.

5. I borrow throughout this section from Steven Starker, *The Oracle at the Supermarket: The American Preoccupation with Self-Help Books* (New Brunswick, N.J.: Transaction, 1989).

6. Delarivière Manley, *The New Atalantis,* ed. Rosalind Ballaster (1709; reprint, London: Penguin Books, 1992), 37.

7. Claudius Quillet, *Callipaedia,* trans. Nicholas Rowe (1722; reprint, Los Angeles: Advertisers Composition, 1963), 47–48.

8. *The Educational Writings of John Locke,* ed. James Axtell (Cambridge: Cambridge Univ. Press, 1968), 19.

9. Ibid., 162.

10. George Cheyne, *The English Malady* (1733; facsimile reprint, Delmar, N.Y.: Scholar's Facsimiles, 1976), 139.

11. Ibid., 149.

12. See Samuel Johnson, review of *A Free Inquiry into the Nature and Origin of Evil,* by Soame Jenyns, *Literary Magazine* 2 (1757): 171–75, 251–53, and 301–6.

13. *Lives* 3:309.

14. *Miscellanies* 1:157–58; cf. *Life* 1:69 n. 3.

15. *Miscellanies* 2:297.

16. Hugo Grotius, *The Truth of the Christian Religion,* ed. and augmented by Jean LeClerc, trans. John Clarke, 9th ed. (London, 1786), 76–77.

17. Ibid., 265.

18. Samuel Johnson, *The Vanity of Human Wishes,* l. 158.

19. Grotius, *Truth of the Christian Religion,* 286.

20. *Yale* 1:226.

21. *Life* 5:351–52.

22. William Sherlock, *A Practical Discourse concerning Death* (1689; reprint, London, 1760), 18–19.

23. Joseph Addison, *Spectator* no. 289 (31 January 1712), in *The Spectator,* ed. Donald F. Bond, 5 vols. (Oxford: Clarendon Press, 1965), 3:29.

24. Wendy Simonds, *Women and Self-Help Culture: Reading between the Lines* (New Brunswick, N.J.: Rutgers Univ. Press, 1992), 26.

25. Giovanni Bona, *A Guide to Eternity by Cardinal Bona,* trans. Roger L'Estrange, ed. J. W. Stanbridge (New York: Edwin S. Gorham, n.d.), 2. Johnson's own copy of Bona's *Manuductio ad Coelum* (Cologne: Cornelium ab Egmont, 1671) is now in the Rothschild Collection at Trinity College, Cambridge. There are many marks and comments in the book, and some verse. Not all of the comments were made by Johnson, but he dated his completed reading "Julij 13 Anno 1732," and surely made some of the marks. Among the most interesting are two cross-references to William Law, *A Serious Call to a Devout and Holy Life* (London: Wm. Innys, 1728), 19 and 40, and a bit of verse that sums up Bona's message: "Sat vixit diu / Quem nec paenitet vixisse / Nec piget mori" (He long prevails enough who is not displeased with prevailing and does not regret to die). But more personal sounding is a brief, self-admonishing remark on the blank leaf before the title page: "Malè inoperat, qui praecipit et non facit" (He works badly who plans and does not do).

26. Ibid., 18, 26, 66, 32, 76.

27. Ibid., 33–34.

28. Ibid., 107–8.

29. Ibid., 105.

30. It was first printed in the fifth edition of *Perseus and Andromeda,* a one-act play by Lewis Theobald (London: Tho. Wood, 1731). The printed version has "No grandeur or" in place of Johnson's "Nor power nor."

31. Wayne C. Booth, "The Company We Keep: Self-Making in Imaginative Art, Old and New," *Dædalus* (fall 1982): 34. This issue of the journal appeared as *Print Culture and Video Culture,* vol. III, no. 4, of *Proceedings of the American Academy of Arts and Sciences.*

32. Bona, *Guide to Eternity,* 164.

33. *Life* 1:67.

34. *Yale* 1:307.

35. *Life* 1:68–69.

36. Ibid., 4:215.

37. All the references to Johnson's reading of Law are taken from Hill's notes to *Life* 1:68–69.

38. Ibid., 68 n. 2.

39. Law, *Serious Call,* 193–94.

40. Ibid., 196.

41. Samuel Johnson, "An Account of the life of Peter Burman, the late Professor of History, Poetry, &c. in the University of Leiden," *Gentleman's Magazine* 12 (1742): 206–10; see *Handlist* no. 226.

42. Law, *Serious Call,* 168.

43. Ibid., 25.

44. Ibid., 10, 31, 30, 69, 73.

45. Ibid., 252, 230, 263.

46. Ibid., 145.

47. *Life* 3:292.

48. Law, *Serious Call,* 111.

49. *Lives* 3:227.

CHAPTER 5. MERE READING

1. John Nichols, *Literary Anecdotes of the Eighteenth Century,* 2d ed., 6 vols. (London: John Nichols, 1812), 4:54–55n.

2. Ibid.

3. André Kertész, *On Reading* (New York: Viking Penguin, 1971).

4. Nichols, *Literary Anecdotes,* 4:109.

5. Samuel Johnson and William Oldys, eds., *The Harleian Miscellany,* 8 vols. (London: Thomas Osborne, 1744–46), 1:vi.

6. Nichols, *Literary Anecdotes,* 4:38–39.

7. Ibid., 42–47.

8. Ben Jonson's play *The Staple of News* shows that the mania began no later than the early seventeenth century.

9. Nichols, *Literary Anecdotes,* 4:86–87n.

10. For a history of Johnson's appearances in journalistic literature, see Helen Louise McGuffie, *Samuel Johnson in the British Press, 1749–1784: A Chronological Checklist* (New York: Garland, 1976).

11. *Letters* 1:249.

12. Ibid., 4:241.

13. *Lives* 2:94–97.

14. *Yale* 2:22.

15. *Life* 3:332.

16. Ibid., 318.

17. *Yale* 2:23.

18. Ibid., 94.

19. Ibid.

20. Ibid., 95.

21. Ibid., 22–24.

22. For Johnson's writings on the Byng affair in 1756, see *Yale* 10:213–60.

23. Ibid., 2:26.

24. "London," *Public Advertiser,* no. 7405, 12 May 1758.

25. "Admiralty Office, May 13," *London Gazette,* no. 9790, 9–13 May 1758.

26. *Yale* 2:25.

27. "Admiralty Office, May 13," *Whitehall Evening-Post, or, London Intelligencer,* no. 1895, 13–16 May 1758.

28. *Gentleman's Magazine* 28 (1758): 242.

29. *Yale* 10:227–33.

30. John Woodruff, "Johnson's *Rambler* and Its Contemporary Context," *Bulletin of Research in the Humanities* 85 (1982): 27–64.

31. *Letters* 1:119.

32. Samuel Johnson, "Preface," *Gentleman's Magazine* 10 (1740): iii–iv.

33. Ibid., viii.

34. Ibid., iv.

35. Michael Schudson, "The Politics of Narrative Form: The Emergence of News Conventions in Print and Television," *Dædalus* (fall 1982): 108.

36. Perhaps he meant Fort Duquesne, on the confluence of the Allegheny and Monongahela Rivers, where the English had been defeated on 9 July 1755.

37. See Brown, *Knowledge Is Power,* 90–91 and passim.

38. Lennard Davis, *Factual Fictions: The Origins of the English Novel* (New York: Columbia Univ. Press, 1983).

39. *Yale* 2:124–25.

40. Terry Castle, *Masquerade and Civilization* (Stanford, Calif.: Stanford Univ. Press, 1986), 3.

41. *Yale* 2:125.

42. Ibid.

43. Ibid., 126–27.

44. See Johnson's "Memoirs of Frederick III, King of Prussia," *Literary Magazine* 1 (1756): 327–33, 383–90, and 439–42.

45. *Yale* 2:127–28.

CHAPTER 6. CURIOUS READING

1. Zoltan Haraszti, *John Adams and the Prophets of Progress* (Cambridge: Harvard Univ. Press, 1952), 16, citing a letter of 27 December 1810.

2. Cited by Richard Beale Davis, *A Colonial Bookshelf: Reading in the Eighteenth Century* (Athens: Univ. of Georgia Press, 1979), 123.

3. *Miscellanies* 1:319.

4. Ibid., and *Life* 3:43.

5. *Life* 2:121.

6. In *A Natural Perspective* (New York: Columbia Univ. Press, 1965), 1–3, Northrop Frye credits Coleridge with making the distinction between Iliad and Odyssey critics.

7. *Life* 4:218 n. 1 and 5:313.

8. Ibid., 3:284–85.

9. Ibid., 5:88, 2:226, and 3:32.

10. *Letters* 4:108.

11. See *Miscellanies* 2:192 and *Life* 2:195.

12. Edward Bernard, ed., *Catalogus librorum manuscriptorum, Angliae et Hiberniae,* 2 vols. (Oxford, 1697). See, e.g., *Letters* 1:112–13.

13. *Miscellanies* 1:332–33.

14. For an account of Johnson's reading throughout the genre, see Eithne Hensen, *The Fictions of Romantick Chivalry: Samuel Johnson and Romance* (Rutherford, N.J.: Fairleigh Dickinson Univ. Press, 1992). As noted above, a book said to be Johnson's copy of *Seven Champions* recently surfaced in the Lichfield bookshop of Peter Stockham; it is not a chapbook version but a complete text.

15. For a history of chapbook versions of these books, see Margaret Spufford, *Small Books and Pleasant Histories* (London: Methuen, 1981).

16. *Life* 1:49.

17. *Yale* 1:312.

18. Charlotte Lennox, *The Female Quixote*, 2 vols. (London, 1752), 2:309.

19. Ibid., 307–8.

20. Ibid., 317.

21. See my *Life of Samuel Johnson,* 184–93, and Donald D. Eddy, *Samuel Johnson, Book Reviewer in the Literary Magazine; or, Universal Review, 1756–1758* (New York: Garland, 1979).

22. *Yale* 4:21.

23. Ibid., 153.

24. *Life* 2:175.

25. Ibid., 174.

26. Ibid., 49 n. 2.

27. *Lives* 2:214.

28. Henry Fielding, *Amelia* (Oxford: Clarendon Press, 1983), 44.

29. Ibid., 267.

30. Ibid., 245.

31. For a full discussion of the masquerade in the eighteenth century and its importance in *Amelia,* see Castle, *Masquerade and Civilization.* I am indebted to Castle's reading of *Amelia* throughout.

32. Fielding, *Amelia,* 263.

33. Ibid., 362.

34. Ibid., 184.

35. Ibid., 71.

36. Ibid., 108 and 142; cf. 435 and 527.

37. *Letters* 1:119.

38. Fielding, *Amelia,* 313.

39. This is an important feature of many of the books that Robert Darnton describes in *The Forbidden Best-Sellers of Pre-Revolutionary France* (New York: Norton, 1995).

40. "A fancy that has sometimes occurred to me in dreaming over the works of Richardson is that I had bought an old chateau. In exploring its rooms one day, I saw in a corner a bureau that no one had opened for a long time, and that, having forced it open, I found the assorted letters of Clarissa and of Pamela." Tom Keymer, *Richardson's* Clarissa *and the Eighteenth-Century Reader* (Cambridge: Cambridge Univ. Press, 1992), 83.

41. "At last, suddenly, it seems to me, I was all alone." Ibid.

42. Cited by Bruce Redford in *The Converse of the Pen* (Chicago: Univ. of Chicago Press, 1986), 20.

43. *The Complete Letters of Lady Mary Wortley Montagu,* ed. Robert Halsband, 3 vols. (Oxford: Clarendon Press, 1985), 1:313–14; in this and succeeding passages, I have regularized a few of the more surprising spellings in the manuscript faithfully followed by Halsband.

44. Ibid., 314.

45. Ibid., 349–50.

46. Ibid., 351.

47. Ibid., 350.

48. Ibid., 351.

49. J. Paul Hunter, *Before Novels* (New York: Norton, 1990), 34–35.

50. Ibid., 35.

51. I cannot locate this reference, but Johnson's diaries are full of resolutions to stop his sensual and vain imaginings; see the index to Johnson's *Diaries, Prayers, and Annals* in *Yale* 1, s.v. "Imaginations, vain or tumultuous" and "lust."

52. Montagu, *Complete Letters,* 1:383.

53. The abridgement was edited by O M Brack and reprinted for the Samuel Johnson Society of Southern California (1993), but I cite the edition that Johnson read, rather than the one he wrote.

54. *The History of Thamas Kouli Kan* (1740; reprint, London, 1775), 1.

55. Montagu, *Complete Letters,* 1:415.

56. *The Turkish Spy,* first published as *L'esploratore Turco* by Giovanni Paolo Marana (Paris, 1684), translated, expanded, and often reprinted through the first half of the eighteenth century.

57. *History of Thamas Kouli Kan,* 101.

58. Ibid., 15.

59. William Jones, *Poems consisting Chiefly of Translations from the Asiatick Languages* (1772) rpt. *Works,* 13 vols. (London, 1807), 10:199.

60. Preface, *Yale* 7:62.

61. Herbert Croft, *Love and Madness: A Story Too True In a Series of Letters between Parties, whose Names would perhaps be mentioned, were they less known, or less lamented* (London: G. Kearsly, 1780), 14.

62. Ibid., 72.

63. Fielding, *Amelia,* 329.

64. Benjamin Victor, *The Widow of the Wood* (London, 1755), 2.

65. Richard Dorment, review of *Hogarth,* by Ronald Paulson, *New York Review of Books,* 27 May 1993, 18.

66. *Letters* 4:352.

67. *Yale* 1:167, 195, and 198.

68. *Life* 5:302.

69. Ibid., 1:465.

70. Martyn Lyons, *Australian Readers Remember* (Oxford: Oxford Univ. Press, 1992).

CHAPTER 7. SAMUEL JOHNSON AND THE
FUTURE OF READING

1. Among the best is Sven Birkerts, *The Gutenberg Elegies: The Fate of Reading in an Electronic Age* (New York: Ballantine, 1994).

2. Michael Joyce, "(Re)placing the Author," electronic manuscript, personal correspondence with author.

3. Carlo Ginzburg, *The Cheese and the Worms: The Cosmos of a Sixteenth-Century Miller* (Baltimore: Johns Hopkins Univ. Press, 1980).

4. J. David Bolter, "Literature in the Electronic Writing Space," in *Literacy on Line: The Promise (and Peril) of Reading and Writing with Computers,* ed. Myron C. Tuman (Pittsburgh: Univ. of Pittsburgh Press, 1992), 33.

5. According to George Landow, a practitioner and theorist of hypertext at Brown University, decentering is one of the effects of hypertext, and one of many in which the new form makes "embarrassingly literal" the view of texts and reading taken in postmodern literary criticism.

6. *Life* 1:71.

7. Ibid., 4:308.

8. Ibid., 2:346.

9. Ibid., 3:37.

10. Ibid., 2:226.

11. Ibid., 4:21.

12. Ibid., 3:43.

13. See chapter 3 above.

14. John Locke, *A Paraphrase and Notes on the Epistles of St. Paul,* ed. Arthur W. Wainwright, 2 vols. (Oxford: Clarendon Press, 1987), 1:110–14.

15. Joyce, "(Re)placing the Author."

16. Late in life he even collected portraits; in keeping with his love of literary biography he collected portraits of authors. For a discussion of Johnson's interest in the visual arts, see Morris R. Brownell, *Samuel Johnson's Attitude to the Arts* (Oxford: Clarendon Press, 1989).

17. *Life* 4:236.

18. Ibid., 92.

19. Ibid., 218.

20. *Yale* 2:459.

21. Johnson, *Universal Visiter and Memorialist,* 162.

22. See, e.g., *Lives* 3:441.

INDEX